The Powhatan Indians of Virginia

The Civilization of the American Indian Series

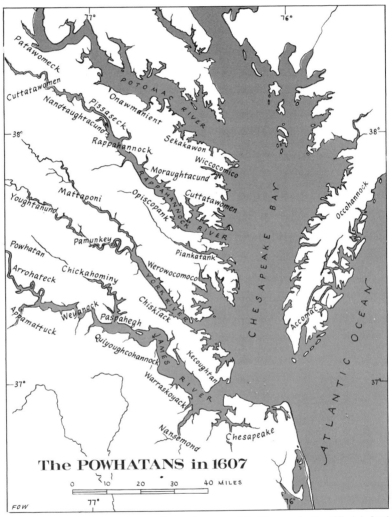

The Powhatans in 1607. Base map after *Bathymetry of the Chesapeake Bay* (Virginia Institute of Marine Science, 1977).

THE POWHATAN INDIANS
OF VIRGINIA

Their Traditional Culture

By

Helen C. Rountree

University of Oklahoma Press : Norman and London

To My Teacher, Mentor, and Friend
NANCY OESTREICH LURIE

Library of Congress Cataloging-in-Publication Data

Rountree, Helen C., 1944–
   The Powhatan Indians of Virginia.

   (The Civilization of the American Indian series ;
v. 193)
   Bibliography: p.
   Includes index.
   1. Powhatan Indians.   I. Title.   II. Series.
E99.P85R68   1988   306'.08997   88-27905
ISBN 0-8061-2156-4

This publication has been supported by the National Endowment for the
Humanities, a federal agency which supports the study of such fields as history,
philosophy, literature, and languages.

The Powhatan Indians of Virginia is Volume 193 in *The Civilization of the
American Indian Series.*

Contents

		Page
Preface		vii
Prologue	English Observers and the Indian Groups They Saw	3
Chapter 1	The Land and Its Resources	17
2	Subsistence	32
3	Towns and Their Inhabitants	58
4	Manliness	79
5	Sex Roles and Family Life	88
6	Social Distinctions	100
7	Law, Politics, and War	114
8	Medicine and Religion	126
Epilogue	The Powhatans as a Chiefdom of Coastal Algonquians	140
Notes		153
Bibliography		194
Index		207

Illustrations

Page

The Powhatans in 1607 (map)   Frontispiece

Fig. 1 The John Smith map of 1608   10
2 A tidal "creek": Harris Creek, in Hampton, Virginia   19
3 A meandering river: the Mattaponi, near Walkerton, Virginia   20
4 A straight river cut through high banks: the York, near Yorktown, Virginia   21
5 Salinity of Chesapeake Bay and altitude of surrounding lands   23
6 Detail of the John Smith map   30
7 Bone and turtle-shell implements   33
8 De Bry's engraving of Indian fishing   36
9 Overhead view of modern tidewater Virginia fish weir   37
10 Eiakintomino in Saint James's Park   43
11 Stone cutting implements   48
12 De Bry's engraving of the town of Secota   59
13 Decorated potsherds   64
14 Stone milling implements   66
15 Textiles derived from impressions on ceramics   67
16 Bone weaving needles   68
17 Pearls and copper artifacts   72
18 Shell ornaments   74
19 Shell ornaments found near the site of Patawomeck   75
20 Gribelin's engraving of a priest, a conjurer, and a *huskanaw* pen   83
21 Gribelin's engraving of women and a baby in a cradle board   95
22 The "Virginia Purse"   104
23 "Powhatan's Mantle"   105
24 Detail of the John Smith map showing Powhatan's court   107

Preface

THIS BOOK IS INTENDED as a historical ethnography, that is, a description of a culture of the past based on historical documents. Specifically, it is a time capsule datable to 1607–10. It is intended as a companion volume to my book *The Powhatan Indians of Virginia through Four Centuries* (forthcoming). This volume helps explain Indian behavior in the first century and a half of colonial Virginia history, and the history volume will illustrate Powhatan culture as it affected Indian-English relations.

I am not aware of having any particular theoretical ax to grind in this book. Instead, I hope that it will become the basic preliminary reading for scholars in other areas who want to test their own hypotheses and evaluate the theoretical works of my colleagues. Here, as far as I have been able to discover, is what was and was not recorded about the Early Contact Period culture of the Indian people of eastern Virginia. I discuss my sources of information and my methods of using them in the Prologue.

I am indebted to numerous people for their assistance while I was doing my research and writing preliminary drafts. The staffs of the Virginia State Library, the Virginia Research Center for Archaeology, the Norfolk Public Library, and the Hampton Public Library were generous in helping me find what I wanted and answering occasional questions over the telephone. Ben McCary, formerly of the College of William and Mary, and Barbara Wood, of the Hampton Center for the Arts and Humanities, assisted me with some archaeological data. Mary Ellen Norrisey Hodges, formerly of the Virginia Research Center for Archaeology, helped me with archaeological data and in making photographs of specimens. Martha McCartney, formerly of the same institution, found another photograph I could use. The Center for Instructional Development of Old Dominion University has helped me reproduce my own photographs, maps, and line drawings.

Christian Feest, of the Museum für Völkerkunde in Vienna, commented voluminously on a version of the manuscript in an earlier format, showing me, in effect, "how it should be done." My friend E. Randolph Turner, of the Virginia Research Center for Archaeology, was marvelous in turning me loose in his private library and in commenting on two earlier drafts that I produced over a five-year period. Howard A. MacCord, Sr., also commented on an earlier draft. Nancy O. Lurie, of the Milwaukee Public Museum, my erstwhile doctoral adviser and mentor ever since, waded through two earlier drafts; her encouragement of my efforts, beginning in 1970, has been invaluable.

Over the years several student assistants at Old Dominion University have helped me compile the culture-trait index from which I wrote this book: Steven A. Ellis, William G. Shea, Jerry P. Walker, and W. Jean Homza. I have been assisted financially by Old Dominion University with four grants from the School of Arts and Letters Research Fund and one summer's Faculty Senate Research Grant. My parents have provided me with moral support and loans of camping equipment since I first began my research in 1969. Both my mother and Nancy Lurie functioned wonderfully as critical proofreaders and editors.

HELEN C. ROUNTREE
Hampton, Virginia

The Powhatan Indians of Virginia

English Observers and the Indian Groups They Saw

THE INFORMATION WE HAVE concerning the culture of the Indians of eastern Virginia in the early seventeenth century comes from archaeology (which is still in its infancy in Virginia)[1] and from writings by Englishmen who lived in Virginia or interviewed or corresponded with those who had or met and interviewed Indians who had gone to England. The Indians themselves did not leave written records until much later. That fact alone means that we have to see Powhatan culture primarily through the eyes of people who are removed from us in time and who usually dealt with Indian people for reasons other than pure observation.

Most of the sources on Indian lifeways in Virginia come from the early seventeenth century, when the English colonization effort was new and in a precarious state. The Jamestown settlement, established in 1607 on the James River, was expected to discover precious metals and a Northwest Passage to the Pacific, at the same time that it was poorly supported by England. Colonists therefore viewed Indians as sources of information and providers or hoarders of needed foodstuffs. Their accounts are accordingly weighted toward the James River area and Indians playing certain roles. There are additionally a few late-seventeenth-century writers who knew the Virginia Indians as a conquered people and whose accounts are colored by that fact. In weighing the possible accuracy of what writers tell us, it is necessary from the outset to know the writers' backgrounds and the conditions under which they saw Indian people. The major writers from whose works we can draw are the following:

John Smith (1580–1631). Smith was in Virginia from April 1607 to October 1609, when the English colony was getting started. He was involved in the major exploring and trading expeditions that took place, made extensive firsthand observations, and wrote voluminously about them afterward.[2] His major description of Indian life is "A Map of Virginia," published in 1612 and reissued in 1624 as part of his "Generall Historie." His interests were primarily military and explorational, however, interests which limit the scope of his accounts of Indian life. Smith was a man of yeoman stock who, once in the New World, rose to the presidency of the Virginia Colony through sheer organizational ability. Unfortunately, while he was talented and energetic, he was also abrasive toward both Indians and Englishmen, making him a controversial figure then and now. His yeoman background did not help matters in his dealings with his fellow colonists, many of whom were gentlemen. Scholarly standards were loose then, and Smith was also decidedly egotistical; thus his writings cannot always be trusted, especially his later accounts, when he tended to rewrite history in his own favor.

William Strachey (1572–1621). Strachey was in Virginia from May 1610 to September 1611,[3] a time of greatly worsening relations with the Indians. He spent most of his time in the Jamestown fort, making at least one expedition each to the falls of the James, to Kecoughtan at the mouth of the James, and to Quiyoughcohannock across the river from Jamestown.[4] At the fort he apparently held extensive interviews with two Indian men, Kemps and Machumps. Kemps lived full time with the English until his death (sometime in 1611),[5] and he spoke English very well; Machumps, who had been to England and returned to Jamestown with the same fleet (though perhaps not on the same ship) in which Strachey arrived, came occasionally. Strachey was a gentleman who had studied at the Inns of Court, after which he lived on in London, fraternizing with writers such as Ben Jonson and patronizing theaters. He was not prepared to be an ethnographer in the modern sense, but he had a wider and more detailed curiosity about Indian life than any other writer of his time. Unfortunately, when he came to write his account in 1612, he found that Smith had gotten there just ahead of him. Hurriedly he copied many passages from Smith's "A Map of Virginia" into his manuscript, adding his own embellishments, rather than writing a completely independent account that might have told us much more. We are left to assume, then, that when Strachey copies from Smith in speaking of an Indian practice, either he is corroborating Smith's information or he does not know any better than to repeat it.

Henry Spelman (1595–1623). Spelman was in Virginia from August 1609 to March 1611, from about 1616 to about 1618, and from about 1619 to his death. He lived among the Indians, first with the ruler Powhatan himself at Orapax and then with Iopassus (Japazaws) at Passapatanzy (Patawomeck territory), from September (?) 1609 to December 1610. Spelman was the nephew of the historian Sir Henry Spelman,[6] but because of trouble at home he left England, relatively ill-educated, and went to Virginia. Spelman's young age induced Smith to "sell" him to Powhatan to learn the language, and when Powhatan became hostile, a visiting Patawomeck village chief helped him escape and took him northward. Spelman's account[7] is invaluable because it is the only one written by an Englishman who lived for any great length of time among the Indians. It is unfortunate that he was (by his own account) too young to notice many things and that his writing style was poor. He subsequently became an interpreter for the colony, and at the time of his death at the hands of the Piscataways[8] he held the rank of captain in the colony.

George Percy (1580–1632). Percy lived in Virginia from April 1607 to April 1612. He was the eighth son of the eighth earl of Northumberland and brother to the ninth earl, a major patron of the Virginia enterprise. His background, with its emphasis on class superiority and military achievement, made him a natural rival of Smith in Virginia, and he wrote the second of his two accounts as a rebuttal to Smith's "A Map of Virginia."[9] Percy had little interest in the customs of "savages," since he was expected to be a leader who made the colonization effort work, but the details he gives us of the Indians' initial reception of the English as they explored up the James River are extremely useful.

Gabriel Archer (ca. 1575[10]–winter 1609–10). Archer was in Virginia from April 1607 to April 1608 and from the summer of 1609 until his death. He was a gentleman who had been a law student in 1593 and a member of Bartholomew Gosnold's expedition to the New England coast in 1602.[11] In Virginia he was one of the colony's leaders and apparently stayed mainly at the fort after the initial expedition up the James River. The authorship of the three accounts ascribed to him here is uncertain but probable.[12] The third account, covering the native people of Virginia, is brief but particularly useful.

The Reverend Samuel Purchas (1577[13]–1626). Purchas was never in Virginia. He was a collector and editor of other people's accounts[14] who interviewed returnees from Virginia when possible. Thus he talked face to face with Smith (after 1611), John Rolfe, the husband of Pocahontas, and Uttamatomakkin, the Indian priest whom Powhatan sent to England as his representative in 1616–1617.[15] Purchas was not interested in Indian culture per se; except in the area of religion, he acquired only scraps of information to add to his works as exotic seasoning.[16] Nonetheless, his report on having interrogated Uttamatomakkin provides us with some unique data on Powhatan religion. The 1617 version of his report, in his now-rare *Pilgrimage,* is longer, less anti-Indian, and therefore more informative than the readily available 1625 version (in *Hakluytus Postumus*), which was written after the great Indian attack of 1622.

John Clayton (1657–1725). Clayton was in Virginia from the spring of 1684 to May 1686. He was an Oxford-educated minister with extensive medical training. As rector of the James-City Parish Church in Jamestown, he met the leading lights in the colony. His closest friendship was with William Byrd, who had frequent dealings with the Algonquian-speaking Appamattucks, the Siouan-speaking Monacans, and other Indian groups on the west and southwest. Since Clayton visited Byrd at his plantation up the James and Byrd was a major Indian trader in the region, Clayton made firsthand contact with the Appamattucks and possibly with the others. Clayton was moderately interested in Indian culture and very much interested in Indian medicine. However, his fairly long accounts[17] are flawed, for two reasons. The first was beyond his control: the Indian remnants by that time had been so battered by the English, both materially and psychologically, that they usually refused to answer Clayton's questions simply because he was an Englishman. The second reason was common to all the later writers about Indians: he met several different kinds of Indians, Algonquians, Siouans, and possibly Iroquoians, but he did not distinguish among them in his writings. We who want to sift the Algonquian data cannot always be sure that what Clayton writes is pertinent to our work.

Anonymous.[18] He was an unidentified minister in Virginia in the 1680s. There is no record showing where he lived while he was in the colony, and, therefore, the identity of the Indians he wrote about is uncertain. Like his contemporaries, he knew of Indians other than the Virginia Algonquians; the Tuscaroras are specifically mentioned in his text. His account is moderately long and gives data that no other does, possibly because of the several Indian cultures that he wrote about.

John Banister (1650–92). Banister lived in Virginia from 1678 until his death. He was an Oxford-trained minister who was an avid natural historian. As rector of Bristol Parish, at the mouth of the Appomattox River, he was a friend of Byrd and was able to meet Appamattuck Indians and probably others. He also may have journeyed elsewhere along the frontier, for he mentions the Pamunkey Indians at one point. It is highly likely that he met Siouan-speaking Indians as well. His moderately long account[19] is well rounded, although it probably mixes Algonquian and Siouan data, and is extremely useful in its specific identification of some plants and animals utilized by the Indians.

Robert Beverley (ca. 1673–1722). Beverley was born in Virginia, was educated in England, and lived most of his adult life in Virginia. He was interested in history, natural history, and Indians, as the scope of his book shows.[20] He dealt with Indian affairs first as a clerk in colonial offices and later as a member of the Virginia House of Burgesses. He also lived across the Mattaponi River from Pamunkey Neck, one of the last large Indian-owned tracts in the colony, and when that tract was opened to English claimants in 1693–99, he was assigned the task of representing the Indians and upholding their rights to the remaining lands.[21] Beverley therefore worked closely with the Pamunkey and Chickahominy Indians. His account is a long one, taking up one-fourth of his book. He borrowed many passages from Banister's account "Of the Natives" without giving any credit, but he wrote more than enough original text about the Indians that he can be forgiven. His work does suffer, nonetheless, from mixing Indian cultures; he did all the intermingling that Banister did and added the northern Iroquoians and Algonquians described in Baron Lahontan's *Nouveaux Voyages* (1703) for good measure.

The limitations of the witnesses listed above and their writings require that any reconstruction of the Powhatan way of life must proceed carefully. Even then such a reconstruction must consist of a patchwork of information that is usually not so detailed as an anthropologist would like. Heaviest reliance must be placed, of course, on the early-seventeenth-century sources. Late-seventeenth-century sources are also used in the book—with cautions that they may reflect a changed situation—because they can help make the picture more vivid. The later sources will be used more extensively in another book, which will provide a reconstruction of Powhatan culture as of A.D. 1700.[22]

The people and the way of life described in this book date to the very first years of the Jamestown Colony. The very presence of Englishmen in their territory was a disturbing enough influence on the Indians that it would be foolhardy to attempt to reconstruct the "pristine" scene from English writings. There may, in addition, have been more seriously disrupting influences, such as epidemics and increasing pressures from non-Algonquian Indians, in the protohistoric period (see Epilogue), which means that we would have to go back more than a century before 1607 to find a coastal Woodland culture in Virginia that was relatively undisturbed. The time period of this book is therefore unabashedly the Early Contact Period.

The Algonquian-speaking groups of Virginia's coastal plain are collectively called "Powhatans"[23] in this volume. The alternative, preferred by Feest,[24] is "Virginia Algonquians," which I find accurate enough but cumbersome to use. At the time of which I write, the Virginia coastal plain was occupied by peoples of very similar language and culture (as far as the records show) who either belonged to or were allied in some way with the paramount chiefdom created by Powhatan, the father of Pocahontas. It therefore seems permissible to speak of a "Powhatan" population in eastern Virginia which had a "Powhatan" culture.

The name "Powhatan" is derived from a paramount chief's "empire"—not a confederacy at all—which covered most of the Virginia coastal plain (see below) and which was organized by the man Powhatan, who had in turn taken his name from his natal town, Powhatan, near the falls of the James River.[25] In addition to these three Powhatans (the collection of coastal plain people, the "throne name" of the chief, and the name of his hometown), the term "Powhatan" is also applied to the closely related Algonquian dialects spoken in the region.

The exact relationships among the various Powhatan dialects are not easy to reconstruct. Smith, the principal early explorer of eastern Virginia, stated flatly that all of the Algonquian groups there spoke "the language of [the man] Powhatan," even the more distant Accomacs and Occohannocks on the Eastern Shore.[26] On the other hand, Bartolomé Martínez wrote at third hand in 1610 that the Jesuit mission of 1570 had learned that many "tongues" were spoken along the waterways of the region.[27] Frank Siebert, today's leading linguist of the Powhatan language, examined the limited data available (word lists by Smith and Strachey and a few scattered words elsewhere; the language was never properly recorded and had become extinct by 1800). He cautiously concluded that there were several dialects (i.e., mutually intelligible variants of the same language) in the James-York region alone.[28] Unfortunately, Siebert ended his account with a highly speculative list showing three distinct Powhatan "languages"—Chickahominy, Pamunkey, and Nansemond—for which he gave no supporting evidence, linguistic or otherwise. That list is easy for nonspecialists to follow uncritically, and at least one has already done so.[29]

A safe summary about the Powhatan Indians' linguistic situation is therefore in order. Their language was Algonquian and was related to other Indian languages along the Atlantic coast. It had been spoken in eastern Virginia for at least three centuries,[30] and probably many more,[31] and by 1607 it had many dialects. Dialects develop when segments of a population are isolated, whether the cause is geographical distance or social avoidance. Thus the Powhatan dialects probably correlated with tribal groupings (e.g., Appamattuck), because these groups literally centered their territories on waterways (see chap. 2), always an excellent avenue of communication. Each dialect was probably closer to the ones spoken upriver and downriver (e.g., Chiskiack and Werowocomoco) than to dialects spoken even on adjacent major rivers in the region (e.g., Chiskiack and Paspahegh). The reason lies in the greater number of contacts between waterfront neighbors, which kept speech patterns more uniform. The dialects along the major rivers probably made a north-south continuum, the Virginia Potomac dialects being close to Maryland Potomac dialects, the south-side James dialects being reasonably close to Chowanoc in what is now North Carolina, and the northern and southern extremes having some difficulty understanding each other. "Powhatan" is an arbitrary grouping of dialects, based on political alliances, in the middle of that continuum. In other parts of the world, unless national boundaries and official pronunciation, grammar, and orthography split language communities apart (e.g., German and Dutch) or join them together (e.g., English and Scots), it is difficult to say geographically, just from traveling around and listening to the people, where one "language" leaves off and another begins. So it must have been with the "Powhatan" language. But all the Algonquian dialects in eastern Virginia were mutually intelligible among the Indians, for Smith was able to travel throughout the region in the summer of 1608 using the same interpreter (apparently himself).

As far as we know, all of the ethnic groups under Powhatan's sway were chiefdoms with powerful rulers (see chap. 7). In 1607, however, there was a nation of holdouts, the Chickahominies, who refused to become Powhatan's subjects (they became independent allies of his soon after the English arrived) and who insisted on being governed by a council of eight elders. Nothing further is known of their political organization, for the English colonists were not especially interested in it. Since the same colonists never wrote of the Chickahominy people as being culturally different from their chief-ruled neighbors except in their politics, we must assume that they resembled those neighbors in most respects and can include them in writing generally about "Powhatan" culture. Because the Chickahominies were not a chiefdom, I use the word "groups" (rather than the overworked and nowadays politically limited "tribes") when referring to any of the Algonquian-speaking peoples of the Virginia coastal plain, whether or not they were part of Powhatan's "empire."

The following list of Virginia Algonquian groups is based on the accounts of English settlers, whose interest lay primarily in Indian military power.[32] The locations are those of capital towns, if any, as shown in Smith's map (see fig. 1),[33] and any relevant archaeological reports on these towns are cited. Pronunciations and spellings are the modern ones still found in Virginia place-names, unless otherwise specified. I give a few translations of names in which I feel some confidence (for others see Barbour 1971). The list begins with a north-south sweep down the Eastern Shore, then moves up the southwestern bank of the James, down the northeastern bank of the James, and so on to the Potomac.

Occohannock (originally spelled Accohannock; ah-co-*han*-nock): about three miles west of Exmore (Accomac County); 40 men (i.e., warriors; Smith and Strachey); actually a subchiefdom of Accomac.[34]

Accomac (*ack*-o-mack): at the head of Kings Creek, near Cheriton (Northampton County); 80 men (Smith and Strachey). The name means "across the water."[35]

Chesapeake (*Ches*-a-peak): east of the South Branch of the Elizabeth River (city of Chesapeake); 100 men (Smith). Not originally part of Powhatan's dominions (see chap. 7) and probably exterminated by the time Jamestown was founded.[36] The name means "big salt bay."[37]

Nansemond (*Nan*-sa-mund): at the junction of the Exchange Branch with the Nansemond River proper, near Reid's Ferry (city of Suffolk); 200 men (Smith and Strachey).[38]

Warraskoyack (name now obsolete; possibly *wa*-ra-skoik):[39] on the Pagan (formerly Warraskoyack) River, at or near Smithfield (Isle of Wight County); 40 men (Smith in 1612; not mentioned in his 1624 account) or 60 men (Strachey).

Quiyoughcohannock (name now obsolete; possibly *kwee*-o-co-*han*-nock): at Claremont (Surry County); 25 men (Smith) or 60 men (Strachey). The first three syllables indicate a connection with a deity (see chap. 8); exact translation doubtful.

Weyanock (now spelled Weyanoke; *wye*-a-noke):[40] primary capital on Weyanoke Point (Charles City County) and secondary capital at the head of Powells creek (Prince George County); 100 men (Smith) and 100 men in the northern sector and 50 in the southern sector (Strachey). The name may mean "at the bend."[41]

Fig. 1. The John Smith map of 1608. Courtesy Virginia Research Center for Archaeology, Richmond.

Appamattuck (now spelled Appomattox; ap-po-*mat*-tux): on the western bank of the Appomattox River upstream from Swift Creek (Chesterfield County); 60 men (Smith) or 100 men (Strachey). The name may relate either to trap fishing or to a waiting place.[42]

Powhatan (possibly formerly po-*ha*-tan [see above]; now *pow*-a-tan): on the east side of the James River near its falls (city of Richmond); 40 men (Smith) or 50 men (Strachey). The name may mean "priest's town" or, more likely, "town at the falls."[43] The Powhatan name for the falls was Paqwachowng.[44]

Arrohateck (name now obsolete; possibly ar-ro-*ha*-teck): on the eastern side of the James River ten miles downstream from its falls (Henrico County); 30 men (Smith) or 60 men (Strachey).

Weyanock—northern territory: see above.

Chickahominy (chick-a-*hom*-a-nee): no one capital town (James City, Charles City, and New Kent counties); 200 men (Smith in 1612; 250 in 1624 account) or 300 men (Strachey). An archaeological survey has been carried out.[45] The name means "crushed corn people."[46]

Paspahegh (name now obsolete; probably *pa*-spa-*hay*): west of the mouth of the Chickahominy River (James City County); 40 men (Smith and Strachey). The name probably means "at the mouth [of a stream]."[47]

Kecoughtan (*kih*-co-tan): southeast of the mouth of Hampton Creek (city of Hampton); 20 men (Smith) or 30 men (Strachey).

Chiskiack (or Kiskiack; name now obsolete; probably *chih*-ski-ack): east of Indian Field Creek (York County): 40 or 50 men (Smith) or 50 men (Strachey). Some excavation has been carried out.[48]

Youghtanund (name now obsolete; probably *yo*-ta-nund): somewhere on the upper Pamunkey River (King William or New Kent County);[49] 60 men (Smith) or 70 men (Strachey).[50]

Pamunkey (pa-*mun*-kee): several "capital" towns near the mouth of the Pamunkey River (King William and New Kent counties); 300 men (Smith and Strachey).

Mattapanient (anglicized to Mattaponi [mat-a-po-*nye*]): somewhere on the middle reaches of the Mattaponi River (King William or King and Queen County);[51] 30 men (Smith) or 140 men (Strachey). The name may mean "landing place."[52]

Werowocomoco (name now obsolete; probably weh-ro-wo-*com*-o-co): at Purtan Bay (Gloucester County);[53] 40 men (Smith and Strachey). The capital of Powhatan's "empire" in 1607.[54] The name means "Kingshowse [town]."[55]

Piankatank (or Payankatank or Peanketank; pa-*yank*-a-tank): on the northeastern side of the Piankatank River, just downriver from Scoggins Creek (Middlesex County); 40 men (Smith in 1612; 50 or 60 in his 1624 account).

Opiscopank (or Opiscatumek; anglicized to Piscataway [pih-*scat*-a-way]; originally the accent was probably on the second syllable): on the southwestern side of the Rappahannock River, east of Lagrange Creek (Middlesex County); no warrior count—the group appears only on Smith's map[56] and in Strachey's text in passing.[57]

Nandtaughtacund (possibly anglicized to Nanzatico;[58] nan-*zat*-i-co): east of the head of Portobago Bay (Caroline County); 150 men (Smith and Strachey).

Cuttatawomen (name obsolete in that area): on the northwest side of the Rappahannock River near Popcastle Turn (King George County); 20 men (Smith and Strachey). Excavations have been carried out on or near the site.[59]

Pissaseck (name now obsolete): at Leedstown (Westmoreland County); no population given. Some excavation has been carried out.[60]

Rappahannock (or Toppahannock; rap-a-*han*-nock): apparently two capital towns, one near Neals Point (Richmond County)[61] and one somewhere near modern Tappahannock;[62] 100 men (Smith and Strachey).

Moraughtacund (anglicized to Morattico [mo-*rat*-i-co]; therefore, the original was probably pronounced mo-*raw*-ta-cund): near Simonson (Richmond County); 80 men (Smith and Strachey).

Cuttatawomen (anglicized to Corrotoman [cur-ro-*toh*-man]; therefore, the original was perhaps pronounced cuh-ta-*tah*-wo-man): southwest of White Stone (Lancaster County); 30 men (Smith and Strachey).

Wiccocomico (anglicized to Wicomico [wi-*com*-i-co]; therefore, the original was probably pronounced wi-co-*com*-i-co): north of the head of the Little Wicomico River (Northumberland County); 130 men (Smith and Strachey). The name could mean "house [or town] at the end," perhaps meaning the end of Northern Neck.[63]

Sekakawon (or Secacawoni; anglicized first to Chickacone and then to Coan; the accent was probably on the penultimate syllable): somewhere on the Coan River (Northumberland County); 30 men (Smith and Strachey). Excavations have been carried out.[64]

Onawmanient (anglicized to Nomini [*na*-min-ee]; therefore, the original may have been pronounced o-*naw*-man-i-ent): on the western side of Nomini Bay (Northumberland County): 100 men (Smith and Strachey).

Patawomeck (anglicized to Potomac [pat-*toh*-mack]; therefore, the original may have been pronounced pa-*taw*-o-meck): north of Accokeek Creek (Stafford County); 160 men (Smith in 1612 and Strachey; more than 200 in Smith's 1624 account). Excavations have been carried out.[65] The name may mean "trading place."[66]

It is difficult to ascertain ethnic identities in these groups, since the seventeenth-century English did not ask people about such things. Presumably all members of each of the above groups identified themselves by the names given. The groups which were fully integrated into Powhatan's paramount chiefdom may have begun to take on a higher-level ethnic identity as well. We do not know what the name of that sociopolitical entity may have been, although Strachey recorded the name for the territory it occupied as "Tsenacomoco."[67]

The number of groups over which the man Powhatan ruled in 1607 is a matter of controversy, thanks to the vagueness of the early English accounts. It has been traditional to place the territorial boundaries at the Potomac River on the north, the fall line (a line connecting the places where the rivers cease to be navigable because of falls) on the west, a line somewhere south of the James River on the south, and the Atlantic Ocean on the east.[68] The frontispiece of this book reflects that scheme. However, the absoluteness of the boundaries is now being questioned by most scholars, including myself. Christian Feest takes an extreme position, placing the boundaries as follows: the northern limit along a line down the center of the Middle Peninsula, the fall line on the west, a line somewhere south of the James on the south, and a line through the Virginia Capes and up the middle of the Chesapeake Bay on the east. Thus Feest considers the Indian groups of the Eastern Shore and the Rappahannock and Potomac rivers to be "Virginia Algonquians" outside the "Powhatan group," and he considers "Powhatans" only the truly hard-shelled loyalists in the paramount chiefdom.[69] Fausz also takes a limited view, though he includes the southern bank of the Rappahannock and excludes the southern bank of the lower James (the Nansemonds; I discuss them below).[70] Most other scholars, notably Turner[71] and I, put the boundaries of the "empire" in their traditional places but also note that the people farther from Powhatan's inherited heartland in the York and upper James valleys were not fully integrated into his dominions. That is, the Powhatan "empire" was extensive but not monolithic. I take this position for both historical and anthropological reasons.

The Algonquian-speaking groups along the southern bank of the Potomac sometimes followed Powhatan's orders and sometimes defied him;[72] the English received the impression that those groups were more or less part of the "empire." There is even some evidence that the Moyaones (or Piscataways) based on the Maryland side of the Potomac may have been allied with or even under the sway of the Virginia paramount chief toward the end of his life: in 1617, Powhatan was said to be visiting a town called "May—umps" on that river[73] (possibly Moyaone, near Pomonkey Creek), and we know that he never went outside his own dominions.[74] The Rappahannock River chiefdoms are less well documented in the early seventeenth century than those of any other river, but Smith's having been taken there while he was a captive[75] may indicate their membership in Powhatan's organization. The Eastern Shore Occohannocks and Accomacs were said by Smith, who met them firsthand, to "speak his [Powhatan's] language, who over all those doth rule as king."[76] Geographical distance may have made them autonomous within the "empire," but they found a nominal submission to Powhatan to be useful in keeping the peace (they were less warlike and more sedentary than the mainland peoples).[77] Altogether, it is historical evidence of this kind that points to Powhatan's strongly influencing, though not absolutely dominating, the peripheral chiefdoms. And that situation appears to be normal in human societies.

Anthropological studies of ethnicity in recent years have shown that most if not all ethnic groups, whether dominant or subordinate members of a larger society, are far from being monolithic entities. They may claim to be absolutely one united people. In reality, however, they are core-and-fringe groups, consisting of a core of people who indubitably belong to the group (and often live in its heartland) and a fringe of varying dimensions containing outsiders who have married in, core people who have drifted away, and people who have always shared some traits with insiders and some with certain outsiders ("permanent" transitionals, who sometimes form distinctive groups in themselves, e.g., Reform Jews).[78]

The fringe is always there, especially during the decades (and even centuries) while a chiefdom or a state is forming and then growing. I suggest here that the groups of the Eastern Shore, the Rappahannock River, and the southern bank of the Potomac River were in 1607 the fringe of the new ethnic identity that Powhatan had tried to create within his "empire." As such they were still technically part of his organization, for in the very early years of the English colony they told Englishmen that they belonged to it. It did not matter that they were not always obedient or that the English were later able to break their allegiance (such as it was) to Powhatan's successors. For an ethnic fringe, that is a normal state of affairs.

Some scholars have placed another Virginia Algonquian group outside Powhatan's organization, although it was less peripheral geographically than the groups already discussed. This group was the Nansemonds. No early English writer even hints that they were independent of Powhatan, though that can also be said for the Accomacs and the Patawomecks. However, Lewis Binford wrote that the Nansemonds were independent,[79] and at least one historian has followed him.[80] Binford regarded the Nansemonds as outsiders because they did not seem to him to participate in the "redistributive network of the Powhatan Chiefdom." He cites no evidence for that statement. As I shall show in chapter 6, there was no genuine redistributive chiefdom in Virginia. Thus the records are silent on Nansemond participation in a redistributive system because the records say next to nothing about *anyone's* participating in one. Binford also notes that Strachey named their chief and three of his subchiefs,[81] showing a structure that paralleled Powhatan's organization. As I shall show in chapter 7, the existence of chiefs with subchiefs was the norm throughout Powhatan's organization, so the Nansemonds' having them is as good proof of their belonging as of their being independent. After all, Strachey also gave the names of a chief and subchief among the Appamattucks,[82] who have always been regarded by scholars as members of Powhatan's paramount chiefdom. And he says elsewhere that "the Weroances of *Nandsamund Warraskoyack* and *Weanock* are now at peace with [Powhatan]."[83] The latter two groups are also regarded by everyone as having been loyalists, especially the Weyanocks, whose chief went trading into the Chowanoc area as Powhatan's representative (see chapter 6). On the whole, I think the evidence is strong that the Nansemond were part of the paramount chiefdom.

The aboriginal population of eastern Virginia is difficult to calculate, given the conflicting estimates of fighting men that we have to work with. Both Feest and Turner have dealt with the subject exhaustively and arrived at approximately the same conclusion: 13,000[84] or a minimum of 14,300[85] people in the very first years after the English arrived. The coastal plain of Virginia contains about 16,500 square kilometers (about 6,350 square miles); thus its population density was at least 0.79 persons per square kilometer (2 persons per square mile). Before the natives were exposed to European diseases, there may have been many more people than that.[86]

The distribution of settlements shown on the Smith map (fig. 1)[87] and the estimates of fighting men for the various Algonquian-speaking groups show that there were two overlapping areas on the coastal plain with a low population density. The first area is a zone along the western rim of Chesapeake Bay. The explanation is probably threefold: (1) the land had less than prime soil for horticulture, (2) it was more exposed to northeasterly storms than was land farther inland, and (3) the rim of the bay was too accessible to northern Indian enemies traveling by canoe (see chap. 7 and the Epilogue). The second zone of lower population is the entire lower half of the Middle Peninsula, occupied only by the Werowocomocos and the Piankatanks (both small groups). Here the explanation probably had to do with Powhatan himself. Werowocomoco was Powhatan's capital. He was known to be jealous and aggressive when he was in his prime, and it is likely that many of his subjects thought it best to keep their distance from him. Powhatan also lived and entertained luxuriously. One major element of Indian feasting was venison, but the deer of eastern Virginia had been seriously overhunted near the Indian towns (see chap. 2). It therefore seems likely that Powhatan discouraged occupation of the lower half of the Middle Peninsula to keep it as a hunting preserve.

I have used native words sparingly in this book. The Powhatan language was poorly recorded before it became extinct in the eighteenth century, and we are not sure of the precise meaning of most of the words that have come down to us. Siebert identified only 263 words from Strachey's list that were authentically Powhatan.[88] Even the pronunciation of words that are definitely Algonquian is uncertain, and proper presentation of them in this book would require a minor dissertation on sources at each use. I have chosen to leave for my next book an account of the Algonquian words, place-names, and personal names that are found in the Virginia records.[89]

I do, however, use two Powhatan terms frequently: *mamanatowick* or "great Kinge," the title of the paramount chief, Powhatan,[90] and *weroance*, the term for district and petty chiefs, which actually means "commander."[91] The meanings of both words are reasonably well established by early-seventeenth-century sources, and as my description of Powhatan culture proceeds, they will become clear.

Writing about the entire lifeway of a people is difficult, for every aspect of their lives is connected in some meaningful way with every other aspect. Verbal descriptions must follow an order, and it is hard to know where to begin and how to proceed when everything to be described is interconnected. Arbitrary decisions about ordering the data must be made. I have begun by listing the Algonquian-speaking groups on Virginia's coastal plain, along with their locations, to orient the reader geographically. Next I shall describe the natural area and its resources and how the people divided it (chap. 1). After that I shall explain how the people procured and prepared their food (chap. 2) and how their towns and houses and the people themselves looked (chap. 3). In chapter 4 I shall attempt a reconstruction of what the men were like and how they were trained to be that way. Then I shall describe other aspects of Powhatan culture which were less easy for short-term visitors to observe: family life and village recreations (chap. 5); social distinctions among the people (chap. 6); legal, political, and military affairs (chap. 7); and reactions to illness and the view of the supernatural (chap. 8). Finally, in the Epilogue, I shall sum up the culture of the chiefdoms on the coastal plain (which means excluding the Chickahominies) in a way more useful to political anthropologists, showing the relations among subsistence and production, political authority, and religious sanctions in Powhatan's paramount chiefdom.

The picture of Virginia Algonquian culture that I am presenting is a skewed one. Any scholar is at the mercy of the surviving documents and of the limitations of archaeology in Virginia, where preservation is usually poor and where the modern cities are growing rapidly. Most of our historical data on the region come from the James and York river basins. The chiefdoms in the "peripheral" areas are underrepresented, and they may have had differing practices. Archaeology shows that their economy matched that of their southern neighbors; the sparse documents about them indicate that their social and religious life differed in some respects, which I shall point out as I go. Nonetheless, this book about the "Powhatan Indians" represents most closely the people who lived near Jamestown, those whose lives were the first to be disturbed by the intrusion of aliens.

The Land and Its Resources

THE POWHATAN PEOPLE occupied the coastal plain of Virginia, located roughly between 36°30′ and 38°40′ north latitude and 75°35′ and 77°25′ west longitude. It includes the area east of the fall line, plus the southern half of the Delmarva Peninsula (known locally as the Eastern shore). All of these territories had at least been claimed by the man Powhatan in 1607. Because of the region's latitude, its climate, plants, and animal life are transitional between those of the "northern" and "southern" Atlantic coasts, terms that modern scholars would use but native Virginians would not.

Eastern Virginia's climate is relatively mild.[1] The ocean ameliorates the seasonal extremes, causing cooler summers and warmer winters. The average annual rainfall is forty to fifty inches, usually distributed throughout the year; however, droughts sometimes occur during the summer. Long, mild springs and falls are the rule, the former occasionally punctuated by severe "northeasters" and the latter by hurricanes. Summers are humid, with temperatures in the upper seventies to lower nineties Fahrenheit, while winters, which normally begin after Christmas, are humid and moderately cold. It is rare for the smaller waterways to be frozen solid, and only once in living memory (1918) has the harbor of Hampton Roads frozen over so solidly that people could walk on it.

Virginia's climate is not now exactly as it was when the English arrived. In 1607 the Northern Hemisphere was in a slightly cooler period known as the "Little Ice Age."[2] In that period, from about 1430 to 1850, annual temperatures averaged about 3½ degrees lower than at present, and West European records indicate that the difference was manifested mainly in more severe winters. Early English settlers' accounts of Virginia winters report more ice in the waterways than is now the norm. There would also have been fewer than today's average of 180 frost-free days per year in which to cultivate crops.

Eastern Virginia tilts downward toward the ocean. At Norfolk the land is fifteen feet or less above sea level, whereas at Richmond, ninety miles to the northwest, the elevation is nearly two hundred feet. The underlying bedrock tilts even more sharply: at the edge of the continental shelf, sixty miles east of Norfolk, it is estimated to be twelve thousand feet down; at

Norfolk it is about twenty-two hundred feet down; and from Richmond (and Fredericksburg and Washington) westward it reaches the surface in outcrops.[3] These outcrops create falls in the rivers, hence the term "fall line" for their eastern edge. The fall line marks the natural end of navigation in the rivers, necessitating the depots which eventually grew into modern cities. The soil of the piedmont, west of the fall line, consists of wind-blown and runoff-carried deposits; the soil of the coastal plain consists of all of that plus thick marine deposits laid down by the Atlantic during the many periods of higher sea level.[4]

In geological terms, Virginia's is a "flooded coastline." Chesapeake Bay is in reality the ocean-flooded valley of the Susquehanna River and its tributaries, with the separate James River valley added in the south.[5] The "rivers" and "creeks" of the coastal plain are therefore tidal estuaries (see, for example, the "creek" in fig. 2), and the tidal pulse can be felt nearly up to the fall line. The larger rivers' previous history during periods of different sea level can be seen today both in floodplains and meander scars (see fig. 3),[6] representing higher seas, and in straight stretches with steep, clifflike banks (see fig. 4), representing cutting during times of lower seas. Straight stretches with high banks reach closer to the bay in the more northerly rivers. There are four major rivers in all, the Potomac, Rappahannock, York, and James, none of them more than twenty miles from another, flowing in parallel courses from northwest to southeast.[7]

The Potomac, the most northerly as well as the largest and longest of the rivers, rises in West Virginia, crosses the fall line at Washington, D.C., and is joined only by minor tributaries as it flows toward the sea. Its width ranges from less than half a mile at Washington to seven miles at its mouth, and its depth in its lower course is about eighty feet.

The Rappahannock River rises at the foot of the Blue Ridge and crosses the fall line at Fredericksburg. It has only minor tributaries, a width on the coastal plain ranging between five hundred feet and three miles, and a moderately deep channel.

The land between the Potomac and the Rappahannock is colloquially known as the Northern Neck, while the land between the Rappahannock and the York is called the Middle Peninsula. Both of these fingers of land are pierced from the east by moderately large tidal estuaries: the Great Wicomico River cuts into high, rolling ground of the Northern Neck, while the Piankatank River and its headwaters, Dragon Swamp, slash deeply into the Middle Peninsula.

The York River has several heads, which rise in the piedmont and merge into two major heads: the Pamunkey and the Mattaponi.[8] Neither river is big enough near the fall line to have been important for English navigation, so that no cities have developed between Fredericksburg and Richmond. The land between the two rivers is known as Pamunkey Neck. The Pamun-

Fig. 2. A tidal "creek": Harris Creek, in Hampton, Virginia.

Fig. 3. A meandering river: the Mattaponi, near Walkerton, Virginia.

Fig. 4. A straight river cut through high banks: the York, near Yorktown, Virginia.

key and Mattaponi meander, but the York is nearly straight, with high banks and a channel nearly seventy feet deep; its width varies between one and two miles.

The James River, Virginia's second largest, rises in the Appalachians and crosses the fall line at Richmond. On the coastal plain it is joined by the Appomattox, Chickahominy, Nansemond, and Elizabeth rivers, three of which are still used in local shipping. The channel of the James varies from twenty feet deep near the fall line to seventy feet near its mouth. The river is less than a quarter of a mile wide at the falls and about a mile wide at Jamestown Island, after which it expands considerably. The mouth of the James is four miles wide, and because of its northeastward curve just as it joins the Chesapeake, it forms the world's largest natural harbor, Hampton Roads. The finger of land between the James and York rivers, which was the first area of Virginia settled by the English, is still known simply either as The Peninsula or the Lower Peninsula. The region south of the James is colloquially called Southside Virginia.

The Delmarva Peninsula, or Eastern Shore, is, in its Virginia extent, low and flat. Its eastern edge is bounded by barrier islands such as Chincoteague near the northern state line and by a several-mile-wide marsh as one moves south. The western edge of the peninsula is somewhat higher and is indented with numerous tidal "creeks," which still bear the names of the Indians who once lived on them.

Coastal Virginia is unique in the world for the combined size, number, and proximity of its major estuaries. Within fifty miles of the Virginia Capes, as the crow flies, there are entrances to four big "rivers," three of them capable of carrying large European craft—not to mention large Indian canoes—more than a hundred miles northwestward into the interior. Considering richness of marine food sources and the ease of communication by water, it is not surprising to find that among the chiefdoms formed by various Algonquian-speaking Indians along the Atlantic coast, the Powhatan "empire" of eastern Virginia was by far the largest.

Each "river" on the coastal plain has "creeks" or smaller "rivers" tributary to it, and these tributaries have their origin in swamps and marshes, which are freshwater or brackish, depending on their elevation and distance from the Chesapeake Bay (see fig. 5). Tributaries of the rivers usually cut into higher, rolling land away from the rivers; only to the south and east of the bay is the land flat. There are also flat areas bordering interior stretches of the major rivers; these are unflooded parts of old floodplains and contain the richest soil in eastern Virginia. These rich areas were the first to be taken by the English, which explains why the first "hundreds" on the James River (1610s) and the first land patents on the Rappahannock and Potomac rivers (1640s) were for lands well upstream, though farther by water from Jamestown. The flood plains are sometimes separated from the rolling country inland, which is colloquially called "the ridge," by a

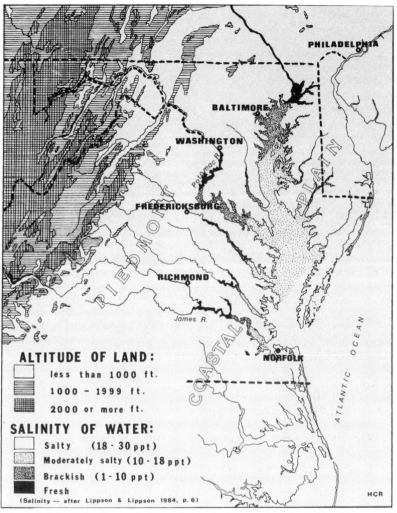

ALTITUDE OF LAND:
less than 1000 ft.
1000 - 1999 ft.
2000 or more ft.

SALINITY OF WATER:
Salty (18 - 30 ppt)
Moderately salty (10 - 18 ppt)
Brackish (1 - 10 ppt)
Fresh
(Salinity --- after Lippson & Lippson 1984, p. 6)

HCR

Fig. 5. Salinity of the Chesapeake Bay and altitude of surrounding lands. After Lippson and Lippson 1984, p. 6.

well-defined scarp. U.S. Route 17 crosses such a scarp near Camden, east of Port Royal on the Rappahannock River.

The predominant direction of storm winds carrying salt spray is from the northeast. Therefore the bay itself is bordered on its westerly and southerly rims by either beaches or large saltwater marshes (analogous to the eastern fringe of the Eastern Shore). Neither kind of environment was preferred for occupation by Indian farmers, and that is why only the Great Wicomico and Piankatank rivers had major towns located near them. (The Chesapeakes had had a major town near the bay's southern rim, on Lynhaven Bay,[9] but their capital town in the early 1600s was on the Elizabeth River, a richer and more protected site.)

Eastern Virginia's configuration of land and water provides a very wide spectrum of slightly different environments for plants, animals, and people. These environments can be classified, by the plants native to them, as follows: beach, dunes, dune forest, salt marsh, freshwater marsh, pine barrens, mixed forest, oak flats, "juniper" swamp, and "cypress" swamp.[10]

The beach zone consists of sand and salt tides and tough grasses above the high-water line. The dune zone is somewhat richer in plant life, for among the scattered live oaks, loblolly pines, Spanish oaks, and American holly trees grow persimmon trees and two species of grapes. The beach and dune zones were little used by the Powhatan Indians, as far as the records show, except when people camped there temporarily while fishing or gathering shellfish.

The dune forest is found only among the inner, higher dunes of Virginia Beach, where again Indian habitations were sparse. The predominant tree there is the loblolly pine, with yellow pine intruding in some places, and there are also laurel oaks, live oaks, Spanish oaks, black locust, and pignut hickory, the last of which produced gatherable nuts. There are also persimmons, sand blackberries, and chickasaw plums available. In the swampy area among the high dunes are cypress trees hung with Spanish moss.

The saltwater marsh zone can occur anywhere that land is covered intermittently by salt water. Various species of rushes and grasses grow there, some of which could have been used by the Powhatans in making textiles. Where the covering water is either brackish or fresh, either because of distance from the bay or because of regular, concentrated runoff of rain, cattails are common. Some Indian tribes (not necessarily the Powhatans) used the leaves of cattails for mats, ate the young shoots in the spring, and ate the rootstock either raw or dried, pounded, and made into bread.[11] Saltwater marshes were extremely valuable to the Indians because of the animal life that existed there: periwinkles (an emergency food); sand fiddlers (small land crabs); oysters, which grew along the shores as well as on shallow bars in the streams; and two kinds of clams. Hard clams (or quahogs) live on sandy bottoms, whereas the others, called maninose, or soft-shelled claims,[12] live on either sandy or muddy bottoms. The saltwater marshes, together with the streams and the bay itself, are also the habitat of blue crabs and many varieties of fish and migratory ducks.

The freshwater marsh zone occurs where very shallow fresh or slightly brackish water covers the land intermittently. In Virginia's coastal plain, the rivers become fresh in their upper reaches near the fall line, so that the shores and the heads of some streams in those areas have such marshes. The rushes and grasses in them differ from those of saltwater marshes, and in addition there are edible root plants such as cattails, arrow arum, broad-leaved arrowhead, and golden club. Animal life includes freshwater mussels and various fish, including great runs of anadromous fish (shad and herring) in the spring, and migratory ducks.

The pine barrens are a zone found all along the coastal plain of the southeastern United States, wherever the land is low and relatively flat. In Virginia, the zone occurs mainly along a very narrow margin of the bay's rim, but it becomes wider and more common to the south. Some of the wide, flat region south of the James is in the pine barrens zone.

The predominant trees of the pine barrens are loblolly, pond, and yellow pines in the lower elevations and longleaf pines in the higher inland elevations. North of the Rappahannock River, the pine barrens are dominated by the pitch pine. The pines, which also colonize cleared areas in the region before being replaced by mixed forest, make up an "upper story" of the woods that is between seventy and one hundred feet high. A "lower story" consists of shrub oak and red cedar, and below that, if the shrubs are not too thick, are broom grasses and a variety of herbaceous plants. The Powhatan Indians considered the pine barrens to be foraging territory, and not the best foraging territory at that. Neither people nor animals nor shrubs can make a good living on land coated with pine straw; there are not enough grasses for many herbivorous animals, and the pine straw does not decompose fast enough to make rich farmland. There is no record of any Powhatan village existing in the pine barrens zone.

The mixed forest is the most extensive zone in eastern Virginia and, with the oak flats zone, the richest in animals and edible plants. The mixed forest zone spreads over eastern Virginia from the fall line down to lowlands with an elevation of four feet or more above mean sea level; thus it reaches right down to the rivers' edges in most parts of the region. The vegetation of the zone includes an upper story, reaching up to one hundred feet, of pines (usually loblolly), sweet gum, southern red oak, white oak, cow oak, Spanish oak, and willow oak. In less well-drained areas, the forest also includes red maple, mockernut, and tulip trees. There is an under story of up to thirty feet consisting of American holly, persimmon, black gum, flowering dogwood, hackberry, pignut hickory, black walnut, red cedar, red mulberry, American elm, chinquapin, sassafras, black cherry, and a host of oaks. Depending on the nature of the soil, there may also be wax myrtle, high-bush blueberry, horse sugar, inkberry, and even mountain laurel. Underneath the shrub cover may grow blueberries, dewberries, and deerberries.

Areas of immature mixed forest and the pine barrens often look like jungle because of the many vines and briers climbing the trees. Also found there are a myriad of flowering plants used by various Indian tribes, probably including the Powhatans.[13] Edible roots were produced by the bugleweed (*Lycopus virginicus*), the toothwort (*Dentaria diphylla*), the downy yellow violet (*Viola pubescens*), the trout lily (*Erythronium americanum*), and the Indian cucumber root (*Medeola virginiana*), among others. The berries or leaves of the checkerberry (*Gaultheria procumbens*), the trout lily, and the sunflower (*Helianthus annuus*) could be eaten. Dyes could be made from goldenseal (*Hydrastis canadensis;* yellow) and wild indigo (*Baptisia tinctora*; blue), as well as the bloodroot or puccoon, which we know the Powhatan used (see chap. 3).

Many plants could have had medicinal uses among the Powhatans, though the following were not actually observed in use: foxglove (*Penstemon digitalis*) for a laxative and antidote to snakebite; white trillium (*Trillium grandiflorum*) for snakebite, diarrhea, and childbirth difficulties; mayapple (*Podophyllum peltatum*) as a laxative and a treatment for syphilis;[14] partridgeberry (*Mitchella repens*) for speeding childbirth (hence its nickname, "squawberry"); Queen Anne's lace (*Daucus carota*) for liver disease, chronic coughs, and dysentery; white avens (*Geum canadense*) for digestive disorders; Indian pipe (*Monotropa uniflora*)for eye problems; Bowman's root (*Gillenia trifoliata*) as an emetic; wild strawberry (*Fragaria virginiana*) for eye problems and gonorrhea; trumpet honeysuckle (*Lonicera sempervirens*) for sore throat, coughs, and asthma; trout lily leaves for swellings, ulcers, and vomiting; spotted touch-me-not (*Impatiens capensis*) for poison ivy and fungus-caused skin disorders; and Indian paintbrush (*Castilleja coccinea*) for burns. The Powhatans used several other plants, according to the English records, and these will be dealt with in chapter 8.

The Powhatans preferred the mixed forest zone to all others. It was rich in gatherable nuts and berries and in the animals which fed on them. It also extended down to the tidal rivers in many places, so that its inhabitants could have easy access to fish and shellfish. And when the forest was cleared, the soil beneath was rich, a feature with obvious appeal to a horticultural people.

The oak flats zone makes up a border for both "juniper" and "cypress" swamps, standing between the swamps and the level pine land beyond. The upper story of eighty to one hundred feet is composed of water oak, several other oaks, elm, maple, sycamore and black gum, with the lower story consisting of Spanish oak, ironwood, and tulip. There is little undergrowth. The yearly production of acorns in this zone makes it fairly rich in animal life, and the Powhatans used it as a hunting territory.

The two varieties of swamp—the "juniper," or white cedar, swamp and the "cypress," or black gum, swamp—were used by the Powhatans exclusively as hunting territories. The "juniper" swamp, which is a less wet outer swamp, has as its dominant tree the juniper,[15] with shorter species of sweet bay, red maple, American holly, and gum. On somewhat higher ground, water oak, cow oak, and beech trees appear. Cane is the dominant ground-level plant. The "cypress" swamp, the deepest and wettest kind, is the archetypal swamp, exemplified by the Great Dismal Swamp near the North Carolina border. The dominant tree is the black gum, with the bald cypress a close second; both have trunks that thicken near water level, though only the cypress has "knees." Other common trees are the red maple and the willow oak, while in swamps smaller than the Dismal Swamp the swamp cottonwood, the tulip tree, and the sweet gum can be found. There are also numerous vines such as yellow and blue jessamine, supplejack, fox grape, and horse brier. Spanish moss lives on the cypress branches in parts of the Dismal Swamp, and mistletoe is abundant in the branches of the water gums and red maples. On the ground is a wide variety of liverworts, mosses, ferns, and other plants.

A large number of native animals still live in Virginia,[16] but there were more before the English came. Some the English found so strange that they adopted Powhatan words to name them: "opossum" and "raccoon." All were theoretically edible, though the Powhatan showed a decided preference for deer and turkey.

Among the carnivores, coastal Virginia has black bears, raccoons, opossums, long-tailed weasels, mink, fishers, river otters, striped skunks, red and gray foxes, and civet cats; only the raccoons, opossums, skunks, and foxes extend their territories to saltwater areas. There were also wolves, which the English and their Indian employees later exterminated. Martens lived within range of Powhatan hunters or traders.[17] The carnivores feed on deer and other smaller mammals such as woodchucks, squirrels (four species, including flying squirrels), mice (six species), rats (two species),[18] voles (two species), moles, shrews, rabbits (two species), muskrats, and beavers. Of these, the woodchucks and beavers live inland along the freshwater streams. Reptiles on the coastal plain include lizards and snakes (black, king, garter, moccasin, rattlesnake, and copperhead), and there are several varieties of frogs and toads as well.

The only hoofed animal native to eastern Virginia is the white-tailed deer. Bison may have existed in the piedmont in small numbers through the seventeenth-century,[19] but their presence is not attested archaeologically[20] and there is no record of Powhatan warriors hunting them. The Powhatans, like other North American peoples, had no domesticated draft animals. Even when the English brought horses to Virginia, the canoe-oriented Indians took little interest in them.[21] The only domesticated animals that the

Powhatans had were dogs. These were likened by one observer to "our wariners hey dogges,"[22] i.e., rabbit-hunting dogs, and they appear to have been closely related to wolves, since they "cannot barke but howle [instead]."[23] They were used strictly as work dogs (see chap. 2).

There are a great many birds in coastal Virginia that neither modern people nor, apparently, the aboriginal people bothered to eat. There are dozens of species of songbirds, some of them new to the English settlers, for example, the cardinal. Other species were named for European birds that they resembled but were not actually related to, e.g., the robin (actually a thrush). Some "common" Virginia birds today are European imports, notably, the English sparrow and the starling. Two native birds, the Carolina parakeet and the passenger pigeon, have become extinct. Virginia also has multiple species of owls, hawks, and predatory water birds like herons, terns, and gulls. The birds that the Powhatans used for food were the larger nonpredators. The premier game bird on land was (and still is) the wild turkey; others that could have been hunted included the quail, various species of grouse, the mourning dove, and, until it became extinct, the passenger pigeon. Among the water birds, the ones available for eating were Canada geese, snow geese, and many ducks: mallards, black ducks, teals (three species), widgeons (two species), shoveler ducks, wood ducks, redheads, ring-necked ducks, canvasbacks, scaup ducks (two species), goldeneyes, buffleheads, old-squaws, scoters (three species), ruddy ducks, and merganzers (three species).

The fishing in coastal Virginia waters is naturally varied due to the number of different environments to be found in the region.[24] Strictly freshwater fish include smallmouth bass, largemouth bass, and white and black crappie. The yellow perch, channel catfish, white catfish, brown bullhead, chain pickerel, redfin pickerel, and gar prefer fresh water but venture down into slightly brackish waters, while the bluegill and pumpkinseed venture down into moderately brackish stretches of the rivers. Eels live in waters of all salinities but migrate to the ocean to spawn (i.e., they are catadromous). In the spring, the Chesapeake Bay is invaded by millions of anadromous herring and shad seeking spawning grounds in the freshwater reaches of streams and rivers. Semianadromous fish such as white perch and striped bass (also called rockfish) leave the lower, saltier part of the bay for the same spawning grounds. Sturgeons, both shortnose and Atlantic, have a longer cycle of migration: they spawn in fresh or slightly brackish water, and the juveniles then spend their first five years or so well up the rivers before slowly moving down toward the ocean, where they spend their maturity. Mature sturgeon, aged ten years or more, weigh at least 150 pounds; the largest Atlantic sturgeon on record weighed 811 pounds and was fourteen feet long.[25] These, obviously, are the biggest fish of the Chesapeake region. Many Chesapeake fish are most at home in salty water: spot, Atlantic croaker, silver perch, weakfish, spotted sea trout, red and black drum, southern and northern kingfish, bluefish, summer flounder, black-check tongue fish, and hog chokers inhabit even the shallow regions of the bay during the warm months (spot and croaker venture far up the rivers into slightly brackish waters as well) but retreat to deeper bay or ocean waters in the winter to avoid the cold. Winter flounders partially reverse this procedure: they enter the bay in the winter, staying in deep waters, and spawn in the shallows in the spring.

Fishing was better in Powhatan times than it is today. Strachey wrote in 1612 about an abundance of shad "a Yard long";[26] today's fishermen are lucky to catch an eighteen-inch specimen. In most rivers there were also sturgeons that could pull a fisherman overboard.

Shellfish were abundant in Virginia's waters before pollution decimated them. There were blue crabs, clams (six species worth gathering in salty waters and one in brackish waters), conches (two species, in salty waters), oysters (*Crassostrea virginica,* in salty and saltier brackish waters), and mussels (two species in salty waters and two genuses in fresh waters). The Powhatans are known to have eaten oysters and mussels, but they usually drew the line at horseshoe crabs.[27]

In sum, the coastal plain of Virginia has a temperate climate and enough rainfall to have allowed it, in aboriginal times, to support dense forests of varied character. Both then and in recent times the region has been a very good one for farming, gathering wild plants, hunting, and fishing. The land was capable of supporting a substantial number of Indian people, who practiced a mixed economy of collecting and horticulture. The wealth of the region and the size of its population made possible the protohistorical development of the complex political unit that the chief Powhatan ruled over.[28]

All of the Virginia Algonquian groups lived on the banks of the major rivers or their larger tributaries (see fig. 6), and they demarcated their territories in a standard eastern Algonquian way.[29] Watercourses and their drainages were at the center of Powhatan groups' territories, because of the Indians' reliance on them for food and communications. Even major rivers formed the center of tribal territories in their narrower reaches;[30] in the outer coastal plain, Indian territories centered on the tributaries of rivers (e.g., the Nansemonds).

Arable land adjacent to waterways provided living and farming areas, and the woods beyond were used for hunting and foraging. Boundaries between the territories of various groups were situated back in the relatively unpopulated forest and were correspondingly vague. From the few names that we can translate (see Prologue), Powhatan groups appear to have taken their names either from their eating habits (e.g., Chickahominy, "crushed-corn people") or from the characteristics of the places in which they lived

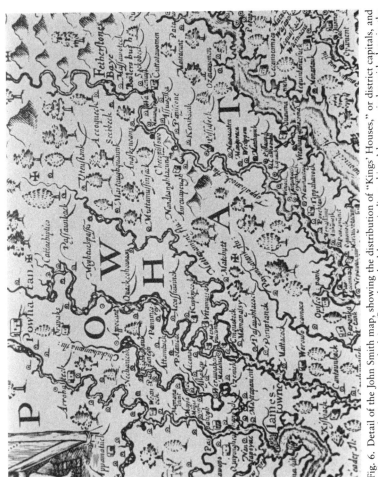

Fig. 6. Detail of the John Smith map, showing the distribution of "Kings' Houses," or district capitals, and villages on the inner coastal plain. (Barrel-vaulted houses indicate kings' houses; circles with dots in the middle are villages; trees indicate that most of the region was forested; river names are followed by "flu:" an abbreviation of the Latin word for river.)

(e.g., Accomac, "across-the-water people"). Among the chiefdoms, the name of the capital town often determined the name of both the group and the watercourse on which it was situated. The same naming principle applied to the major rivers of the region: the dominant group on a river gave the river its name. Thus in aboriginal times the James was called the Powhatan, the York was the Pamunkey (and the modern Pamunkey was the Youghtanund), and the Potomac was the Patawomeck. Names of major rivers could change with the political fortunes of the groups living on them: in 1607 the Rappahannock had its modern name, but until shortly before the English arrived, it had been known to the native people as the Opiscatumek.[31]

CHAPTER 2

Subsistence

THE POWHATANS HAD LITTLE or no economic specialization, as far as the historical and archaeological records show. Thanks to the easy access to waterways, farmland, and forest throughout eastern Virginia, each village appears to have been able to produce everything it needed except certain luxury goods (see below and also Epilogue). And the nature of Powhatan technology was such that each family with at least one male and one female adult could live in comfort entirely by its own labors.

The Powhatans were "Stone Age people" in a region where stone is not plentiful and most of the trees are hardwoods. This fact is central to an appreciation of their technology. Quartz, quartzite, and some kinds of flint for knives, arrowheads, and hatchet blades were available by trade from the fall line[1] or by gathering from certain sediments exposed along some waterways. Otherwise, before "thousands" of iron hatchets were acquired from the English (by 1610),[2] the enterprising toolmaker sometimes had to use other things to cut with: sharpened reeds,[3] spurs from wild turkeys, bills from sharp-billed birds, beaver teeth hafted in a stick (a stone projectile point hafted in bone has been found in the piedmont; see fig. 7), or the very sharp edges of mussel shells.[4] None of these materials could hold a sharp edge for long without chipping or breaking.

The nature of the Powhatans' cutting tools affected their entire way of life and resulted in the English observing two things when they arrived. First, the Powhatans' desire for iron tools was extreme and sometimes led to nasty incidents. Second, Powhatan woodworking, house building, and field clearing, which depended in part on cutting tools, looked "primitive" (see the descriptions below). This second observation, together with incomprehension of the Powhatan men's lack of involvement in farming and yet real appreciation of the Indians' mastery of their environment, gave rise to an opinion among the English that the Indian people were clever but not very industrious.

The most expensive objects, in terms of labor, that the Powhatans produced were dugout canoes. Early English sources omit mention of the wood used, but a few waterlogged cypress canoes have been found, dating to the seventeenth century, one of which bears evidence of Indian manufac-

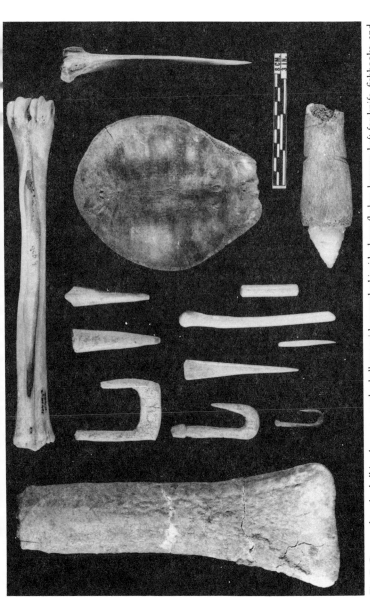

Fig. 7. Bone and turtle-shell implements: turtle-shell cup with smoothed inside; bone flesher, beamer, heft for knife, fishhooks, and awls. Although these implements came from the piedmont, they are analogous to coastal plain artifacts (except possibly the hafted knife, which is not documented for the Powhatans). Courtesy Virginia Research Center for Archaeology.

ture.[5] A big log was hollowed out either with stone axes or by gradually charring patches and scraping them away with "stones & shells."[6] The finished dugout was a long, round-bottomed, thick-walled craft that Henry Spelman described crudely as "an Hoggs trowgh."[7] The biggest canoes were about four feet deep and up to fifty feet long,[8] with a carrying capacity of some forty men. However, most canoes were smaller, with room for between ten and thirty people with baggage.[9]

Canoes were propelled by paddles or, in the shallows, by poles. They were capable of going faster than the English "barges," or larger rowing boats,[10] though sailing ships could and did outdistance them when the wind was right.[11] Besides paddles and fishing tackle, Powhatan canoe gear often included mats for a temporary shelter if a sudden squall drove the party ashore.[12] Materials for shelters were also carried on long trips, for the Powhatans did not travel on the water at night.[13]

Fishing was primarily men's work among the Powhatans, and the most common methods were angling, netting, shooting, and trapping in weirs. The only English writer to mention poisoning (actually, stunning) is one from the late seventeenth century, and he provides few details;[14] juice from "an herb" was cast on the water and caused fish to rise to the surface, where they could be caught by hand.

Likewise, the only records of using fire in a canoe to attract fish at night come from later writers. In one account of 1676,[15] the fire was made at the bow of the canoe, and the canoe was paddled through shoal water near the shore. The fish which gathered about the canoe were speared. Robert Beverley wrote, perhaps from Powhatan information or else from reading Theodore de Bry's edition of Hariot, that the fire was kept in a raised hearth in the center of the canoe, while men at either end poled the canoe ahead with the butt of their spears and, when fish appeared, speared them.[16] In yet another account, of 1687,[17] Indian fishermen caught "little fishes" in canoes manned by three persons. One tended a fire (its location is not mentioned); one knocked rapidly on either side of the canoe; and the third paddled as fast as he could. The combination of noise and fast-moving light attracted the fish and caused them to "jump into the canoe." The fish were probably mullet, colloquially called "jumping mullet."

Angling was done with rods, lines, bait, and fishhooks. The rods were "small," just "little stick[s]," with a "clift" at the end where the line was fastened.[18] There is no record of the length of line or of the bait and sinkers used. Fishhooks were either a piece of bone ground into a hooked shape (see fig. 7) or else "the splinter of a bone." The bait was tied onto the hook with the end of the line.[19] Sturgeon were also caught in the freshwater reaches of the rivers by lines lassoed around their tails; the fisherman then played his fish (while swimming, if the fish pulled him off the bank) until he could land it.[20]

The Powhatans made fishnets variously from deer sinew, "bark" (probably bast from under the bark), or Indian hemp cordage that had been spun by the women between their hands and thighs. The latter kind of cordage was also used for fishing lines, fabric making (for leather mantles), and lashings for house frames,[21] so the women gathered large quantities of it at certain seasons and kept "great . . . bundells" of it on hand "the whole yeare."[22] The makers of nets, whether men or women, were not described by the English writers, and the only reference to net making is a passing remark that the nets were "as formally braded as ours."[23] Some of the net impressions on the pottery of the region (see chap. 3) may have been made with fishnets.

Fish were occasionally shot with long arrows tied to a line; the Accomacs and possibly others also speared fish in the shallows with "staves like unto Javelins headed with bone."[24]

The remains of fish traps have been found in the shallow upper reaches of the Potomac, Rappahannock, and James, barely within Powhatan territory; they consist of stones laid close together across the river or between islands, in the shape of one or more Vs with the points heading downstream.[25] The point itself was left open, and a trap was placed in it, consisting of a long wickerwork cone, three feet wide at the opening and about ten feet long. Fish swimming downstream would be directed by the dam into the trap, where they would become helplessly wedged in by those behind them.[26]

Fish weirs in the lower Tidewater were not described in great detail by the Jamestown settlers. Pictures from the Pamlico region show reeds placed close together to make a fence (see fig. 8); however, Powhatan weirs may also have used poles and nets. Weirs were made like a maze, with "divers Chambers or bedds" to trap fish; they were more or less permanent structures, placed in water "a fathome deepe" (probably at high tide). Harvesting was done at low tide, when the fisherman paddled out in his canoe and scooped the fish out of the trap "with a nett tyed at the end of a pole."[27] The Pamlico pictures are probably inaccurate, however. The John White painting[28] has the wrong shape (see below), and the de Bry engraving based upon it, from which figure 8 is taken, shows a less incorrect "head" but also a man harvesting fish at the wrong place.[29]

The exact shape of Powhatan weirs is not recorded, and their location and flimsiness have precluded our finding archaeological evidence of them. Since Indian men built weirs on contract for Englishmen in the mid-seventeenth century, however, it may be safe to use modern fish weirs as an approximate ethnographic analogy to aboriginal Powhatan ones.[30]

Today's weirs (also called fykes or pounds)[31] are made of poles with nets fastened between them (see fig. 9). A "running net," or "hedgine," is placed at a right angle to the shore and terminates at the entrance to the first set of "bays," called large bays. Fish swimming parallel to the shore encounter the running net, and some of them, in attempting to swim around it, head

Fig. 8. De Bry's engraving of Indian fishing. Based on John White's painting of North Carolina Algonquians, the engraving repeats to a lesser extent White's mistake in depicting a fish weir (White shows only a fence and a square "head"). The people in the canoe are fire fishing, an activity normally carried on at night. Courtesy Dover Publications.

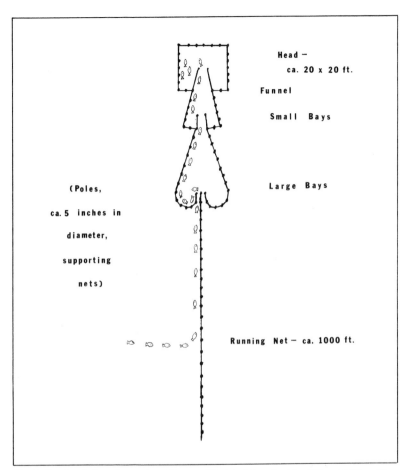

Fig. 9. Overhead view of a modern tidewater Virginia fish weir. After Elliott 1976, p. 47.

into deeper water along the net and into the large bays. Once in, they rarely find their way out and instead head into the second set of bays, called small bays. The same attempt to escape then takes them through the "funnel" and into the "head" of the pound, where they stay until the fisherman comes and dips them out with a net on a pole,[32] in the same fashion the Indians used. The Tidewater fishermen who set up pounds today install the bays carefully, for the arc has to be just right to maximize the catch. Even now, the teaching of that delicate art is done by oral tradition.[33] It is probably that fact which made seventeenth-century Englishmen willing to hire Indians to build weirs for them.

Nothing was recorded about the Powhatans' means of gathering of shellfish, but archaeologists have found large middens of oyster and clam shells throughout the Tidewater. In the freshwater reaches of the rivers, at least, mussels were taken by boys who dived for them,[34] and they were often boiled together with oysters in a stew.[35] The English colonists noted the hordes of migratory birds that visit the Cheaspeake area, but they neglected to write anything about how the Indians hunted them.[36]

Fishing activities put food in the pot with great regularity, but truly high-status food had to be hunted. Hunting supplied a large part of the protein in the Powhatan diet and provided all but the poorest Indians with clothing as well. Hunting was made an even more serious business by the social pressures put on the men. Not only did they have to prove themselves as hunters in order to be "real" men (see chap. 4), but they had to pay tribute to Powhatan in deerskins, among other valuables.[37] According to William Strachey,[38] the *mamanatowick* Powhatan expected to receive 80 percent of his subjects' "income," and payment was not voluntary. All deerskins the men acquired had to be placed before Powhatan, who took what he liked, Strachey wrote. That may be a biased view, taken by colonists anxious to paint Powhatan as a tyrant and break up his "empire," but considering the possibility of much tribute merely being claimed, not paid (see chap. 6), the figure may be fairly accurate. In theory, therefore, a man had to kill five deer in order to cover his nakedness or that of his family with one deerskin. It may have been possible to substitute foodstuffs for deerskins, but the English observers say nothing about that.

Powhatan men therefore considered hunting to be a deadly serious business as well as an "enjoyable" activity.[39] Powhatan hunters were professionals in every sense of the word, a fact that the English settlers were reluctant to appreciate. They did, however, admire the Indian men's woodcraft. Professional hunting required an intimate knowledge of the local terrain and the plant cover that attracted certain animals, knowledge that Powhatan boys began picking up as toddlers. To Strachey and his colleagues it seemed "a Marvayle how [the Indians] can so directly passe and wander in those desartes [wildernesses], sometimes three or fower dayes Iourneys," when there were no human habitations and no glimpses of the sun through the thick forest canopy to give them their bearings.[40]

Deciding where to hunt depended partly on woodsmanship and partly on what omens were observed. The omens came from the deity Okeus, the god who policed people's behavior (see chap. 8). This god would "by some knowne signe manifest himselfe, and direct them to game: they all with alacritie acknowledging that signe, and following."[41] Regrettably, no one recorded what the omens were.

The hunting of land animals was done in three principal ways: trapping, stalking, and surrounding. The first method was used for smaller game, and little was recorded about it except that beavers and otters were taken that way (the beavers for their meat and especially their tails, which were considered a great delicacy by the Powhatans).[42] Late in the seventeenth century John Banister recorded that beaver traps were smeared with a "medicine" to attract the animals;[43] he was unable to identify the substance, though he was sure it was not castoreum. It may have been a pulverized form of the "hunting root" that John Clayton identified as angelica (see below). Muskrats were taken regularly by boys, at least among the Patawomecks.[44] The other two hunting methods, stalking and surrounding, were used in deer hunting, a source of great prestige for males and a subject on which they willingly expounded to the English. No record was made of how bears were hunted, although the English knew that their meat was considered a delicacy[45] and that their oil was frequently used as a base for paints (see chap. 3).

Deer stalking was done by lone hunters and demanded tremendous skill; therefore, it probably brought a successful hunter the greatest prestige. Stalking was done with a dummy deer, made of a deerskin with the head stuffed and the body slit on one side to admit the hunter's arm. The hunter "wore" the skin as he approached a browsing deer, creeping from one tree to another. If the deer became wary and stared at him, the hunter moved the head in a natural, deerlike way, "also gazing and licking himselfe." There was an element of danger in stalking stags, who might charge the hunter. However, a skillful hunter would make deerlike movements and allay the suspicions of the deer, which would then allow the hunter to come near enough to shoot. If the hunter only wounded his victim, a chase would ensue during which the hunter pursued the animal wherever it went until it collapsed or he shot it again.[46] (Bows and arrows are described later in this chapter.)

Considering the pressure that was put on a man to bring home game, a hunter chasing a wounded deer must have been a picture of single-minded determination, heedless of where the pursuit took him or how long it went on. In later years Powhatan men got into trouble when the chase took them onto Englishmen's patented land, for the English, thinking that hunting was sport and that the hunters were trespassing, were angry that the chase did not stop at their fence lines. Bloody incidents sometimes resulted.[47] There is no evidence in the seventeenth-century English records of individual hunting territories among the Powhatans:[48] Land that was not in cultivation was common ground, at least within the boundaries of each chiefdom in Powhatan's "empire."

Surrounding, or "fire hunting,"[49] required more people and killed more deer. There were two variants. In one, a group of men would find a herd of deer and then spread themselves in a circle around it. (Banister wrote later that men set fires in a circle "four or five miles" in diameter, presumably to be certain of enclosing a herd.)[50] They built fires between their stands and begin shouting. (Banister added that then "they step Ten or Twelve Paces in, each at his due distance, & put fire to the Leaves again, to accelerate the Work. This they Repeat till the Circle be almost clos'd.") Panicked, the game fled the fires, only to find that between the fires were shouting, shooting men. Soon the deer would be running in a circle (Banister spoke of a small circle of men and fires in which the herd stood, "panting and almost stifled with heat and smoke"), while the men picked them off one by one until the herd had been killed. The bag, according to John Smith, might be "6, 8, 10, or 15 at a hunting" (Strachey says "in a morning"), and in the annual fall hunt the hunters would move on to another area the next day and go through the same procedure again.

The other variant of surrounding was used in the lower Tidewater, when a herd of deer was sighted near a point of land. The animals' escape to landward was cut off, and they were then driven down to the point and out into the water, where men in canoes moved in for the kill.[51]

The daily pressure put on Powhatan men to hunt successfully put a corresponding pressure on local populations of game. Deer of both sexes and all ages were killed, without regard for conservation,[52] until few deer were left anywhere near most Indian towns. Strachey said that all animal species felt the pressure, for "at all tymes and seasons they destroy [deer] . . . Hares, Patridges, Turkeys, fatt or leane, young or old[,] in eggs[,] in breeding tyme, or however, they devowre, at no tyme sparing any that they can katch in their power."[53] However, the only animal that seems to have declined seriously by 1607 was the deer.

Turner[54] has calculated deer populations and human pressures on them and concluded that deer began to be overhunted in the lower Tidewater as early as the late Archaic Period. This seems the place to respond to Calvin Martin,[55] who postulated a Postcontact change in Indian attitudes that allowed for serious overhunting in the fur-trade era. The evidence from eastern Virginia, allowing for English bias, shows no such change. Powhatan hunters held a fairly exploitive attitude toward animals, at least from the very earliest years of the Jamestown colony. That attitude was probably exacerbated by the demands of a newly formed paramount chiefdom. But neither modern-style conservation nor a fear of punishment by animal powers for overhunting was recorded at any period for the Powhatans.

The Powhatans solved the problem of hunted-out territory from year to year by organizing large-scale hunts near the fall line in the winter, after the crops were in and the thanksgiving festivities had concluded (see chap. 8).[56] The hunts' proximity to Siouan territory and the probability of some trespassing may help explain the enmity that existed between the two peoples (see chap. 7); the warfare, in turn, helped keep the area a buffer-zone hunting territory for both sides.[57]

Whole families left their towns in the late fall and went westward, to areas where the Powhatan settlements were farther apart and the deer had not been overhunted. Decisions about where to hunt were made each morning by the "principall men" of each group that participated; for the six-group hunt mentioned below, twenty to thirty men were involved.[58] While the men hunted by day, the women and children carried equipment, set up temporary households at previously arranged places (probably on the way to the site of the following day's hunt), and processed the carcasses as the men brought them in.[59] Living conditions in the camps closely approximated those in the towns. Housing was similar (see chap. 3), and so was the cuisine, for the women brought their mortars and supplies of dried corn and acorns and (probably) cooking pots into the wilderness with them.[60]

Some communal hunts involved two or more Powhatan groups. John Smith was captured in 1607 when he blundered into a hunt that involved three hundred men from Paspahegh, Chickahominy, Youghtanund, Pamunkey, Mattaponi, and Chiskiack.[61] The number of groups involved and the fact that the last four were in the *mamanatowick's* personal inheritance make one wonder whether that particular hunt was being conducted for the benefit of Powhatan.

Dogs were used only in hunting wild turkeys and other "land fowles," as far as the English records show. The dogs were purely working dogs, not pets, for the Indians were observed to "keep nothing tame about them."[62] Turkeys were lured close to a hunter with callers made of turkey wing bones.[63]

The English colonists neglected to observe whether the Powhatans had rituals connected with hunting. It is very probable that they did, considering that deer play an important role in their creation story (see chap. 8). Other Algonquian speakers are known to practice conservation through ritualistic rather than practical means,[64] and it is likely that the Powhatans did likewise. However, the English settlers were attuned to Indian lifeways only to the extent of one of them noticing that the Powhatans possessed a "hunting root." In the 1680s Clayton, a minister with a deep interest in medicinal plants, heard through an acquaintance about an Indian hunting deer with the root, which he identified as angelica:

The Indian contrary to his usual custom went to windward of [the deer], &
sitting down upon an old trunk of a Tree, began to rub the root betwixt his
hands, at which the Deer toss[ed] up their heads & snuffing with their noses
they fed towards the place where the Indian satt, till they came within easy
shot of him whereupon he fired at them, & killed a large buck.[65]

For a Powhatan hunter, full shooting gear consisted of a bow, arrows, a
quiver, and a wrist guard and shooting glove (see fig. 10).[66] Bows were
made either of witch hazel or of locust;[67] English records say nothing of
sinew backing or other strengthening devices. As with other forms of
Powhatan woodworking, the wood for a bow was worked by scraping it
with a shell.[68] Bowstrings were made from deer gut or from twisted thongs
of deer hide.[69]

There were at least two kinds of arrows. John Smith wrote of arrows
made of "straight young sprigs" headed with a bone head two or three
inches long, which were used against squirrels and birds,[70] and George
Percy observed that arrows could be made of "Canes or Hasell."[71] Smith
also noted that some arrows were in several parts: a reed shaft, a wooden
foreshaft, and a head.[72] Arrowheads were variously made of "splinters" of
"christall" or stone, wild turkey spurs, sharp bird bills, splinters of deer
bone, "an oysters-shell," or "the ends of Deeres hornes."[73] Stone arrowheads were described in detail only by Strachey, who said they were "in the
forme of a heart" barbed and jagged.[74] The majority of points from that period that have been found archaeologically are small and triangular.[75] Stone
projectile points were "made" (probably finished after knapping) "quickly"
with a small piece of antler that hung from the hunter's wrist guard, and
they were bound onto their shafts or foreshafts with deer sinew and then
glued with a waterproof glue made of deer antlers boiled down into jelly.[76]
The overall length of Powhatan arrows was about forty-five inches,[77] and
they were fletched with turkey feathers cut to shape with a sharpened reed
knife.[78] The nock of the arrow was grated in, using a hafted beaver tooth.[79]
Arrohateck hunters, at least, used poison on their arrows, but the sole Englishman to write about the practice identified the source of the poison only
as a root.[80]

Powhatan bows were strong enough to shoot "forty yards . . . leuell, or
very neare the mark, and 120 [yards] is their best at Random."[81] They were
also better for piercing English wooden shields than English pistols were.[82]
They were less impressive compared with English muskets, which could kill
men in armor at two hundred paces, kill unarmed men at six hundred
paces, and shoot several hundred yards at random,[83] but they could be re-
loaded much faster than muskets could.

Quivers are only implied in English descriptions of Powhatan hunting
gear.[84] They probably resembled those of the Carolina Algonquians, which
were tubular containers more than two feet long[85] and made of "small
rushes."[86] Wrist guards (called "bracers" or "vambraces" in the seven-

Eiafintomine?

Fig. 10. Eiakintomino in Saint James's Park, one of two Indian figures on a lottery broadside of 1615–16, adapted from a lost original (Feest 1967a, pp. 8–13). Another copy, in watercolor, is in the Michael van Meer autograph album, now in the Edinburgh University Library (Feest 1972, p. 305; illustration in Feest 1978, p. 260). Courtesy Society of Antiquaries of London.

teenth century) and probably also shooting gloves were made of the tanned hides of wolves, raccoons, or foxes.[87]

Once the Powhatans had killed animals with their weapons, the carcasses had to be divided and butchered and the skins tanned. Early-seventeenth-century English visitors to the Indian towns recorded nothing of Powhatan customs in these matters, with one exception: among either the *mamana-towick*'s courtiers or the Potomac *weroance*'s, tanning of hides was a summer occupation for men.[88] Allotting that task to men was unusual in the New World, and Spelman was probably wrong. Later in the seventeenth century Banister, who knew the Appamattucks, the Souian-speaking Monacans, and possibly the Pamunkeys, wrote that tanning was women's work and that deer brains were used in tanning that animal's hide.[89]

Foraging activities went on practically year round on a fairly large scale. A substantial number of Powhatan recipes called for wild plant foods, and the bulk of Powhatan technology used plant materials. Because of the intermittent and far-flung nature of the activity, however, as well as the sex difference between the female foragers and the male foreign visitors, English observers learned little about Powhatan uses for wild plants.

The gathering of useful plants required a detailed knowledge of which parts of which plants could be used for what purposes, in what season the plants ripened or reached their peak of usefulness, and where each species grew locally. Cultural anthropologists working with twentieth-century foraging peoples have found a working list of a hundred plant species to be not uncommon. Therefore, a competent Powhatan gatherer of plants probably required long training and practice, as well as a keen memory. It is a pity that the English did not see more.[90]

Dealing with food plants, wild or domesticated, was primarily women's work among the Powhatans. Medicinal plants were gathered by men (see chap. 8), and tobacco cultivation was probably also their prerogative (no Virginia English source says so specifically). The Powhatans practiced a mixed economy of horticulture and collection of wild plant and animal foods. The importance of women in producing food—especially a high-prestige plant food like maize—probably guaranteed them a high status in society (see chap. 5). However, the amount of maize that the women produced and the length of time it lasted each year are open to dispute.

The Powhatan diet varied considerably in the course of a year:

> In March and April they live much vpon their [fishing] Weeres, and feed on Fish, Turkeys, and Squirrells and then as also sometymes in May [John Smith adds: "and Iune"] they plant their Feilds and sett their Corne, and live after those Monethes most[ly] of[f] Acrons [*sic*], Wallnutts, Chesnutts, Chechin-quamyns and Fish, but to mend their dyett, some disperse themselues in smale Companies, and live vpon such beasts as they can kill, with their bowes and arrowes. Vpon Crabbs, Oysters, Land Tortoyses, Strawberries, Mulberries and such like; In Iune, Iuly, and August they feed vpon the rootes of Tockohow-

berryes [wild potatoes], Grownd-nuts, Fish, and greene Wheat [corn], and
sometyme vpon a kynd of Serpent, or great snake of which our people likewise vse to eate.[91]

A later writer added that turtles were considered "delicate meat," while the
meat of snakes, especially rattlesnakes, was highly esteemed.[92]

The Powhatans made two major dispersals out of the towns, one for foraging while the crops in the fields were ripening, and one, as noted, for
hunting in the late fall. Their pattern resembled New England Algonquian
subsistence practices. Carville Earle has, as part of a fascinating piece of
detective work on disease in the Jamestown colony,[93] postulated that the
Indians dispersed in the summer at least in part because they knew to avoid
the middle reaches of the rivers (the oligohaline zone) in the summer. At
that time the water is salty-brackish and relatively stagnant, since the tides
more than equalize the diminishing freshwater flow from the mountains;
the water is also prone to retain human effluents, thanks to the effect of a
"salt plug" slightly downriver.[94] Earle credits Smith with learning, from observing the Indians, to disperse and rely upon fresh water elsewhere during
that season, as shown by his sending people to establish new settlements at
the falls of the James and on the fringe of the Nansemond territory in 1609.
Given the well-documented Powhatan focus on food procurement, however, and also given the correspondence of their annual round with that of
even much more northerly Algonquians whose rivers differed greatly from
the James, I doubt that the Powhatans had consciously any idea of dispers-
ing in the summer for sanitary reasons. Strachey's wording also indicates
that Indian towns that were near brackish or salty rivers were located near
springs for drinking water throughout the year,[95] not just in the summer, as
Earle says.[96] Smith, for his part, probably sent his people so far afield because the Indians living closer to Jamestown were all too obviously hostile
by 1609.

The leanest time of year was late spring and early summer, when the previous fall's stores of corn were gone and the spring's berry crop was not yet
ripe. People became thin at such a time: "It is strange to see how their
bodies alter with their diet, even as the deare and wilde beastes they seeme
fat and leane, strong and weake."[97]

If we can believe the English, the Powhatan diet contained domesticated
plant foods for only about half the year. If this is true, it may have been due
to the tribute demands of Powhatan and his petty *weroances,* to a preference for a varied diet, or to both. On the other hand, Turner[98] has calculated that the Powhatans actually raised more corn than the English real-
ized (an estimated 75 percent of their annual subsistence needs). They hid
the full extent from the English colony, which was perennially hungry and
usually dependent on the Indians. However, Turner's figures are based on
field sizes that are at the high end of the Powhatan spectrum, whereas I feel

that ordinary people cultivated smallish fields (see below). In any case, there was always a shortfall of some kind for the ordinary people. Only the *mamanatowick* and his subordinate *weroances* had domesticated plant foods available for feasts all year.[99]

There is ample evidence that the English colonists tried to persuade the Indians to raise more crops, both for trade and for their own consumption (a "civilizing" effort),[100] and that the Powhatans refused to cooperate. The men would not have been willing to do women's work (sex roles were rigidly separated; see chap. 5), and the women probably preferred to spend the traditional amount of their working time in gathering the wild foods that their politicians did not want and their Indian and English enemies could not destroy easily.

Powhatan fields were square and were usually located near the houses of the women who worked in them. English witnesses disagree about their extent. Strachey and Spelman reported that the majority of fields were small, varying between one hundred and two hundred feet square.[101] Smith said Indian gardens were "small" and estimated their sizes at from twenty to two hundred acres,[102] the word "acres" appearing in his later edition but not his first, so that he may originally have meant "feet" and thus have been in accord with the other witnesses. *Weroances'* fields, which were tended by whole towns (see chap. 6), were larger. A field belonging to the *weroance* of Weyanock was estimated at one hundred acres.[103] Ownership of fields was apparently based on usufruct (see chap. 7).

The practice of building houses near the fields resulted in a dispersed settlement pattern, unless nearness to enemies, such as those across the fall line, necessitated a stockaded town, as at Patawomeck. The practice of letting fields go fallow while clearing and working others resulted in a continual movement of families. Turner[104] has estimated that Powhatan fields had to be left fallow after about two years, because of a decline in fertility caused by leaching, weed infestation (and rudimentary tools to combat it), and the establishment of insect pests in cleared soil after the first year of cultivation. A palisaded town would have to move whenever most of its fields in cultivation were inconveniently far away. In dispersed settlements, the moving was probably done gradually, family by family. The net effect in either case was that whole villages within groups' territories changed location. Snow has estimated that Eastern Woodland towns moved at intervals of five to twenty years,[105] and Iroquoian data indicate that fifteen to twenty years was normal.[106] Powhatan "towns" and the local names that applied to them were therefore temporary entities.

Clearing land for gardens was arduous work in which men probably participated. English observers have left us incomplete descriptions, which seem to concern differing methods of clearing virgin forest and reclaiming old plots gone fallow. Both kinds of clearing, however, required preparation long in advance of planting, a standard procedure in slash-and-burn farming. Clearing virgin forest was described by Spelman. Small trees were easily killed by girdling them with fire, but larger trees were cut down, presumably either by chopping with a stone ax (see fig. 11) or by alternate burning and chipping away of the charcoal, "sum half a yard" above ground.[107] The entire field was later burned over.[108] Old gardens overgrown with saplings were reclaimed by debarking or simply chopping all around the trees' roots. The next year, when the trees were dead, people uprooted them with levers of "crooked peece[s] of wood" and planted crops in the soft earth of the depressions left by the trees' roots.[109] The trees themselves were presumably dragged away and used for firewood.

Powhatan fields must have looked messy by European (and Anglo-American) standards, for they were peppered with burned tree stumps and had surfaces that were far from smooth. But to the Powhatans, who lacked draft animals, plows, and fertilizer,[110] a "garden" was just a temporarily worked space where enough of the forest cover had been removed to allow the sun to reach the ground.

All the other farming tasks were women's work, in which children and, possibly, old men were expected to help.[111] There is only one (ambiguous) record of Powhatan men cultivating a separate tobacco patch by themselves: at Paspahegh "there was a Garden of Tobacco, and other fruits and herbes."[112] The only early-seventeenth-century reference to tobacco's growing and preparation is a statement that it was dried over a fire, after which it was smoked predominantly by married men.[113]

Planting was done by digging holes between the tree stumps with "a crooked peece of woode being scraped on both sides in fation of a gardiners paring Iron" and then dropping in several corn kernels and beans.[114] (This wooden digging tool was rapidly replaced by English iron hoes.)[115] The planting holes were spaced about four feet apart.[116] From each hole, a corn plant emerged first; by the time it had a good stalk, the beans came up and twined around it.[117] Four kinds of corn were planted, two that ripened late (flint corn and she-corn) and two that ripened early (in May), so that two crops per year could be raised.[118] The beans were of two kinds: a larger sort like chick-peas and a smaller sort the Powhatans called *assentamens* and the English called "pease."[119] Squash, including gourds and muskmelons, and "maracocks," or passionflower plants (a semidomesticate), were planted between the corn-and-bean clumps and allowed to run along the ground,[120] giving Powhatan fields an even more cluttered appearance.

Corn and beans were planted each month from April through mid-June, so that in a good crop year there was ripe corn to eat from August (or May, according to Beverley[121]) through October. Each cornstalk bore two ears, on the average, with between two hundred and five hundred kernels per ear.[122] The squash ripened from July until September, and the passion fruit ripened from August through October.[123] With berries and nuts also available, late summer and early fall were times of plenty for the Powhatans.

Fig. 11. Stone cutting implements. Found in Suffolk (formerly Nansemond County). Old Dominion University Collection, Norfolk, Virginia.

Weeds flourish in Virginia, so weeding had to be frequent.[124] The Powhatans may also have followed the North Carolina Algonquian practice of putting children into small covered scaffolds in the fields, to serve as live scarecrows.[125] In the late seventeenth century Banister[126] recorded practices that may or may not have been aboriginal:

> They keep the crows from their corn, by tying strings of bark from pole to pole round the field, which is all the fence the outward [frontier] Indians make where there are no hoggs: they also hang Gourds on the top of poles, in which build small birds, of the swallow or Martin kind, that . . . will not let them rest near the place of their aboad."

Halfway through the corn's growing season the women and children would "hill it about like a hop-yard,"[127] that is, they would pile earth around the base of each cornstalk to preserve moisture during a potentially dry summer. When the crops were ready to be harvested, they were gathered into hand baskets, the loads being transferred into large baskets and eventually stored in huge baskets in the houses[128] or in storage pits "in the woods,"[129] for use later in cooking.

Like many other horticultural people, the Powhatans had a fairly sophisticated numbering system, which allowed them to evaluate their harvests. According to Smith, there were numbers from one to ten, after which "they count no more but by tennes" to one hundred; there was also a word for "one thousand."[130] However, a later English writer remarked that "their numbering beyond an hundred is imperfect, and somewhat confused."[131] The Powhatans' calendar was relatively simple and was based on the annual cycles of the plants around them. They recognized five seasons:

> Their winter some call *Popanow* [later writers say Cohonks[132] or Copahunks[133]], the spring *Cattapeuk*, the sommer *Cohattayough*, the earing of their Corne *Nepinough*, the harvest and fall of the leafe *Taquitock*. From September untill the midst of November are the chiefe Feasts and sacrifice.[134]

The list above reflects the fact that the Powhatans considered their year to begin with the return of the migratory geese in the early winter.[135] People's ages were calculated by "returnes of the Leafe,"[136] although John Rolfe, the husband of Pocahontas, told Samuel Purchas that they "reckon[ed] euery Spring and euery Fall seuerall [separate] yeeres."[137] Travel time was calculated as "day's journeys," reflecting the practice that even on canoe trips the Powhatans camped ashore at night. The priest Uttamatomakkin, crossing the Atlantic in 1616 with Englishmen who sailed day and night, added up twice as many "days" as the English calculated for the trip.[138]

Little was recorded of Powhatan astronomical knowledge, beyond the fact that they called the constellation around the North Star the "great bear" (Manguahaian).[139] However, they recognized lunar months,[140] such as "the Moon of Stags, the Corn Moon, the first and second Moon of *Cohonks*, Etc." and adjusted the names in order to "make them return again by the same name."[141] They also believed that the world was circular and flat, like a plate, with themselves in the center.[142]

Around 1670 John Lederer observed that some Powhatan groups had a "winter-count." Painted skins were divided into sixty sections, each one representing a year and the whole resembling a "wheel." The "wheel" may have been a circle divided into sixty sections, which would require fine painting technique, or it may have consisted of sections arranged in a spiral, as in Plains Indian winter counts.[143] In each year's section a drawing was made representing the most remarkable occurrence of that year. One section on the Pamunkey chiefdom's wheel showed the arrival of the English, who were represented by "a swan [whose white color represented the paleness of English skin] which expelled smoke and fire from its beak." These "hieroglyphic wheels" were kept in temples and called "*Sag Ko Ko K. Quejacasong*, which means *the memory of the gods*."[144] The wheels may not have been in use in the early seventeenth century; Lederer is the only European writer of any period to mention them. The Powhatans possessed other, simpler mnemonic devices: notched sticks,[145] "little sticks" as a tally (recorded for the Eastern Shore only),[146] knotted strings, and corn kernels or small stones in a group.[147] There were also "altar" stones,[148] which were placed away from the towns "where they have had any extraordinary accident, or incounter"; the events memorialized by the stones were related orally by one generation to the next.[149]

Food gathered in any season could be prepared in a variety of ways. Foods taken on long-distance trips consisted of dried meat, which was eaten with "bears oyl, [or] oyl of Acorns," and "Rocka hominy, that is Indian corn parched & beaten to flower."[150] Men who journeyed away from home usually expected to live mainly off the game they could shoot, and if they failed to find game and their provisions ran low, they "girded up their Bellies" (i.e., tightened their belts) and kept on walking.[151]

Nuts, berries, oysters, and the juice from green cornstalks were often consumed raw. The cornstalk juice, which was sucked out, was as sweet as cane juice.[152] All other foods were cooked. Oysters, clams, and mussels were roasted; fish were roasted, ungutted and unscaled,[153] either on a "hurdle" (a pole-and-slat frame)[154] over the fire or else on a spit. Drying these foods was accomplished simply by placing them farther from the fire. Fish and shellfish alike were smoked as they were dried, a necessary combination in a humid climate; thus prepared, they kept for "a month or more without putrifying."[155] The Powhatans dried oysters and mussels by hanging them "vpon strings . . . in the smoake, thereby to preserve them all the year."[156] Shellfish were also boiled in a bisque that was thickened with cornmeal, while fish were frequently boiled in a stew, the broth of which, like the broth of meat stews, was drunk with relish.[157]

Venison was the Powhatans' favorite meat, and it is the only meat whose preparation the English described in any detail, a fact that reflects the early colonists' status as honored guests in the Indian villages. Like fish, venison could be either dried in smoke or boiled for immediate consumption. Among the groups of the upper James River, however, preparing fresh venison for eating involved roasting and then boiling.[158] An English observer later in the seventeenth century wrote of "Venison *barbecuted,* that is wrapped up in leaves & roasted in the Embers."[159] Another later observer mentions a very good stew made with deer's heads and entrails, "which they put in the pot all bloody."[160]

The favorite and most prestigious plant food used by the Powhatans was maize, for it was a domesticated plant that produced abundantly for the amount of labor expended on it. Possession of corn in great quantities in late winter and early spring, when most people's stores were gone, was a status symbol (see chap. 6). When corn was in season, however, everyone ate it in quantity.

Fresh green corn was either roasted in the fire and eaten or beaten to flour in a mortar, rolled in cornhusks, and boiled "for a daintie."[161] Any corn that had not ripened by the end of the harvest season was gathered and roasted in hot ashes, "the heat thereof drying it." It was then kept for winter, when it was boiled with beans "for a rare dish, they call *Pausarowmena.*"[162]

The Powhatans were less fond of the taste of fully ripened corn. However, they let a substantial part of their crops ripen, both for seed and for ease in drying for winter. The ears to be dried were laid out on thick mats in the sun by day and piled up and covered by night. When dry, they were shelled by women working them "betwene ther hands"; the kernels went into "a great Baskett."[163] Dried corn would keep almost indefinitely, but it had to be soaked overnight "in hot water" (or lye, according to later writers) before being cooked.[164] Perhaps it was for this reason, if not also for ritual ones, that women kept fires burning continually in their houses.[165]

After dried corn had been soaked, it could be boiled gently for ten or twelve hours to make hominy,[166] boiled with beans, or made into meal. The Powhatans normally pounded corn into meal in a wooden mortar,[167] sieved it to discover how many hard nubs were still left, and then pounded the nubs again. The sieve was a loosely woven basket, and a wooden platter beneath it caught the flour.[168] Most of the kernels became meal in this process, but there were always hard pieces left over in the mortar. These pieces were saved, cleaned by winnowing, and then boiled in water for three or four hours. The result was "a straunge thick pottage, which they call *usketahamun;*[169] and is their kynd of Frumentry."[170]

Cornmeal was either used to thicken stews or made into bread.[171] Some women, "more thrifty then cleanly," stretched their cornmeal by burning corncobs to powder, called *pungnough,* and adding it to the meal.[172] Cornmeal and water were mixed to make dough, which was then fashioned by hand into one of several shapes. "Flatt broad" cakes were either baked in the ashes of the fire (and washed off with clean water before eating) or boiled in water, in which case both bread and water were consumed.[173] Some of the people on the James River worked their dough into "round balls and Cakes," boiled them thoroughly in water, and then laid them on a smooth stone to harden.[174] These dumplings might be "of the bignesse of a tenise ball."[175] Baked bread was eaten either "dry" or greased with deer suet.[176] For a saltier taste, bread and meat were boiled in water to which ashes had been added, the ashes coming from the roots of hickory, stickweed, or any other plant that would produce a salty ash.[177]

Beans were generally boiled, both varieties together, with corn added. This dish, the ancestor of our succotash, was a staple of the Powhatan diet.[178] When it was made with roasted unripe corn, it was called *pausarowmena* and was usually eaten with relish during the winter.[179] A pot of succotash was kept ready so that family members could dip in whenever they were hungry.[180]

Squash was boiled for eating; often it was added to "walnut milk" (see below) to "make a kynd of toothsome meat."[181] There is no contemporary record of whether any of these boiled vegetables were seasoned or of how passion fruits were prepared. A later writer says the Indians had no salt and speaks of the ashes of stickweed being used to season meat.[182] There were probably wild greens that Powhatan women could have used to season their stews;[183] wild onions also grow plentifully in cleared ground, though Strachey's informants, at least, could "not abyde to eate of them."[184]

The most succinct list (though not a complete one) of wild plants eaten by the Powhatans was written by Gabriel Archer: Virginia's soil "naturally yeeldes mulbery trees, Cherry trees, vines [in] aboundance, goosberyes, strawberyes, hurtleberryes, Respesses, ground nuttes, scarrettes [carrots], the roote called sigilla Christi, certaine sweet thynn shelled nuttes, certain ground aples, a pleasant fruit."[185]

Red mulberry trees (*Morus rubra*) grow naturally in Virginia. The Powhatans liked their fruit so well that they sometimes built their houses near the trees.[186] The berries ripen in May and June, at which time the Indians ate "wheate [corn] beanes and mulberryes sodd [boiled] together."[187]

Wild strawberries (*Fragaria virginiana*) grow in grassy areas and ripen in April. There are also several kinds of wild plums in Virginia, which the English settlers called both plums and cherries, as well as wild raspberries, grapes, and crabapples. The Powhatans ate gooseberries either raw or boiled,[188] and perhaps they did the same with the other fruits. Persimmons (*Diospyros virginiana*)[189] can be eaten raw only if they are fully ripe; the Powhatans are known to have dried them on "hurdles on a mat" like prunes.[190]

Another fruit was called *ocoughtamnis* by the Powhatans, later Anglicized to *cuttanemons*. This was "a Berry . . . very much like vnto Capers" that was part of a species of arum.[191] The berries were sun dried in the summer for storing, and before they could be eaten they had to be boiled "neare halfe a daye, for otherwise they differ not much from poyson."[192] The tuberous root of the same[193] or a related arum species (*Peltandra virginica*, arrow arum or flag root), called "*Tockawhoughe*,"[194] became known to the English as "tuckahoe," or wild potatoes. Tuckahoe grows in abundance in freshwater marshes, and in the months before the corn became edible, it was a staple of the Powhatan diet. The roots were either sliced and sun dried or laid on a bed of leaves, covered with earth or sand, and baked for twenty-four hours, to rid them of the acid they contained. Then, pounded into meal and boiled or baked, they made a passable bread.[195] Groundnuts (*Apios americana*) were also gathered and consumed.[196]

Several species of nuts were gathered and processed each fall; because they contained oil, they were used in medicines as well as food (see chap. 8). According to the English settlers, the Powhatans used the acorns of only one species of oak; the species is uncertain, for descriptions say only that its bark was "more white" than that of other oaks. The tannic acid was leached out of this oak's acorns by boiling them for half a day "in several waters." The meats were then made into bread "and otherwise" prepared. The oil boiled out of them, called *monohominy*, was stored in gourds for medicinal purposes.[197] The oil, after being boiled out in a lye solution,[198] was also consumed with cornmeal on journeys.

The chestnut and its close relative, the chinquapin,[199] produced nuts greatly favored by the Powhatans for eating. Chinquapins were eaten off the tree as "a great daintie."[200] Chinquapins and chestnuts were boiled together four or five hours to make "both broath and bread, for their chiefe men, or at their greatest feasts."[201] Hazelnuts, on the other hand, were not eaten.[202]

English observers wrote of several kinds of walnuts, which in reality were one walnut species (*Juglans nigra*); a bitter pecan; and several unidentified species of hickory nut. The nut of one kind of hickory was used to make oil for medicinal purposes, and another kind of hickory nut was used to make "walnut milk," or *powhicora*.[203] The nuts were first broken up with stones (see fig. 14, chap. 3),[204] after which they were dried "againe upon a mat over a hurdle." Then they were beaten fine in a mortar, and water was added to make the shell matter sink to the bottom. A later observer wrote that the mixture was then boiled until it was thick, like "hasty pudding."[205] "Walnut milk" was a great delicacy among the Powhatans,[206] who occasionally added squash to the mixture to make it especially good.[207]

The seeds of numerous wild grasses were gathered, ground into flour and made into bread, probably by either baking or boiling. English accounts are too vague to allow identification of the species, but bread made from the ryelike seeds of the grass the Powhatans called *mattoume* was considered a treat when "buttered with deare suet."[208] John Clayton wrote later in the century that the squeezed juice of wood sage or wild marjoram was consumed as a "diet drink."[209]

The English recorded very few dinner menus from their visits to Powhatan towns. A feast given at Arrohateck on May 23, 1607, included mulberries, boiled corn and beans, corncakes, and venison which had been roasted and then boiled. Two days later another Arrohateck dinner featured cornbread, "parched meale," a boiled concoction of beans, strawberries, and mulberries, and a cooked "land turtle."[210] A more complete account of feasting menus is given in chapter 6. Liquid refreshment at all Powhatan meals was either water[211] or broth, and people preferred their water lukewarm.[212]

From these fragmentary sources alone it is difficult to reconstruct statistics on crop yields and calorie counts, which are of interest to economic anthropologists. Turner has used field size, maize productivity records, human population figures, and the like to reconstruct Powhatan subsistence. He has calculated that maize cultivation and weir fishing alone could have yielded 78 percent to 93 percent of the Indians' caloric needs annually,[213] though as mentioned before, his estimates of the size of Powhatan fields are much more generous than mine.

The Powhatans seem to have been well nourished for most of the year, except for the lean times in late winter and early spring. According to English observers, the *mamanatowick* and "some others" (probably his *weroance* subordinates) were "provident," but most people preferred to live more or less from hand to mouth, eating their fill when food was available and worrying about the future later, a common feeling among competent foragers.

Powhatan eating habits were irregular: they ate "night & day" when they were hungry and could get food, and if they could not find food, they were "patient of hunger."[214] There was an etiquette for eating, at least among the "better sort" of Powhatans, when they sat down to a communal meal. Powhatan and some of his *weroance*s and their families washed their hands before and after eating, the washing being converted into a ceremony in Powhatan's case (see chap. 6). The washing made sense among a people who had only knives and ladles as eating utensils.[215] A thanksgiving prayer was also proper before eating. Strachey heard it but forgot it before he could write it down, but he noted that the first bit of food taken was thrown into the fire at the same time,[216] presumably as an offering.[217] Spelman, on the other hand, remembered Indian diners murmuring their prayer of thanks after meals.[218]

The seating order for formal meals, as well as for diplomatic conferences, was subject to rules of precedence. Mats were laid down in a square; the ruler of the host town sat down on one side of the square, and the honored guests sat down on the opposite side. Local dignitaries might then seat themselves on the remaining sides.[219] When only family members were present, seating was less formal, but men and women sat separately.[220] Food was served by women (servants, in the higher status families) in individual dishes, not the large communal ones used by "common" families every day.[221] Ordinarily all the food was served at once, if the meal was well organized, and the contents of one's dish was all one got. As the diners finished, they set aside their dishes, which were gathered up by the women

serving the meal. Among the "better sort," leftovers were either kept for
the next meal or given to any poor persons present. In the *mamanatowick*'s
household, and possibly those of his subordinate *weroances*, all food served
was expected to be consumed, probably as a form of conspicuous consumption (see chap. 6)

The Powhatans were accustomed to gorging when food was available, an
ability common among foragers. Their eating capacity astounded the English ("they be all of them huge eaters"), who then agreed to feed Indian
employees at Jamestown Fort twice the rations given to Englishmen.[222] It is
unlikely, however, that those Indian men really "needed" the extra food.
They probably considered their employers' supplies to be "available" and
loaded up accordingly.

Powhatan families lived self-sufficient lives for the most part, according
to the accounts left us by the English colonists. Thanks to the richness of
the region, every family had access to seafood, garden produce, and game,
as well as hides for clothing, various materials for cutting tools, and plant
products for houses and canoes.

Some movement of goods did take place within eastern Virginia, however; we can infer it from fragmentary English sources and from the nature
of the region itself. The materials that we know were handed around, usually
as tribute to the *mamanatowick*, were all inedible luxury goods: copper,
iron, antimony ore, puccoon, shell beads, and pearls. Powhatan also demanded deer hides from his people, as well as corn, though all of the corn
may have been produced specially for him in separate fields (see chap. 6).
Saltwater mollusks for eating may have been traded among people, as may
bark for sheathing houses. And venison, fish, and horticultural produce
may have been traded in times of need, though there is no documentary
evidence of it.

Copper was imported into Powhatan's domain from three sources: a mine
in Monacan country where the James River divided into two branches,[223] a
source far to the northwest for which the Pocoughtaonacks were either the
miners or the middlemen,[224] and, of course, European visitors and (later)
settlers. All of the English copper was bought by Powhatan himself and
used for his own benefit (see chap. 6); the recipients were mainly other
weroances. The decorative items into which copper was made are described in chap. 3.

A "goodly Iron myne" was found by the English on the "Pembroke"
(north) side of the York,[225] and "iron" was observed set into swords among
the Appamattucks.[226] That iron, which required smelting, must have been
European iron. Possible sources are the French traders in Canada (through
Indian middlemen); Carolina Indians, who still retained goods from the
Roanoke Colony; and the Chesapeakes (newly exterminated), who har-
bored Roanoke colonists in 1585 and may have done so again after 1587.[227]
The Powhatans considered iron tools to be extremely valuable, as shown

by the rate of "thefts" from the English fort at Jamestown.[228] The things stolen were always turned over to the *mamanatowick*.[229] English weapons were obviously desirable, but steel axes may also have been much wanted, for the trade axes ordinarily available were "poore ones of Iron."[230] Indians experimenting with both kinds must soon have seen the difference. Iron trade hoes, and possibly stone ones as well (Strachey is not specific about either), were among the items that people hid in caches out in the woods.[231] And in the very early days of the English colony, even bullets were prized by the Indians. In a story that forms the only English account of gift exchange practiced by Indians who were not chiefs (outside of the marriage ceremony; see chap. 5), we see the contents of two missing bullet bags returned to an English party at Powhatan town, near the falls of the James. Recovering the contents was not easy, for the thieves had already shared them among at least a dozen persons in the town and on an island in the river.[232]

Antimony was mined in Patawomeck territory and sold all over the "country" for face and body paint (see chap. 3). Since the English originally learned of the mine from a Wiccocomico named Mosco[233] and the only Indian recorded as wearing it in the English documents was the *weroance* of Rappahannock,[234] the "country" in question may only have been the Northern Neck.

From puccoon (*Lithospermum caroliniense*) came the most valuable pigment known to the Powhatans (see chap. 3). However, the plant occurs primarily in pine barrens, an ecological niche found in Virginia mainly south of the James.[235] People living north of the James were observed wearing puccoon, and these would have had to buy it.

Shell beads among the Powhatans were made from quahog and whelk shells. Whelks occur only in salty bay waters,[236] and they could have been gathered only by the Chesapeakes, Kecoughtans, Chiskiacks, or Werowocomocos (if they traveled downriver), Piankatanks, Wiccocomicos, Accomacs, and Occohannocks. Quahogs occur in salty and moderately salty waters and could therefore have been gathered by the above-named groups plus the Nansemonds and Warraskoyacks on the James; the Opiscatumeks, Moraughtacunds, and lower Cuttatawomens on the Rappahannock; and the Sekakawons and Onawmanients on the Potomac. The various shell ornaments used by the Powhatans will be described in chapter 3.

Pearls came from freshwater mussels, which do not tolerate anything but fresh water;[237] they would therefore have been available to the town of Powhatan, the Arrohatecks, Appamattucks, Weyanocks, Paspaheghs, and Chickahominies in the James River basin; the Youghtanunds and the upper part of the Mattaponis in the York River basin; the upper Cuttatawomens, Nandtaughtacunds, and possibly Pissasecks on the Rappahannock; and the Patawomecks if they went upriver a short distance. The preparation and use of pearls by the Powhatans is described in chapter 3.

Local shellfish from salty or fresh waters were eaten throughout eastern Virginia, but there was apparently some movement of them between peoples. In May 1607 an Arrohateck man followed an English exploring party up the James, asking to buy English goods with "basketes full of Dryed oysters." [238] We assume that the writer's identification of the oysters was correct, though we cannot be sure. Oysters cannot live in the James above the mouth of the Chickahominy River.[239] It is equally uncertain whether the Arrohateck man had bought them or gone downriver through friendly territory to gather them himself. It may be significant that none of the *weroance*s of the upper James River offered visiting Englishmen dried shellfish of any kind as a delicacy.

Bark appears to have been the preferred material for sheathing houses on the coastal plain.[240] Bark from chestnut, black walnut, tulip poplar, elm, and oak trees could have been used (see chap. 3). All five of these trees grow (or grew, before the chestnut blight arrived) in mature deciduous forests, away from the Chesapeake Bay. Black walnut and elm trees additionally do not grow very large unless something such as the clearing of a field adjacent to them allows them to have plenty of light.[241] Thus it is understandable that Strachey spoke of expense in "purchasing" enough bark to cover a house.

Other goods may occasionally have been produced in surplus and traded without the English being aware of it. English writers agree that the Indian territories nearer the bay were overhunted, as far as deer were concerned.[242] Therefore many Indian groups went on a communal deer hunt each fall. Those groups living nearer the fall line would have had more venison available all year long, and they may at times have dried and traded it. Deer suet was normally made into cakes for future use, and on some occasions, at least, it was traded to Englishmen.[243] The Eastern Shore people, on the other hand, were said to rely less on deer and more on fishing, fowling, and domesticated plants.[244] They may have produced a surplus of these things at times in order to trade across the bay, particularly if local droughts were causing a scarcity that threatened the corn supplies of mainland *weroance*s. There were also more bears "towards the Sea-coasts," [245] and their meat and oil may have been traded inland.

Altogether, the Powhatan economy was a relatively unspecialized one, which nevertheless produced a comfortable living for the majority and a truly noble lifestyle for the ruling families. Except for a few nonperishable luxury goods, "wealth" among the Powhatans consisted of foodstuffs and hides. It was not easily inheritable, and it was accessible to all, since the land was owned in common (see chap. 7). Although chiefs' families had an advantage through the tribute they collected, the land was so rich that everyone had a chance to prosper. The resultant channeling of men's ambitions will be discussed in chap. 4.

CHAPTER 3

Towns and Their Inhabitants

THE CUTTING TOOLS of the Powhatans made large, permanent dwellings laborious to build, while the mild climate made such dwellings unnecessary. And the practice of most of the Powhatan groups of living out among fields that were only in temporary use made for a settlement pattern that was both dispersed and constantly fluctuating, rendering permanent housing even less desirable. Powhatan settlements were "towns" only because they were named, territorial entities in the minds of their inhabitants.

Powhatan settlements, as opposed to hunting camps, were always located near waterways of some sort. When the waterways were brackish or salty, the towns were sited near springs that provided drinking water.[1] The springs, of which there are many in eastern Virginia, did not need to be very large to serve their purpose. The Powhatans' practice of dispersed settlements and of bathing even in salty streams meant that they needed less fresh water than English settlements did. There is no record of Indians in eastern Virginia digging a pond to catch rainwater, as Thomas Hariot said inland Carolina people did.[2] Streams were an integral part of Powhatan towns because of their use in food procurement and transportation and also because the Indians bathed in them daily.

The Powhatans also preferred to locate settlements on high ground overlooking the water, so that everything and everyone approaching the town could be seen.[3] Those few towns which were palisaded[4] were surrounded with stout, tall poles set into the ground close together. Later in the century, when extra security was needed, "the Indians" (perhaps not the Powhatans) used "two three or four thicknesses of timber, coverd with earth, perhaps least they should be fired [set on fire]."[5]

The houses in most towns were scattered, "without forme of a street, far and wyde asunder."[6] (See fig. 12; the artist has Europeanized that town, giving it features that are too neat and regular.) Interspersed among the houses and fields were groves of trees.[7] These provided the houses with shade from the sun and shelter from the wind and rain.[8] Some of the trees were mulberrys, from which fruit was easily gathered.[9] The woods near Indian settlements were cleared of underbrush, both to prevent the unobserved approach of enemies and because the "small wood or old trees"

Fig. 12. De Bry's engraving of the town of Secota, based on John White's painting. The town is Europeanized in its straight streets and field boundaries. Tobacco and squash are shown planted in separate gardens (*E* and *I*, respectively), while corn is shown in its own field, both newly planted (*H*) and mature (*G*). The dancing ground (*C*) and the "praying" plot (*B*) are shown as separate places, which may not be accurate. The building in the foreground (*A*) is a temple, while in the far background is a river (*L*). Courtesy Dover Publications.

were gathered for firewood. The clearing was so effective that "a man may gallop a horse amongst these woods any waie, but where the creekes or Rivers shall hinder." [10]

Most Powhatan settlements had relatively few houses. John Smith placed the number at "from 2 to 100," [11] and the number actually recorded for most settlements fell between those extremes. [12] However, Smith's estimate of six to twenty people living in each house [13] makes the population of each settlement more impressive. For all that, no town was really large by English standards. Henry Spelman wrote that the largest towns did not have more than "20 or 30 houses" in them, [14] while Gabriel Archer estimated that most towns were hamlets of "families of kindred & allyance some 40 tie or 50 tie [people]" to a town, the towns being "not past a myle or half a myle asunder in most places." [15] Not all figures can be trusted at face value. William Strachey, who was present in 1610 when the town was conquered, [16] wrote that the town of Kecoughtan had one thousand "Indians" living in three hundred houses [17] and went on to talk about tremendous fields ready for the English to begin tilling. On the other hand, Smith, who actually went into the town several times before the English took it, described it as being eighteen houses on three acres of ground. [18] Strachey may have been speaking of Kecoughtan's size before Powhatan conquered it in the mid-1590s (he is our source for that conquest), but then most of the fields would have been left to revert to first-growth forest by the town's fewer new inhabitants. Strachey's other estimates of large "towns" on the Pamunkey River are equally suspect. [19] On the whole, even the principal towns on the Virginia coastal plain seem to have been rather small, with most of the population living in hamlets.

A Powhatan house was called a yi-hakan (yeee-ha-cahn), not a "wigwam." [20] Houses were neither large [21] nor very solid by our standards, even when they belonged to rulers, but they were eminently practical. [22] They were made "like gardein arbours," with saplings set into the ground at one-foot intervals [23] in two rows, and then bent over and lashed together at the top to make a barrel-shaped roof. Sapling cross-pieces were lashed on after that. Callahan's experiments [24] showed that saplings of red maple (Acer rubrum), black locust (Robinia pseudoacacia), and red cedar (Juniperus virginiana) proved most useful, the maple for horizontal beams and the cedar and locust for vertical posts. Lashing could be made of "fibrous Roots" or of the "green Wood of the white Oak, which will rive into Thongs." [25] In his experiments, Callahan found root cordage, especially roots of yellow pine (Pinus virginiana or echinata), to be best, followed by cordage made with bast from locust trees; vines proved to be overly brittle in the long run. [26] In addition, deerskin lashing was recorded at Portobacco town late in the seventeenth century. [27]

The house's framework was then covered either with bark or with mats made of marsh reeds. [28] Strachey had the impression that bark sheathing was more difficult to acquire—enough bark to cover a house was "long tyme of purchasing"[29]—and that bark-covered houses were therefore a sign of wealthy owners. Strachey got his information from Indians who came from near Jamestown Island (see Prologue); Archer, on the other hand, noted that most houses in the upper James River valley were covered with bark.[30] Callahan did not experiment with the elm bark favored by the Iroquois[31] or the oak bark used by the Mahicans;[32] confining himself to the trees available on the modern Pamunkey reservation, he found that the best bark, in order of usefulness, came from chestnut (*Castanea dentata*), black walnut (*Juglans nigra*), and tulip poplar trees (*Liriodendron tulipiflora*).[33] He also found that bark might be better than reed mats or thatching when it was newly flattened and applied but that it had a distressing tendency to curl at the edges as it dried out, necessitating regular chinking.

Light could enter a Powhatan house only through the smoke hole in the center of the roof or through the mat-covered door located at each end of the house.[34] Therefore, artificial light was provided by the fire in the central hearth and by the continual use of lightwood torches[35] a foot long.[36] The smoke from the latter did not sting the eyes, but it blackened the skin of the house's inhabitants.[37]

English accounts from Virginia do not say whether the house ends into which the doors were set were rounded or squared off. Most of the houses shown in the John White paintings from the Pamlico region are clearly rectangular in shape (see fig. 12).[38] Doorways were small ("a litell hole to cum in at").[39] Lashed to the framework of each house was the only permanent furniture the Powhatans possessed, the bedsteads.

Powhatan temples and houses for rulers were built in the same manner as ordinary houses, but they were longer, were often covered in bark instead of mats, and were partitioned inside with "Mats, and loose Poles"[40] (see chaps. 8, for temples, and 6, for rulers' houses).

Sapling-and-mat and sapling-and-bark houses were not perfectly weatherproof, especially during a gale, so the Powhatans built them in tree-sheltered places.[41] Once protected from the worst weather, however, the houses could be comfortably heated by their central fireplaces. Smith described them as "warme as stooves, but very smoaky,"[42] and he had fond memories from 1608 of "the drie warme smokie houses of Kecoughtan."[43] The relative flimsiness of the sapling construction, coupled with the smallness of the doors, could also be a protection against unwanted intruders trying to squeeze in the small doors while the family slept. Such intruders could make the whole house shake, waking up its occupants.[44] In the heat of summer, walls made of mats could be rolled up or removed, though considering the number and pertinacity of Virginia's mosquitoes, it is likely that the Powhatans spent summer nights inside their smoky houses.

Powhatan houses were cheap to build and easy to move. A family wanting to change its residence could dismantle the house completely in a few hours, as the Narragansetts did,[45] and reassemble it in a new location. However, references to "old Indian cabins" in the Virginia colonial land patents[46] indicate that the framework, at least, was left behind when the family moved. Temporary shelters during canoe voyages and hunting trips were treated the same way. Mats were carried along on the trip, and a new framework (though "not so laboured, substanciall nor arteficiall [clever] as their other" houses at home) was erected each night in "twoo or three howres."[47] Most, if not all, of the labor of house building was done by women.[48]

The furnishings in Powhatan houses were simple in the extreme. The only large pieces were the bedsteads,[49] which were built in along both long walls of the house. These consisted of "thick short posts, stak't into the grownd, a foote high and somwhat more," with "smale poles" lashed to them. This framework was about four feet in width.[50] "A hurdell of reedes" was placed over that, and then "a fyne white Matt or twoo" was added for bedding, with more mats or some skins for blankets (and a rolled mat for a pillow).[51] People slept "heads and points [head-to-feet] one by the other" on these beds or else lay either rolled in bedding or "stark naked on the grownd." Bedding was folded up and stored during the day. All other furnishings in the house were easily and often moved: clothing, cooking utensils, and hunting and fishing gear.

English observers differ on the standard of cleanliness in Powhatan houses, perhaps because observations were made in different places and different times. Two Englishmen staying in Powhatan's capital in 1614 were run out of their sleeping quarters by the fleas in the bedding.[52] John Clayton, who knew the more southerly Powhatan remnants in the 1680s, said the Indians "keep these houses very sweet & neat."[53] And John Banister claimed that the Indians had to wear oil and paint to keep "lice & fleas & other like troublesom vermin from coming near them with which otherwise by the nastiness of their cabbins they would be very much infested."[54]

Fires were kept going all the time in the houses, as part of the women's work, and "yf at any time yt goe out, they take yt for an evil signe." The household fire was immediately rekindled by chafing "a dry pointed stick in a hole of a little square piece of wood" until the heat generated caught some moss or leaves on fire.[55] There is no record of an annual rekindling from a temple fire, as was practiced in some southeastern tribes.

The Powhatans sometimes also built a ramadalike shelter of small saplings, with a mat-covered roof which at times served as a loft for laying out corn and fish to dry. These shelters were well-lighted, shaded places for summertime living; some sleeping went on in them in spite of the mosquitoes.[56]

Each town also contained at least one sweathouse, whose uses are described in chapter 8. The ovenlike building was built "in some bank near the water side"[57] and was made of saplings and mats. The mats were probably laid on in two or three thicknesses, for the roof was "so close [airtight] that a fewe coales therein covered with a pot, will make the [person] sweat extreamely."[58]

The last major structures that the Powhatans built were bridges. Given the nature of Indian cutting tools, the bridges were rickety by European standards and could span only shallow water and marshy land. Forked stakes were pounded into the mud, and "three or foure" connecting poles were lashed to them with "barkes of trees."[59] There is no record of anything to serve as a handrail. Bridges like these were adequate for moccasin-clad people traveling light, but the English, with their boots and heavy woolen clothes, found crossing them a harrowing experience.[60]

The equipment used in men's subsistence pursuits has already been described. The equipment used by the women, unfortunately, was poorly recorded by male English observers. Banister, with his botanical interests, noted that gourds were used for "Dishes, spoons, Ladles, funnells, Tobacco boxes &c." as well as cups and "flagons," and dishes and other spoons were made of wood.[61] One of the White paintings from the Pamlico region shows a gourd container that could have held several gallons of water.[62] Shells were sometimes used as spoons.[63] Cups made out of turtle shells, with the interior smoothed, have been found archaeologically (see fig. 7). The digging sticks used in farming were mentioned in chapter 2; hoes were also used. Aboriginal hoes might be made of stone or clam shells or animal bone, e.g., deer scapulae.[64] However, the English writers said nothing about which of these Powhatan women used, except for Strachey, who remarked that when the Powhatans hid their valuables in caches in the woods, those valuables included hoes,[65] probably the iron ones bought from the English.

Ceramic pots were used daily for boiling food, but we have to turn to a White painting[66] or to archaeology for a description of them. Powhatan pots often had rounded, conical bases which were meant to be wedged in among the coals of a fire for efficient heating.[67] The other prevalent shape in ceramics was a round-bottomed pot. Pots were coil-made, usually tempered with crushed shell, and left unglazed. Early in the Contact Period they were decorated with impressions of textiles (see fig. 13), which were sometimes partially smoothed over. Since the clays occurring in the region contain iron and an oxidizing environment was used in firing, pots usually came out with a rusty color. Ceramic smoking pipes were also made. These were usually whitish in color,[68] somewhat larger than English pipes, occasionally decorated with copper or designs made with sharks' teeth.[69]

The other heavy, cumbersome utensils in Powhatan households were the wooden mortars; these and possibly also cooking pots were taken along on the annual communal hunting trips.[70] No archaeological evidence of mortars has come to light, and the only historical observation about them was that the pestles used in them were long and also made of wood.[71] Archaeologically, shallow, basin-shaped grinding stones, stone pestles, and hammer

Fig. 13. Decorated potsherds from the Woodland Period in eastern Virginia, incised, stamped, and fabric-impressed. Virginia Research Center for Archaeology Collection.

stones are common throughout the region (see fig. 14). Strachey wrote of breaking hard-shelled nuts "with stones,"[72] which he does not describe. Banister, writing of the Indians he knew near the fall line, is the only English writer to mention stone pestles even in passing.[73]

The rest of the inventory of Powhatan household goods consisted of bags (Eiakintonomo carries a decorated one in fig. 10), baskets, and mats, about which the English colonists recorded little and of which nothing has been found archaeologically on the coastal plain. Impressions of textiles are, however, preserved in some ceramic finds,[74] showing that the techniques of twining, coiling and netting were used (see fig. 15). Textiles were made with the aid of bone weaving needles, which have been found by archaeologists (see fig. 16).

Baskets were made from "the straw whereon ye wheat groweth," i.e., cornhusks,[75] as well as from "the barkes of trees" (probably the same trees that yielded house sheathing) and a "grass" erroneously called "Pemmenaw."[76] *Pemmenaw* means merely "rope" or "thread";[77] the grass was actually a "naturall hemp and flax"[78] that the English commonly called "silk grass." Banister identified the plant late in the seventeenth century, when he wrote that the beaten dried peel of an *Apocynum* species (actually *Apocynum cannabinum,* Indian hemp) made a soft, shiny fiber called "silk grass," which the Indians dyed and wove "into Baskets & Cohobbes [tumplines], [which were] a thing about a hands breadth in the middle which comes upon their breast, & is prettily wrought terminating in two long strings with which they bind up their truck [trade goods] at their backs."[79]

Baskets and mats must have shown considerable variety, since they were put to a wide variety of uses. Baskets were used for sieving, gathering corn (and probably also wild nuts and berries), and storing foodstuffs (see chap. 2). Mats were used for covering houses and their doors, covering sleepers within the houses, wrapping corpses for burial (see chap. 8), making a clean place for drying foodstuffs (see chap. 2), and making a smooth, clean place on which to sit, a practicality for a people whose women wore only aprons. Some baskets and mats were decorated, but we know only that the designs were made with bloodroot.[80]

The Powhatans, like other American Indians, had sallow-white skin, darkened by exposure to the sun, that turned coppery when painted red; coarse, straight, black hair; scanty body hair; dark brown or black eyes; heavy jaws; and, frequently, wide faces due to prominent cheekbones with fatty deposits over them (common to Amerinds and Asiatics). The English thought them "tall" and "straight"[81] and admired the strength and agility that their life as hunters and warriors brought them. The anonymous writer of the 1680s remarked that "the Indians" "come sooner to their full growth than here in Europe,"[82] which probably was a result of their better-rounded diet.

Fig. 14. Stone milling implements: shallow grinding stone, hammer stone, crusher with indentation on both sides, and two pestles. Found in Norfolk and Suffolk. Old Dominion University Collection.

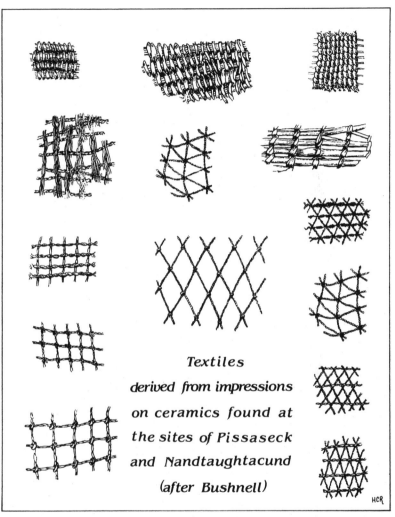

Textiles

derived from impressions

on ceramics found at

the sites of Pissaseck

and Nandtaughtacund

(after Bushnell)

HCR

Fig. 15.

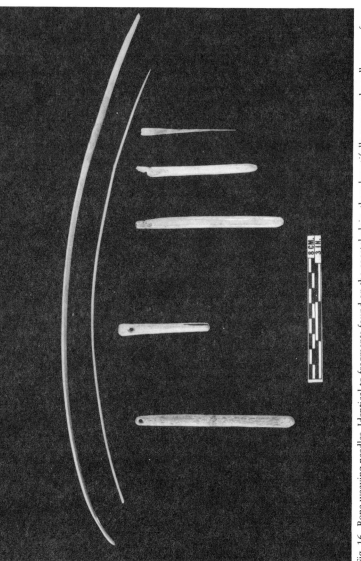

Fig. 16. Bone weaving needles. Identical to fragments found on the coastal plain, these beautifully preserved needles come from the Trigg site in the piedmont. Courtesy Virginia Research Center for Archaeology.

Clothing was worn by everyone except prepubescent girls[83] (and possibly boys when at home). The women's aprons (Strachey's word is "semicinctum"), were often fringed. The normal material used was deerskin, though some aprons were made of closely woven "silk grass."[84] Men wore loincloths which were passed between the legs and lapped over their belts. Those who could not afford leather for these garments thrust grass and leaves into their belts for coverings before and behind.[85] Some loin coverings were decorated with "little bones [probably shell beads], or beasts teeth,"[86] and others were painted with puccoon.[87] Wealthier people added long, fringed, deerskin mantles, dressed with the hair on for winter and without the hair for summer wear. These were fastened over one shoulder (see fig. 10) and were often decorated with paint, "copper" (copper beads?), and shell beads.[88] The painted designs were often of animals: "beasts, fowle, tortoyses, or other such like Imagery."[89] When people went into the forest, they wore long leather leggings and moccasins or "sandals."[90] The only description of Powhatan moccasins is from the late seventeenth century: they were made of a single piece of buckskin, with a one-inch flap sewn down around the opening so that they could be tied tightly around the ankle with a drawstring.[91]

The Powhatans, being active outdoor people, dealt with winter cold as long as possible by merely acclimatizing and oiling themselves. Smith was amazed at the men's ability to go about nearly naked in weather such that "a dogge would scarse have indured it."[92] However, when they finally bundled up they wore fur cloaks called "matchcoats."[93] These were the forerunners of Indian trade blankets (one of the latter is shown on the woman at left in fig. 21). Wealthy people also wore feather mantles. These apparently had a woven or netted fiber base into which feathers were worked, overlapping so that only a smooth sheen of feathers was visible; the best-described example is the blue- or purple-feathered mantle of the wife of the *weroance* Pipsco (see chap. 6).

The rest of Powhatan attire consisted of necklaces, bracelets, earrings, various kinds of headgear, tattooing, and painting. "Dressing up" usually meant adding ornaments instead of clothing.

Hairstyles could be elaborate among the Powhatans. Before puberty, girls had their hair cut very short ("shaven") except for the locks at the back of the head, which were worn in a very long braid.[94] Accounts of women's hairstyles differ, possibly because of the differing locations where the observations were made. The ruler of one Appamattuck town wore her hair loose down to her waist,[95] while some married women along the James River wore their hair in a single long braid[96] with short bangs in the front.[97] Other James River women wore their hair "all of a length shaven [cut], as the Irish by a dish."[98] Later in the century, at least, both women and men plucked the hair of "the other parts of their Body [i.e., armpits and pubic region] for Cleanliness sake."[99]

Men's hairstyles were more elaborate and frequently included ornaments. Powhatan men "shaved" (plucked) the right side of their head, let
the other side grow long, and cut their top hair moderately short in a roach
(see fig. 10, which was actually printed in reverse).[100] The "shaving" was
done by their women, who used two shells as tweezers.[101] The reasons for
such a drastic measure were both practical and religious. Very short hair
does not get caught in bowstrings,[102] and the Powhatans believed that the
style had been given them by their severe deity, Okeus (see chap. 8), as
being "proper" for all "human" males.[103] On special occasions a man's
roach might be replaced by a stiffer version made of deer's hair. Priests'
hairstyles were slightly different from other men's (see chap. 6).

The hair on the left side of the head was "an ell" long (forty-five inches)
and was usually combed[104] and oiled into sleekness with "walnut" (hickory)
oil. The hair was then done up into a "well laboured" knot[105] and stuck
through with ornaments such as a deer antler, "the hand of their enemy
dryed," copper crescents, the wings of birds, or "the whole skyn of a hawk
stuffed, with the winges abroad." Some men attached rattles from rattlesnakes to feathers in the knot, while others attached various kinds of shells
to it by threads, so that they tinkled as the wearer moved.[106] However, men
merely stuck long feathers in their knots most of the time.[107]

Powhatan men, like most American Indian men, had light or no beards.
Custom appears to have decreed that all but old men and some priests (the
ones referred to may also have been old men) should pluck their whiskers.[108]
Powhatan himself had a thin, gray mustache and beard.[109]

On special occasions Powhatan men augmented their roaches or knots
with deer's hair dyed red.[110] These artificial roaches were not always worn
alone. George Percy met an Indian ruler in 1607 who wore "a Crown of
Deares haire colloured red, in fashion of a Rose fastened about his knot of
haire [on the left side of his head], and a great Plate of Copper on the other
[shaved] side of his head, with two long Feathers in fashion of a paire of
Hornes placed in the midst of his Crowne."[111]

Deer antlers were occasionally worn as a headdress; the precise significance of the act was not recorded. Two lesser rulers were observed to wear
antlers when meeting English visitors. During the preliminaries of the
huskanaw (see chap. 4), the "keepers of boys" wore "horns," which may
have been antlers. And some young women wore them while imitating
hunters or warriors in a dance given for English guests in 1608.[112]

Both sexes commonly pierced their ears in two or three places, but
Powhatan men wore more elaborate earrings than the women did. Ornaments included

> chaynes of stayned perle, bracelette[s] of white bone [i.e., shell], or shredds
> of Copper, beaten thin and bright, and wound vp hollow, and with a great
> pride [on the part of the wearer] certayne Fowles leggs, Eagles[,] Hawks, Tur-
> keys, etc., with Beasts Clawes, Beares, Arrahacounes [raccoons], Squirrels,

etc., the clawes thrust through, they lett hang vpon the Cheeke to the full view; and some of their men there be, who will weare in these holes, a smale green and yellow couloured live Snake neere half a yard in length, which Crawling and lapping himself about his neck oftentymes familiarly he suffers to kisse his lipps, others weare a dead ratt tyed by the Taile, and such like Conundrums.[113]

For variety, that list is hard to surpass.

The "claws" were not always plain claws; Percy saw as a pair of ear ornaments "a Birds Claw . . . beset with fine Copper and Gold [lighter copper]."[114] Strachey also took a string of "Lyons"—probably cougar—claws from an Indian house at the falls of the James River.[115] These had very probably been traded eastward from the mountains.

The "stayned" pearls were not stained intentionally. The local freshwater mussels (one or both of the two local *Anodonta* species)[116] produced small, low-grade pearls (the largest as big "as pease"),[117] which were neither so perfectly formed nor so consistently pearlescent as European tastes demanded (see fig. 17). The "stayned" pearls were those discovered in mussels that had been cooked,[118] a process which turned them purple.[119] Then the pearls had to be drilled with the tools the Powhatans had, which led to their being "burnt thorow with great hoales & Spoyled."[120] Pearls were strung for necklaces and the like and were also embroidered onto clothing (where they may have been taken for "white beads") and even moccasins.[121]

Copper was used for earrings (the "shredds" mentioned above), head ornaments (the "great plate" mentioned above), and necklaces. The wife of the *weroance* Pipsco wore a necklace consisting of "a Chayne with long lynckes of Copper";[122] these "lynckes" may in fact have been long tubes. Long tubes, short, delicate tubes, and conical tinklers have been found at a few piedmont locations (see fig. 17 for particularly well-preserved specimens).[123] The former two types have also been found in a Middle Woodland status burial in Virginia Beach.[124] The large tubes in that burial were an inch and a half long and about half an inch in diameter (fatter than the ones in the figure), and the short tubes were about one-fourth inch long and one-eighth inch in diameter (like the ones in the figure).

Before the advent of European glass trade beads, the Powhatans made beads from conch and quahog shells. Given the Indians' cutting tools, such beads were laborious to make and valuable once made, which is why Powhatan took part of his tribute in shell beads, as well as copper, hides, and foodstuffs.[125] The early-seventeenth-century writers speak of only white shell beads (Strachey always calls them "white coral"),[126] but three kinds were recognized by late-seventeenth-century authors, and four distinct kinds have been found archaeologically.

The three bead types in the historical literature are *peak*, *runtees* (a term from the "Southern Indians," according to Banister; also called *rounda*), and *roanoke*.[127] *Peak* was made from quahog (*Venus mercenaria*) shells

Fig. 17. Pearls and copper artifacts: copper beads in two sizes, copper "fishhook" pendant, conical copper tinkler, rectangular copper pendant, and four pearls from freshwater mussels. Various coastal plain sites. Virginia Research Center for Archaeology Collection.

and came in white or dark purple ("black") forms. Beads of *peak* were highly polished and cylindrical, with an average length of one-third inch and diameter of one-quarter inch (see the strung beads in fig. 18). The purple *peak*, known to later writers as *wampum peak*, was more valuable because of the lesser area of the shell with that color. Powhatan himself drew an analogy between *peak* and European trade beads. When he sold corn for beads for the first time in February 1608, he valued blue glass beads much more highly than beads of other colors,[128] and the ownership of them soon became a "royal" prerogative.[129] Early-seventeenth-century writers mention only *peak*, used in necklaces and embroidery; later writers mention the other kinds of beads, as well as coronets for the hair and collars of *peak*.[130]

Runtees was made from the central columns and adjacent areas of conch shells (both *Busycon carica* and *Busycon canaliculatum* are found in Chesapeake Bay).[131] It consisted of large, polished pieces made variously into oval pipe beads drilled lengthwise, fat round beads, or coin-shaped pendants an inch across and one-third inch thick, drilled at the edge. (See the tubular shells in fig. 18; the smaller disks, centrally drilled, can also be called *runtees*.) Larger shell disks (see fig. 18) have been found in the piedmont, where preservation is better, and near the Contact Period site of Patawomeck (see fig. 19). Robert Beverley mentioned four-inch disks on which were engraved "Circles, Stars, a Half Moon, or any other figure suitable to their fancy," which people wore "before or behind their Neck."[132] One disk from near Patawomeck (fig. 19), often called the "Bruff mask," although it is far too small to be worn, has a humanoid face engraved on it and appears to be the kind of item Beverley refers to. Late in the seventeenth century, at least, the fat, round *runtees* beads were strung for necklaces[133] and bracelets,[134] and the pipe beads were hung from the ears.[135]

Roanoke was made from mussel and other thin shells (Banister writes of its being produced on the Eastern Shore, which is in the saltwater zone) and consisted of small, disk-shaped pieces drilled through the center; as it was easier to make, its value was less. It came in two forms, "rough or cragged on the edges" and "worn" (i.e., the edges ground smooth to make perfect disks), the latter of which was more valuable. Roanoke was always strung. In the late seventeenth century a "fingers length of smooth Roanoak" was hung from the ears,[136] and arm's lengths of it were used for certain kinds of payments.

The fourth type of decorative shell, used in embroidery,[137] was *Marginella roscida*, about one-half inch long. These were abraded on one side of the large end, making a hole. Sinew thread was then passed through the hole and out the open aperture of the shell. The embroidery on the so-called "Powhatan Mantle" (see fig. 23, and description in chap. 6) utilizes these shells, in both full- and half-sizes.

Tattooing was a women's form of adornment among the Powhatans.

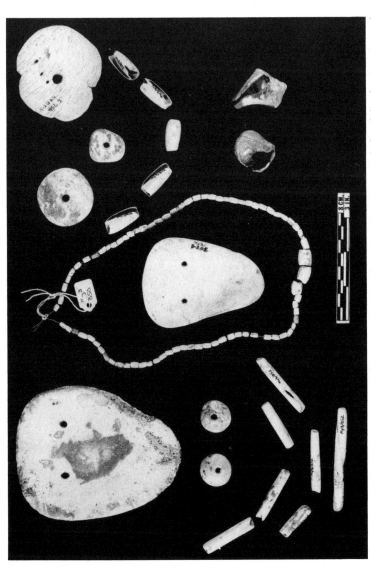

Fig. 18. Shell ornaments: *peak* beads with three *runtees* beads on the string; other *runtees*, including disks of various sizes and the long pipe beads; five marginella shells; and two unidentified shells. These specimens came from the Trigg site in the piedmont, where preservation is better, but they are analogous to finds on the coastal plain. Courtesy Virginia Research Center for Archaeology.

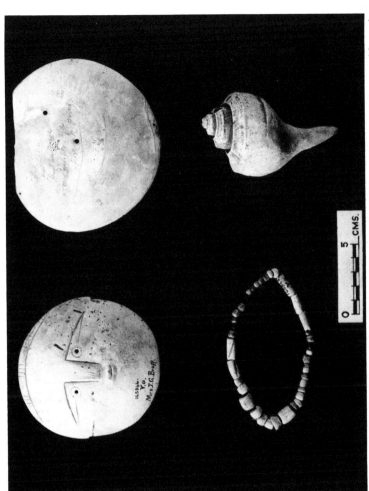

Fig. 19. Shell ornaments found near the site of Patawomeck. The "maskette" at the upper left is one of five such items found in 1869 with a burial on the Lewis Ashton farm on Indian Point, Accotink Creek (Potter n.d.). Smithsonian Institution Collection. (Courtesy Stephen R. Potter.)

Arms, breasts, shoulders, faces, and thighs were "cunningly imbroydered" by puncturing the skin with a heated "Instrument" (Percy called it a "sharp Iron")[138] and then dropping "sondry Colours" on the holes. The designs were of "flowers and fruicts of sondry lively kyndes, as also Snakes, Serpents, Efts [lizards], etc,"[139] as well as "Fowls, Fish or Beasts."[140] No further details were recorded, such as the age at which the tattooing was done.[141]

Painting of the shoulders and face was both an everyday and a dress-up activity for both sexes among the Powhatans. The favored color was a mulberry red, produced by pulverizing certain roots and mixing in either "walnut" (hickory nut) oil or bear grease. The oily mixture was believed to shut out winter cold and summer heat and mosquitoes.[142] Constant experimentation went on among the people to achieve an ointment "better" in color and consistency; those who improved the recipe shared it freely with others.[143] When the ointment dried in the sun on one's skin, it became a dye. Due to the lack of smoothness in stirring and applying the mixture, however, it made the Indians' skin "(besyde the Coulour more black and spotted, which the Sun kissing oft, and hard, addes to their paynting) the more rough and rugged."[144]

The roots used to produce a red color are usually called "puccoon" in the English records. However, several roots were used. "Real" puccoon (*Lithospermum caroliniense*)[145] grows rather infrequently in the southern pine barrens as far north as Virginia south of the James.[146] Its rarity and its beauty when made into body paint made it the valuable commodity that was sent to Powhatan as tribute, and it was also felt by the Indians to have medicinal qualities (see chap. 8). Another root that produced red dye was *musquaspenne,* which was probably the bloodroot (*Sanguinaria canadense*)[147] that grows throughout Virginia in rich soils.[148] This was the red used for painting "Mattes, Targets [shields], and such like."[149]

Black pigment was produced either from the juice of the inkberry or from swamp mud that contained decaying alder leaves.[150] The methods of producing other colors were not recorded.

A dressy addition to paint was a yellowish-silvery dust, collected from an antimony-rich ore called *matchqueon,* located in Patawomeck territory. This ore was mined with "shells and hatchets," washed, bagged, and sold all over "the country" to decorate both people and temple images.[151] The *weroance* of Rappahannock was observed wearing it in 1607. His face was "painted blew, besprinkled with siluer Ore as wee thought."[152]

Other colors of paint were used on different occasions, though the scanty English accounts leave us uncertain about Powhatan color symbolism. Black was associated with death (women mourned twenty-four hours after a funeral, with faces painted "with black cole and oile"),[153] but it may have had other associations, with dignity and solemnity. The first time the Paspahegh ruler met the English in 1607, he came "painted all black, with hornes on his head."[154] Some of the people who danced in the preliminaries of the *huskanaw,* the initiation of boys into manhood (see chap. 4), were also painted black.[155] White paint was sometimes worn by people engaged in social dancing. But it was also the color boys wore when they were first brought forward in the preliminaries of the *huskanaw.*[156] The color may have symbolized either innocence or, since that puberty ritual created men where none had been before, a void.

The Rappahannock ruler wore more than one color to his first meeting with the English: "His body was painted all Crimson . . . his face painted blew, besprinkled with siluer Ore."[157] Ordinary people wore various colors on social occasions, according to personal preference. Kin-group membership may have played a part in the choice, but the English did not think to inquire about such matters. Yellow paint was worn at times, though the source of the pigment and the context of wearing it were not recorded.[158] When several young women did a "warrior"-like dance to entertain English visitors in 1608, they had "their bodies al painted, some white, some red, some black, some partie colour, but every one different."[159] Except for that dance, when the women apparently imitated men, women are recorded as having normally worn tattoos and red paint, leaving the other colors for the men.[160]

Men also painted and bedecked themselves specially for war, when they would "paint and Crosse their foreheades, cheekes, and the right [shaved] syde of their heades diversely, either with *terra-sigillata* [reddish earthy pigment], or with their root Pochone."[161] Later in the century, around 1659, John Gibbon observed Indian men from the Northern Neck (Wiccocomicos or Sekakawons or Cuttatawomens) in a "War-dance."[162] The designs of the men's paint were half red and half black, with either vertical division into two sides of the body or a horizontal division into upper and lower halves. The men carried bark shields painted in those ways and also in three horizontal bars of color.

Men preparing for war added other substances to their paint before it dried.[163] One was "the soft downe of sondry Coloured birdes, or blew birdes, white herenshews [herons] . . . as if so many variety of laces were stitched to their skyns."[164] Another substance applied to the body was "the hair of Beasts,"[165] presumably long hair which may have been dyed.

The most elaborate decoration for war was one that led the English to dub the wearer, Nemattanew, with the name "Jack of the Feather." This man was an aggressive, flamboyant warrior who "used to come into the felde all covered over [with] feathers and Swans wings fastened unto his showlders as thowghe he meante to flye."[166] One historian, Fausz,[167] has taken that appearance, coupled with the man's later behavior, to mean that by 1621 he was a charismatic religious leader.[168] The reason is a third-hand Spanish account saying that the Powhatans' god appeared to them "in the guise of a bird."[169] However, that description is belied by what Samuel Purchas learned from the Powhatan priest Uttamatomakkin in a face-to-face interview: the Indians' Okeus had appeared to his priests in human form and actually taught the men how to wear their hair.[170] The connection between feathers and religious power, at least for the Powhatans,[171] is very poorly documented. Powhatan men wore feathers on many occasions, as we have seen, and Nemattanew's attire accomplished the purpose of making him conspicuous to the point of daredevilry.

Smith wrote in his last account that the priests who had "conjured" over him during his captivity seventeen years before (see chap. 8) were painted.[172] The chief priest was "all painted over with coale, mingled with oyle," while the other priests, arriving in two sets of three, had more elaborate designs. Those in the first set were painted "halfe blacke, halfe red: but all their eyes were painted white, and some red stroakes like [mustaches] along their cheekes." Those in the second set had "red eyes, and white stroakes over their blacke faces."

The English recorded little about the sanitary practices of the Powhatans, probably because they were not much interested in the subject at home.[173] Accounts contain no reference to the trash pits that archaeologists have found in Powhatan settlements. However, the English did notice that the Indians washed every morning in the nearest stream, whatever the weather, after which they staged a prayer ritual (see chap. 8). They told the English that they washed themselves and even their small children in order to make them hardy and inured to cold.[174] Some of them also washed their hands before eating, drying them on "fresh greene ashen leaues"[175] or, in the case of Powhatan himself, on feathers that were dried afterward for reuse.[176]

CHAPTER 4

Manliness

A HUNTING SOCIETY'S DEMAND for toughness and individualism combined with an incipient class system (see chap. 6) to produce Powhatan men who were proud, aggressive, and eager for social advancement. At the same time, Powhatan rulers required absolute deference and obedience from their social inferiors,[1] who were encouraged to channel their aggressions into activities useful to their *weroances*. The evidence for these statements is admittedly fragmentary, but it is indicative.

Ideally, an Indian man was wealthy and was invincible in war. The Powhatans lived in a world where wealth was obtained by acquiring food. So a rich man was successful in the chase at all seasons, and he also had plant foods produced by the wives that his hunting success attracted (see chap. 5). Success therefore required personal skill, endurance, and courage. A man gained prestige, in addition to his wealth, through his *weroance*'s recognition of his great personal exploits in hunting and war. These exploits were a matter of public interest in a population living in small, intimate settlements and constantly warring with some more distant peoples. Thus Powhatan men had to be carefully and continually socialized for the role they were to play.

The English took considerable interest in the initiation rites by which Powhatan men were created, though their Elizabethan background did not make them analytical enough to perceive that that kind of man was a well-integrated adult personality, not an egotistical child.

Boys were trained as hunters by their mothers as well as by their fathers. Mothers normally refused to give their sons breakfast in the morning until they had passed an archery test, in which the mother threw "a piece of Mosse or some such light thing" into the air for the boy to hit.[2] When the boy was proficient enough with his bow, his father began taking him hunting and fishing, teaching him the lore and keeping a close watch on his progress. His parents hoped that the boy would make steady progress and qualify for initiation into "real" manhood by his early teens.

The name a boy carried was in itself a source of pressure on him. Powhatan personal names had meanings that everyone could understand. Every infant was given its first formal name a few days after birth, when the relatives gathered. The father took the baby in his arms and publicly named it, and a feast and dance followed.[3] There is also evidence that children were given secret, very personal names. Pocahontas's "other" name of Matoaka became known to the English only after she converted to Christianity,[4] the name having previously been kept from them "in a superstitious feare of hurte by the English if her name were knowne."[5] But children, especially boys, received more names as they grew up. From pet names (e.g., Pocahontas, or "little wanton" [i.e., mischievous one]; her formal name was Amonute, the meaning of which is unknown)[6] boys, at least, graduated to more serious nicknames that reflected their exploits, and the process continued throughout a man's life. A great exploit in war brought a man a new name, bestowed by his *weroance*[7] in public along with a gift of copper, pearls, or beads.[8] A *mamanatowick* presumably renamed himself when occasion warranted.[9] Thus William Strachey wrote that those "of greatest merritt . . . aspire to many names."[10] A male Indian's current name reminded him and everyone else of how much (or how little) he had done for his people lately.

All Powhatan males were expected to qualify for initiation into manhood at some time,[11] but the most promising young men were publicly recognized by being initiated at the age of ten to fifteen.[12] Until he had passed through the ordeal, no man was eligible for the priesthood or a councillorship[13] or, indeed, for any real recognition from his *weroance*.[14]

The ritual was a rigorous test of endurance which a few youths did not survive. The English colonists were soon made aware that most boys survived and that the "deaths" and "mourning" they witnessed were symbolic rather than real.[15] Nonetheless, the explanation of the boys' deaths originally given the English led the colonists to call the ordeal a "sacrifice of children."[16]

The initiation into manhood was called the *huskanaw*;[17] it was also called "making black boys," for reasons that are uncertain.[18] In the early seventeenth century the whole of Powhatan's "empire" held a *huskanaw* "once in 14. or 15. yeeres" for those who had not previously gone through it, one such being held in 1615.[19] But in any other given year one chiefdom (e.g., Kecoughtan in ca. 1608–10)[20] or a few together (e.g., Quiyoughcohannock and Paspahegh in 1608)[21] might hold a *huskanaw* by themselves.[22] Thus the early English colonists received the impression that a *huskanaw* was held annually, and so it was, somewhere or other.

Proceedings began with a morning-long dance and feast in the woods, in which the entire population of the chiefdoms concerned participated. Two huge dance circles were made around a fire, the people being dressed in their very best. They danced four in rank, led by a *weroance,* and they moved seemingly endlessly, one circle going clockwise, the other counterclockwise. If people became tired and lagged in the dance, one of "foure or fiue principall men" armed with "bastinadoes," or bundles of reeds, came over from the center of the circle and "beat [them] forward." Another group of men, who wore "black hornes" on their heads and held green boughs, were dancing in the circle's center. Twice during the dance these people made "a hellish noise," flung away their boughs, ran up into a small tree while clapping their hands, and then tore the tree to the ground before falling back "into their order againe" in the dance. Their fierceness in this preliminary dance was a foretaste of their fierceness toward the initiates later on, as well as an imitation of the wildness that the boys would exhibit much later. (The men themselves may not have seen it in this light. The symbolism behind the events of the *huskanaw* was never properly recorded.)

When the people had danced themselves into exhaustion, the initiates, in their white body paint, were brought into the circle. The people danced around them and sang. In the afternoon the boys were led to a tree, made to sit down next to it, and guarded by older men armed with reed bundles. Presently the guards formed a lane, down which came five older youths (who may have been young priests). These led the boys one by one through the lane of older men, who acted as if they were furious at the boys' "abduction" and beat at the groups with the reed bundles. The escorts received most of the blows as they took the boys to another tree and seated them. When all the boys were seated, the older men formed another lane near them, and another violent "abduction" took place; there were three such "abductions" altogether. After at least one of these events, the older men furiously tore apart the tree where the boys had been sitting and made wreaths for their hair from its branches.

During all this time, the female spectators mourned loudly from a distance, "weeping and crying out very passionately . . . some . . . singing (as yt were) their dirge or funerall songe." They also had beside them the accoutrements of a funeral: dry wood, mats, skins, and moss for preparing the dead.

The boys were then taken to a "valley" or ravine where their *weroance* (or *weroances*) was waiting, and everyone followed and partook of a feast lasting two or three hours. Then suddenly the older men with reed bundles rose and made another lane, through which the initiates had to pass a fourth time. This time the boys did not "survive,"[23] and we next hear of their bodies being laid "lifeless" under a tree. The older men danced around them for a time, and when they sat down in a circle around the "bodies," the *weroance* (or *weroances*) had the people bring their dry wood, set it up in the shape of a steeple, and set fire to it.

At this point any English observers present were politely asked to leave. The "bodies," the "funeral" preparations, and the garbled translations they got about further proceedings led them to believe that a sacrifice was about to take place.[24] In fact, it is likely that the "sacrifice" explanation was the standard rationalization made by Indian people in the case of boys who did not survive the rigors ahead.[25]

Noninitiates like the English learned only the outlines of what followed. The boys were taken out into the forest for several months,[26] and under the observation of older, initiated men, or "keepers," they were given a "Decoction of some Poisonous Intoxicating Roots," the roots possibly including the jimsonweed (*Datura stramonium*), which grows on waste ground throughout Virginia.[27] The effects of drinking this potion for eighteen or twenty days and of the beatings they received while under its effects[28] made the boys so "stark staring Mad" that they had to be shut up in a cage. This was a tall latticework "in shape like a Sugar-loaf"[29] or a cone (see fig. 20). After a period of total madness, the boys who survived were released from the cage and brought gradually off the drug over a period of several weeks. Before they had recovered completely, they were brought home again, where their zombielike behavior was taken as a sign that they remembered nothing of their former lives as boys. They were now retrained as "men" by their "keepers." If a boy made the mistake of showing any memory of his earlier life, even a recognition of his parents, he was taken to the woods and put through the *huskanaw* again, a procedure that usually killed him.

Thus in the *huskanaw* Powhatan boys seem to have been ceremonially "killed," and they were "reborn" as [real] men. Rebirth is often a leitmotif of male puberty rites, but rarely is it acted out with such long-term violence.

The *huskanaw* was a deadly serious affair for the boys and their "keepers" alike. Absolute secrecy was essential for the regimen to work. Initiated men were tough survivors who shared a secret (the details of what happened in the woods) that bound them together and made them better than noninitiates. Thus the Powhatan *huskanaw* combined two features common to male puberty rituals in other parts of the world: hazing to gain the victims' loyalty and a shared secret to cut the possessors off from others.

Only initiated men were considered sufficiently attuned to the needs of their nation, rather than of their families, to be eligible for positions as councillors to their rulers.[30] This must have been especially true of youths from widely separated chiefdoms who were initiated together in the rare "empire"-wide *huskanaw*s. Councillorships were lucrative positions, as well as responsible ones, because of their nearness to *weroance*s who collected tribute and wives. Therefore, it can be fairly said that success bred success among the Powhatans: boys who were superior hunters (i.e., able to produce much wealth)[31]—and who thus stood to acquire more wealth-producing wives—went through the *huskanaw* earlier and became councillors sooner, which gave them access to yet more wealth and not a little power.

The Powhatan *huskanaw* was a product of chiefdom-level societies living in a state of war with their neighbors, and as such its origin was probably not earlier than that of the chiefdoms it served. The Eastern Shore Accomacs and Occohannocks, who were relatively isolated from enemies, lacked the ritual.[32] And at a later date the Algonquian- and Siouan-speaking

Fig. 20. Gribelin's engraving of a priest, a conjurer, and a *huskanaw* pen. The engraving is based on two John White paintings. The pen is an addition made at the behest of Robert Beverley, whose book the illustration accompanies. Courtesy University of North Carolina Press.

tribes in the Carolinas, all in constant contact with English traders, were found to have an initiation (called the same thing by the English observer)[33] which all young people went through.

The Powhatan boy learned by experience that proficiency, endurance, and reckless courage were necessary to be a professional hunter and warrior and therefore a real man. The consequence of failure as a hunter was poverty; but the consequences of failure as a warrior were ignominy at best and a horrible death at worst. The Powhatans and all their neighbors tortured war captives to death. That raised the stakes in the game of manhood, and for some it became the last and most difficult test of manliness.

English observers in Virginia were mercifully terse in their accounts of Indian torture methods, compared with the writers of accounts from other parts of North America.[34] They tell us how it was done, but not how long it took.[35] The usual Powhatan practice was to build a fire and then strip the captive and tie him either to a tree or to stakes. The execution was then carried out either by the town's women or by a man appointed for the job. Using sharp mussel shells, the executioners gradually flayed and cut off the limbs of the victim, throwing the pieces into the fire before the victim's eyes. At length the victim was disemboweled, which killed him. Accounts differ on the disposal of what remained: it was either dried into a kind of mummy, "which they kept aboue ground in a by-roome,"[36] or burned along with the tree or stakes. The latter seems more probable, with trophies being taken first for drying.

Any show of pain on the victim's part was an occasion for derision by the Powhatans. As was the case in other Woodland tribes, a "real" man died not only stoically but also deriding his tormentors. The Powhatans probably had mocking death songs for their men to sing, like those of other tribes. Death with honor was the only possible end for a captured man, unless he could escape, and Indian men went to war carefully conditioned for such an end. The Powhatans were firmly locked into this way of thinking. After at least four captured Englishmen had died "badly," the Indians near Jamestown began singing a "scornefull song" when Englishmen approached.[37]

Success in war was courted avidly by Powhatan men, in spite of the danger involved, for "they that kill most of ther enimies are heald the cheafest men amonge them."[38] Success was publicly claimed and publicly rewarded. It is likely that the same women who tortured captives could deride any man who did not take enough chances. Men painted and bedaubed themselves garishly in order to startle the enemy, but also to make themselves more visible, a deliberate courting of danger. One of the *mamanatowick*'s most formidable warriors was Nemattanew, or "Jack of the Feather," introduced in chapter 3. This man was said in the early 1620s to have such a reputation among his own people that they believed him immune to English bullets, so that when in 1621 he lay mortally wounded by English firearms, he asked his captors not to return his body to his people or let them know that bullets had finally killed him.[39]

Powhatan men were encouraged to recite accounts of their exploits as hunters and warriors, especially on public occasions with "royalty" present. We know this from a story recorded in 1621.[40] The *mamanatowick* (either Powhatan or his successor) was making "his annuall progress through his petty provinces" and arrived in Patawomeck, where he was entertained lavishly. Part of the festivities consisted of all the young men of the chiefdom presenting themselves one by one and telling the assembled company what great feats they had performed, either as hunters or as warriors. A tall-tale contest soon developed, under the pressure of showing the *mamanatowick* what formidable people the Patawomecks were.[41] No one knew whether the *mamanatowick* had guessed that truth had been left behind, but the man who was last in line felt he was sure to be discovered if he bested the others. So when his turn came he stepped forward, made his obeisance "with a stoute and decent behaviour," and said: "And I my Lorde went this morninge into a great Marshe and there valiently killed six Muske Ratts, w[hi]ch though itt be no more then the boyes doe dailye yett this my Liege is true and most of the rest but fables." At this, the *mamanatowick* and everyone else burst out laughing, and the young man's wit was considered so good that he was "most regarded and best rewarded."

A powerful *mamanatowick* played his part in goading men into great deeds. It was, after all, to his advantage to have such warriors as loyalists if he wanted to defend or expand his holdings. The *mamanatowick* may also have needed to goad his men in order to protect his own power. All Powhatan men were brought up to be touchy and vindictive. After the dissolution of Powhatan's "empire," and probably before his rise to power, it was up to each man to defend himself and his relatives. An English observer noted later in the seventeenth century that revenge for a murder was taken by the victim's family, "though it be two or three generations after, having no justice done amongst them in this respect but what particular persons do themselves."[42] Men who are ever ready to defend their honor can be difficult to mold into a larger political entity, unless they are given incentives for turning their aggressions elsewhere. Getting the men to wage war on non-Powhatans and strive for great reputations as hunters, coupled with making the finding and punishing of wrongdoers primarily a chiefly business (see chap. 7), was an effective method of welding men together without having to change their essentially defensive outlook on life.

The favor of the *mamanatowick* or any lesser *weroance* was able to raise a man almost to the level of "better sort." His wrath, on the other hand, was to be avoided, for his power was such that retribution was swift and violent. The Powhatans deferred completely to their rulers, to hear the English tell it: "It is strange to see with what great feare and adoration all these people doe obay this Powhatan. For at his feet they present what-soever hee commandeth, and at the least frowne of his browe, their greatest spirits will tremble with feare."[43]

The only detailed eyewitness account (from early-seventeenth-century Virginia)[44] that makes a ruler's authority vivid to us involves a "fringe" *weroance*'s wife rather than a male subject in the "core" of Powhatan's "empire." The deference due a ruler was also expected by his wives and children during his lifetime. Henry Spelman found that out while he lived for several months with the ruler of the town of Passapatanzy, a "brother" of the Patawomeck *weroance*. Spelman was an adolescent at the time, and that created confusion about his status in his host's household: he could be either a guest or a (foreign) retainer. One day his host went on a trip, leaving Spelman behind with two of his wives. One of the wives decided to while away her husband's absence by visiting her father, a day's journey away, and she ordered Spelman to accompany her as a servant and carry her child in his arms the whole distance. Spelman, rejecting the status of servant, refused her demand, whereupon the wife began to beat him. Spelman returned the blows. Seeing this, the second wife joined in, and a brawl ensued. The husband returned later, heard Spelman's side of the story first, and promptly clouted the first wife into insensibility, thereby establishing Spelman's status once and for all. When she regained consciousness, the wife's only thought was to appease her husband, which she did.[45] The servility of the wife was probably due more to the "royal" status of her husband than to his being a paterfamilias.

John Smith and other colonists had many occasions to witness the aggressiveness of Powhatan men toward foreigners they suspected of being their "inferiors" as men, as the detailed records of early Jamestown show.[46] A sort of "testing" of foreigners went on continually. Smith and his compatriots were not the only European visitors to North America to perceive Indian men generally as touchy and challenging after the first few meetings. Smith did, however, acknowledge that Powhatan men were not carbon copies of one another when he wrote, with typical European condescension:

> They are inconstant in everie thing, but what feare constraineth them to keepe. Craftie, timerous, quicke of apprehension [comprehension] and very ingenuous [naive]. Some are of disposition fearefull, some bold, most cautelous [cautious and wily], all Savage. Generally covetous of copper, beads, and such like trash. They are soone moved to anger and so malitious, that they seldome forget an injury.[47]

Strachey, in copying this passage, added from his personal experience that some men were "so bould and audatious as they dare come unto our forte, truck and trade with vs and looke vs in the face, crying all freindes, when they haue but new done vs a mischief, and when they intend presently againe, if yt lye in their power to doe the like.[48] "Outsiders" should have expected to be tested, given the testing to which Powhatan men themselves were continually subjected within their own society.

The qualities that the Powhatans thought befitted a "real" man were necessary qualities in men who hunted for a living, waged constant guerrilla war with enemies, and tried to rise in an incipient class system. There was, however, one problem with their belief in being extremely tough in order to survive, a problem which they probably did not perceive themselves: the system was self-perpetuating and potentially self-escalating. Men were brought up to be warlike and proud, and therefore abrasive incidents were likely to occur, sometimes within the paramount chiefdom (see chap. 7). An injury demanded revenge, which was considered by the other side as an injury that demanded revenge in turn, and so on. It took powerful social forces to direct the aggression toward more distant "outsiders," as Powhatan must have discovered when he tried to weld independent chiefdoms into a new organization of "insiders."[49] He was probably aided by the scarcity of game in the more densely inhabited part of his paramount chiefdom, a scarcity itself partially caused by the pressure on men to be "manly." It was necessary to have communal hunts near the fall line, which must have increased the potential for escalation in war with the Siouan-speaking Monacans and Mannahoacs of the piedmont. The "outsiders" to focus on were already conveniently in place.

Societies like the Powhatan one, with very high expectations and limited occupations for their men, can perpetuate themselves for generations, if not hundreds of years. Such cultural systems became common in the eastern woodlands after the introduction of maize horticulture.[50] But systems of this sort balance on a razor's edge between success and failure. A bad drought, an epidemic, or an especially successful enemy raid might deal a tribe a blow from which it could not recover. Not recovering did not necessarily mean physical death to the men; it could simply mean a humiliating loss of independence and incorporation with another, related tribe. The result was that a tribe's continued independence when surrounded by other nations of "he-men" was never assured, and life was fraught with danger, tension, and drama.

Powhatan's new paramount chiefdom did not fundamentally alter its men's lives. It merely changed the geographical scope of their warfare and made their lives more competitive still. It was the English who eventually put an end to the system by forcing the men to adopt what in Powhatan eyes was the peaceful, "feminine," and relatively boring life of farmers. It is little wonder, then, that in the seventeenth and eighteenth centuries, Powhatan men clung to their old ways of making a living as long as they possibly could.[51]

CHAPTER 5

Sex Roles and Family Life

POWHATAN MEN AND WOMEN lived in separate worlds, a common situation in societies which do not allow much overlap between men's work and women's work. Among the Powhatans, the two sexes' work overlapped only in the following areas: both sexes cleared land for gardens,[1] and some women inherited ruling positions in their chiefdoms (see chap. 6). Men and women ate simultaneously but apart in the "better" families. And as among virtually all other American Indian groups, Powhatan women retreated during their menstrual periods to separate houses, near which the men dared not come.[2]

Men's work in Powhatan culture consisted of jobs that were few but demanding. Men who were neither rulers nor priests were responsible for hunting and fishing, no matter what the weather, as well as making war; they also produced and repaired most of the gear for those endeavors.[3] Some men, among either the *mamanatowick*'s household or the Patawomeck people also tanned the hides,[4] an activity which is not attributed to Powhatan men later in the seventeenth century. Englishmen's background colored their views of Indian men's occupations. Because hunting and fishing were sports to which most Englishmen only aspired, whereas farming and housework were ordinary labor, Gabriel Archer wrote that Indian women "do all the labour and the men hunt and goe at their plesure."[5] The English witnesses' inexperience with the hunting life also showed when they wrote that "the women be verie painefull [i.e., burdened] and the men often idle."[6] Professional hunters work in intensive, protracted bursts of physical energy and mental concentration, between which rest periods are a necessity. English visitors to Indian towns normally saw the men during their rest periods.

Women did a wide variety of jobs, some of them requiring great skill and all of them providing necessities that men could not exist without. Women made mats, baskets, pots, cordage, and wooden spoons, platters, and mortars. They planted the corn, harvested it, pounded it, and made it into bread. They were barbers for their men. They carried all the burdens when the family was on the move, so that the men could instantly pursue any game or enemies they sighted.[7] Women erected (and may have owned) the houses[8] and gathered the firewood to keep fires going in them at all times.[9] They prepared and served meals,[10] and they were themselves served up as a form of hospitality to important male visitors.[11] And, of course, women bore and reared the children.

English observers wrote of Indian men "scorning to be seene in any woman-like exercise,"[12] but their view may have been colored once again by their own background, in which women's work was considered "inferior." Powhatan men's "scornful" reaction may have been at least partially an explosive reaction to the ignorant questions (e.g., "Don't you work the farm yourself?") asked by Englishmen. Where men and women live in different worlds, the members of one sex may feel prohibited from "trespassing" in the "territory" of the other, all notions of superiority and inferiority aside. It is likely that Powhatan women's work was not much less prestigious than men's work, as the patriarchal English assumed; it was merely different work.

Women produced corn, which was recognized by everyone as a form of Indian wealth.[13] That alone would have raised their status in society. Controlling wealth—by custom, not just by individual force of character—would raise their status further, and there is evidence of such control. In the early seventeenth century Powhatan women received, processed, and served all foodstuffs. Later in the century, when the Indians had come to use currency,[14] it was observed that "the women . . . keep all the money."[15] The Powhatans apparently saw an analogy between food as wealth and currency as wealth and applied an old custom to new economic conditions.

Women's work was probably not as onerous as the English believed. Where technology is simple, standards of neatness are not high, and people do not live by clock time, life need not be a high-pressure struggle for survival. Even nomadic hunters and gatherers, who are popularly visualized as scrounging hard for subsistence, are, according to some analyses, "literally the most leisured people in the world."[16] Obtaining food requires skill and some hard physical labor, but in a rich natural environment such as Virginia was, it did not take up nearly so much of the people's day as we expect. Powhatan men and women had enough time and energy left for frequent community dances. They probably also had elaborate song cycles, rituals, and the like, but the English writers do not tell us about them.

To the Powhatans, as to all Woodland Indian people, the men's world and the women's world were separate but reciprocal and therefore intertwined. Women had to do the daily housework and field work, but they had a right to be provided with meat for the pot, no matter how poor the hunting or fishing was, and they also had a right to be protected against being kidnapped by enemy warriors. Men had to provide the meat and fight dangerous enemies, but they had a right to have a comfortable household and children successfully borne and reared. This reciprocity is best illustrated by marriage customs. As in so many other cultures around the world, the customs surrounding Powhatan marriages brought the basic expectations of both men and women into the open.

The greatest pressure in Powhatan courtship, as in life itself, fell upon the men. A man could not acquire a wife until he had proved himself as a provider,[17] for he had to attract feminine interest with presents of food, and he had to pay bride-wealth to her parents. The English saw the latter, of course, as a "buying" of wives. However, ethnographic studies have shown that bride-wealth compensates a woman's family for the loss of her valuable labor and child-bearing potential, so the amount paid is a public declaration of value for the woman involved.[18] It is therefore likely that Powhatan women, like those of some better-documented ethnic groups, felt very proud when they commanded a high bride-wealth payment.

A girl became marriageable at puberty.[19] A man interested in her had to persuade her to marry him by giving her presents of meat, fish, or wild plant foods. If she lived with her parents, they had to approve the man as a suitor, which means that he had to convince them, too, of his worth as a provider. Personal attraction between potential spouses was secondary,[20] which is to be expected in a culture in which men's and women's worlds were separate and both spouses had sexual freedom after marriage.

When a girl agreed to marry a man, he went to her parents and negotiated the bride-wealth, after which they all sat down to a feast, presumably at the expense of the bride's family. The prospective groom then went home to accumulate (probably with his kinswomen's help) the accoutrements of a household: a house, a mortar and pestle, mats, pots, and bedding. When all was ready, he took the bride-wealth to his prospective in-laws and returned home. Soon afterward the bride was brought to the groom's dwelling,[21] and her father, guardian, or "chief friend" joined the couple's hands together. The groom's father or "chief friend" then brought a long string of shell beads and broke it over the couple's heads, after which the beads belonged to the bride's father. The couple were now married, and a feast took place.

First marriages like the one contracted above were expected to be for life. Additional marriages may also have been made in that way, especially by *weroances*, who were expected to be possessive of their wives, but there was another, more common form for additional marriages in which spouses were temporarily "hired by Covenaunt."[22] The agreement usually lasted for a year or so, after which the couple could separate if they wished. But if they stayed together longer than the agreed-on time without renegotiating, the union became permanent no matter how ill-suited the couple were.

English observers are silent on the conditions under which Powhatan polygyny operated. William Strachey noted only that "each chief Patron of a famely especially Weroances" wanted many wives in order to father many children to care for him in his old age.[23] There may or may not have been a custom demanding the consent of the first wife, as in some societies. Since "six to twenty" people lived in a house, it seems that co-wives normally shared one house with their husband, although Powhatan himself did not permit all his wives to live with him (see chap. 6). Chiefly husbands, at least, were permitted to play favorites among their wives.

Marriage to even one wife was a symbol among the Powhatans that a man had truly reached maturity. The English recorded, without understanding, that it was mainly married men who smoked tobacco (and, by extension, were participating in political or religious affairs), while unmarried men smoked "little or none at all."[24] Marriage to two or more wives was a status symbol. The husband in question had already proved he could afford them, and he may have acquired one or more of the women from his *weroance* as a mark of favor.

Divorce was possible in Powhatan culture, at the behest of husbands[25] and possibly also of wives. A divorced wife kept the family's stores of wealth to live on, along with her children (though sometimes the boys stayed with their father). When she remarried, the goods became the property of the children or, if there were no children, the ex-husband.[26] Divorce by capture or elopement was also possible, at least in chiefly families; four such divorces were recorded by the English. In one, three wives of the Rappahannock *weroance* were stolen by the *weroance* of Moraughtacund, and after English intervention only one wife was returned.[27] Powhatan's brother Opechancanough lost his favorite wife to the blandishments of Pepiscunimah (called "Pipsco" by Indians and English alike), the *weroance* of Quiyoughcohannock. Powhatan showed his displeasure by deposing Pipsco and replacing him with a "son" of his own, but Pipsco kept the wife.[28] Pocahontas, daughter of Powhatan, was married at puberty in 1610 to a "pryvate Captayn" named Kocoum.[29] After her capture in 1613 she languished in captivity among the English for a year, during which she fell in love with John Rolfe. Their marriage, approved by her father, took place in April 1614 and established peace between the English and the Powhatans.[30] Kocoum's reaction was not recorded. Lastly, the *weroance* of Powhatan town lost a wife by capture to the "King of Chawan" later in the century; he retaliated by ambushing the Chowanoc *weroance* and killing him.[31]

Considerable sexual freedom was permitted to both sexes outside marriage. Strachey reported that men and women alike were "most voluptuous" and that because of it they were "full of their owne country-disease (the Pox [syphilis] very young."[32] Women formed part of the hospitality dispensed to important visitors to the Indian towns. Married women were allowed to conduct affairs if their husbands gave permission. "Adultery" meant an affair not sanctioned by the husband, and it was punished by death for the male offender (but not, apparently, for the female one) if he were caught in the act.[33] Women were therefore careful "not to be suspected of dishonestie without the leave of their husbandes, but he giving his consent, they are like [the "bad" women in European culture] and may embrace the acquaintance of any Straunger for nothing [i.e., no fee], and yt is accompted no offence." [34] Actual prostitution is so poorly attested to as to be suspect. The only reference is by John Smith, who in 1624 mentioned "whores by profession." [35] He may have meant those same wives who had their husbands' permission.

The wives of rulers were apparently an exception to the rule of freedom allowed married women. Their husbands "abide[d] not [their wives] to be toucht before their face," [36] and when Powhatan, an elderly and prodigiously polygynous husband, traveled, he left his less favorite wives behind under guard. [37] Powhatan once made a much-loved but adulterous wife sit "upon a great stone, on her bare breech twenty-foure houres, only with corne and water" every third day for nine days. [38] Male rulers were status-conscious men whose wives' favors remained their exclusive prerogative, along with their other status symbols.

Powhatan men married wives who were "a large distance [away], as well in affinitie as consanguinitie." [39] That and their virilocal marriages ensured that Powhatan towns were comprised of "families of kindred & allyance" [40] related through males. One writer noted a form of "heraldry" among the Indians, in which "every great family has some particular bird or beast that belongs to the family in their nation, the skin whereof they have usually stufft and hung up in their houses, or before their doors, which is as it were their coat of arms." [41]

Virilocal villages or other kindreds may have formed large corporate kin groups among the Powhatans, but most Englishmen remained unaware of them. If they existed, however, they would probably have been "descent lines" rather than "ramages" (see below), and they probably would not have been patrilineal.

Kinship structure (not recorded for the Powhatans) can be linked to the environment in which people live (well established for the Powhatans). Sahlins, in his study of traditional Polynesia, [42] found that islands such as Hawaii with an ecological diversity that favored local specialization tended to develop ramage (internal ranking) systems of kinship so that local settlements were tied cooperatively together and surplus goods could be accumulated and redistributed easily. On the other hand, islands such as Samoa, which had several different ecological niches clustered geographically close together, tended to have economically self-sufficient settlements [43] and descent lines (unrelated lineages) within them. The Powhatans match with the latter. Flannery and Coe have added data from the Village Formative Stage of Mesoamerica. [44] They found that within that stage precursory to statehood (chronologically analogous to the Powhatans of 1607), when populations were growing and new settlements were being established, two different settlement patterns arose, depending upon the natural environment in which they were located. In a "microenvironment reduction" system, the original settlement lies in one ecological niche, and "daughter" settlements are made in different niches, leading to economic specialization and encouraging a ramage system of kinship. In a "contagious distribution" system, original and "daughter" settlements alike were located in the same niche each time, and adjacent niches were exploited independently by each settlement; the authors feel that a descent line kinship system was in operation here.

Smith's map shows plainly that Powhatan settlements were always located along waterways. This means that as the population grew, new settlements were made along the shore, in a "contagious distribution" pattern which would correlate with a descent line (or with several other kinds of kinship system). The nature of eastern Virginia itself, so inhibiting to economic specialization, also leads me to favor descent lines (or something less formally organized) among the Powhatans rather than ramages.

Binford has suggested that the Powhatans had a ramage system, based on the lack of English observations on "a distinct break between the chiefs and non-chiefs";[45] Lurie agrees with him.[46] Yet I feel that the English did, in fact, see such a break and that they phrased it as falling between "the better sort" and the common folk. I also suspect that the English, who were attuned not only to stratification but also to ranking among themselves and others (e.g., the various named ranks of their nobility), would have given us at least some meager evidence of an internal social ranking system if they had heard of it from Indians. Powhatan cited his three brothers and two sisters as his successors, but no English writer indicated that the elder of these people ranked above the younger in wealth and deference before they actually took power. In a true ramage system, birth order means that much. A descent line system, on the other hand, would have been *terra incognita* to the English of the early seventeenth century. English silence on the subject of Powhatan kinship may indicate that a lineage system or something similar to it was present.

Evidence for descent reckoning among the Powhatans is scarce, but the fragments that exist point away from patrilineality. Ruling positions passed from relative to relative in a system of lateral succession within a framework of matrilineality. Powhatan's heirs were recorded precisely: his three brothers in order of age, then his two sisters, then the eldest sister's daughter, and finally the younger sister's daughter.[47] (Women could rule, but they had to outlive their brothers in order to do it.) On the other hand, the common folk seem to have inherited property bilaterally: "what goodes the partye leaueth is deuided amonge his wiues and children. But his house he giueth to the wife he liketh best for life: after her death, unto what child he most loueth."[48]

Another telling bit of evidence against Powhatan society as a whole being patrilineal is English descriptions of the sexual freedom that Powhatan women enjoyed after marriage. Patrilineal societies tend not to allow their women much sexual freedom;[49] the thinking usually is that a father's children should be indubitably his, to keep their loyalty and the ownership of any family estate from coming into question. Yet the English accounts are clear that only the wives of status-conscious "royal" husbands were carefully guarded. Biological paternity was obviously not a major concern among the Powhatans, which argues in some degree against patrilineality among them.

Some kinship terminology systems are roughly correlated with bilateral descent, e.g., the lineal system and others, such as the bifurcate merging system and its variants, correlate with unilineal descent. Unfortunately, the Powhatan word lists that survive do not allow us to use such correlations. There is only one list (Strachey's) that contains any kin terms at all; the ones listed are for parents and siblings.[50] Either the English did not ask for uncle-aunt-cousin terms, or they asked but could not understand the answers.[51]

Strachey, at least, received an impression that the Powhatan birthrate was lower than the English. In accounting for native Virginia's lower population density, he suggested as causes the Indians' "poor" medicine, frequent wars, a high rate of syphilis, and a low birthrate.[52] The last, he felt, might be caused by a combination of polygyny and promiscuity that wore out the men (he speaks of "many women devideing the body, and the Strength thereof"). Being an Elizabethan, Strachey did not look for postpartum taboos or periods of continence before important military or religious events, both of which probably did play a part in lowering the Powhatan birthrate. Seasonal malnourishment may also have been a factor, for as we have seen, some people became thin in the hungry times of late winter and early spring.

The English were led to believe that Powhatan women, like all "savage" women, had an easy time in childbirth, unlike "civilized" women.[53] If that were true, then it was because of the regular physical exercise the women got. The women may also have thought, as Iroquois women did, that childbirth was "the consummation of a healthful process rather than an illness,"[54] an idea that would have reduced their fears somewhat. Childbirth has its dangers for all human females, however, and along with their exercise and attitude control[55] the Powhatans must have had means, practical and magical, of assisting difficult deliveries. The English observers, all of whom were male, recorded nothing about these.

When children were born, they were first dipped into water, however cold the season. During childhood, washing was done daily, followed by oiling and painting of the skin to make children impervious to extremes of weather.[56] Babies were bound onto cradle boards until they were of an age "to crawl about." These boards, which are mentioned only by Robert Beverley in the early eighteenth century,[57] had "a hole fitly plac'd for evacuation," and a cloth was inserted between the board and the baby. The baby was bound on with a cord, as shown in figure 21. Once bound,

How Indian Mothers Carry Their Children

Fig. 21. Gribelin's engraving of women and a baby in a cradle board. The engraving is based on two paintings by John White. The figure on the left has been updated to show a woman in a late-seventeenth-century matchcoat and leggings of duffels, while the depiction of the cradle board is an original based on Robert Beverley's account. Courtesy University of North Carolina Press.

child and board were at various times laid flat, propped upright, hung up
on a tree limb, or carried about. Children able to crawl were carried otherwise. The summertime illustration in figure 21, showing the child with one
leg under its mother's arm, is drawn from a North Carolina Algonquian
prototype[58] and may not apply to Virginia. However, the wintertime illustration in the figure, with the child wrapped in its mother's matchcoat,
probably does apply.[59]

Children were educated informally by their relatives and were shown a
great deal of affection.[60] At the same time the tacit expectations for them
would have been high; in the case of boys learning to hunt, the expectations
were not tacit at all (see chap. 4).

In some ways the Powhatans resembled the stereotypical silent Indian,
and in some ways they did not. John Clayton observed late in the seventeenth century that they were seldom seen to be "affected w[i]th pleasure,
or transported with passion [anger], and even among themselves "they discourse . . . little[,] sit[t]ing several hours & perhaps not one word."[61] Another writer of the same period recorded that people who returned home
from a trip "sit down first and compose themselves; or they take some refreshment of meat, and drink, if it be needfull, before they say one word:
thereafter when they think good they begin to talk."[62]

In their spare time, on the other hand, the Powhatans liked to gather for
lively games, music, and dancing; the latter two were pastimes that people
indulged in most evenings.[63] Several games were recorded for the Powhatans, most of them for adults. One was a stickball game, which Strachey
likened to bandy (a game like field hockey)[64] and which corresponds to the
widespread North American Indian game of shinny.[65] The object of the
Powhatan version was to drive a leather ball stuffed with hair "between
two trees appointed for their goal" by means of hitting with crooked
sticks.[66] Then there were two kinds of football games. In one, played by
women and boys, the aim was to kick a ball to a goal. The players were not
allowed to "fight nor pull one another doune" or "strike vp one anothers
heeles as we doe."[67] In the other game men dropped a "litel balle" from the
hand and kicked it with the top of the foot, with the winner kicking it the
farthest.[68] The last active games, both recorded late in the seventeenth century, were wrestling contests and a footrace in which the winner was the
first to reach a prize hung on a tree.[69]

The Powhatans gambled in a game played with reeds. Strachey's account
of it is regrettably vague: he speaks only of "carding and discarding."[70] He
could be referring to either of two reed games to which "the Indians" of the
late seventeenth century were addicted. One, the less likely, was played
with eighty-one small reeds; the object was to pick up either seven or eleven
reeds, probably in a quick snatch.[71] The other, and more likely, game involved manipulating a handful of reeds rapidly while someone tried to

guess the number displayed. The manipulator would "take a certain number of straws, & spread them in their hands, holding them as if they were cards, then they close them, & spread them again & turn them very suddenly."[72] Practiced players got to "know how to count [the reeds] as fast, as they can cast their Eyes upon them."[73]

Powhatan music and dancing went largely unappreciated by the English, who recorded little about the former and made fun of the latter. Several kinds of songs are mentioned in English accounts: the "scorneful songe" about English prisoners dying "badly" (see chap. 4), an "angry" song that concluded with a petition that the gods plague the English, "conjuring" songs performed during rituals, and "amorous dittyes . . . which they will sing tunable ynough."[74] Strachey remarked that when Indian women sang, "they [had] a delightful and pleasant tang in their voyces."[75] Most English listeners were less kind and described what they heard as "howling."

The accompaniment to singing and dancing was either hand clapping[76] or playing of musical instruments. The principal instruments of the Powhatans were rattles,[77] which were made of gourds and graded in size and pitch into "Base, Tenor, Countertenor, Meane and Trible." Such rattles were even a symbol of priestly office,[78] indicating the essential part that music played in religious ritual. All the other Powhatan instruments were also percussion instruments except for "a thicke cane, on which they pipe as on a Recorder."[79] It was "hardly to be sounded without great strayning of the breath," and they played "certain rude tunes" upon it.[80] These reed instruments were sometimes used ceremonially: the *weroance* of Rappahannock once met a visiting party of Englishmen "playing on a Flute made of a reed."[81]

Drums were used in war[82] as well as in other activities. They were made of deep wooden "platters" covered with animal skin. To the corners of the skins were attached walnuts, which were then pulled beneath the platter and tied with a cord. When the skins were thus stretched tight and beaten upon, the drums "yeild a reasonable ratteling sownd."[83] It was not until later in the seventeenth century that an English writer recorded drums consisting of skins stretched over pots half filled with water.[84] Strachey described another instrument vaguely as "some furre or leather thing in his left hand, vpon which he beates with his right."[85] The "leather thing" may have been analogous to the Lenape folded deerskin drum.[86]

Powhatan men and women frequently danced together, and they always danced in a circle around someone or something.[87] The "welcome" dance with which the early Jamestown colonists were honored resembled ordinary social dances and had a set pattern.[88] Someone stood in the center of a circle of seated people, beating on the (folded?) leather instrument and singing. Each dancer got up in turn and danced a solo until relieved by the next person, whose place he or she took in the seated circle. When everyone had had a turn, all the dancers got up and danced in a ring at "an equall distance" from one another,[89] the men alternating with the women.[90] Thus the dance ended, the performance having lasted about half an hour.[91]

Only three other dances are recorded for the Powhatans. The dance that began the *huskanaw* (see chap. 4) involved whole populations of chiefdoms, moving in two immense circles around a group of male dancers who wore "black hornes" and held green boughs. This dance continued so long that people became tired and had to be forced back into order by "principall men" armed with reed bundles.

When Smith was taken prisoner in December 1607, his male captors marched him into their hunting camp and then put on a victory dance, or rather three identical dances.[92] The men's heads and shoulders were painted red and oiled ("which Scarlet-like colour made an exceeding handsome shew"), and they wore fox- or otter-skin wrist guards, quivers and clubs at their backs, and "a peece of copper, a white shell, a long feather," or a rattlesnake rattle tied in their hair. Carrying their bows, they danced "in severall [different] Postures," all the while "singing and yelling out . . . hellish notes and screeches." Smith was newly captured and uncertain of his future, and he found the dance disquieting.

In the fall of 1608, English visitors at Werowocomoco were entertained for nearly an hour until Powhatan's arrival by thirty young women who danced for them and the assembled townsmen.[93] Making a "hideous noise" (probably in imitation of men's war cries), the women rushed from the adjoining woods into the field, where a fire had already been built for them to dance around. They wore body paint of various colors, "some white, some red, some black, some partie colour, but every one different." They wore loin coverings of green leaves, held in place with "girdles," and they had stag horns on their heads. Each woman also carried a weapon, such as a club or sword. The leader carried a bow and arrows and wore "an otter skinne at her girdle, another at her arme," and a quiver of arrows on her back. The dance itself is poorly described, but each woman appears to have alternated singing and less active dancing with very active "fancy-dancing," which Smith described as falling into "infernall passions."

Powhatan dance movements required keeping strict time with the feet while improvising with the body. Strachey called these body movements "frantique and disquieted *Baccanalls*." In fact, the movements sound much like modern pan-Indian "fancy dancing." Interestingly enough, Henry Spelman compared Powhatan dancing to the English "darbysher [Derbyshire] Hornepipe."[94] He was the only Englishman to recognize the kinship between English and Powhatan dancing: both cultures featured active dances in which the whole community could participate.

The Powhatans considered dancing to be a necessary part of life and one which they enjoyed "almost as frequent[ly] . . . as their meat and drinck."[95]

Every evening a fire was made at the dancing ground, and anyone who wanted to could come and participate.[96] Music making and dancing used up excess energy and promoted cohesion among people (especially those aggressive men) who might otherwise have aggravated each other. The English in rural districts had community dances for similar reasons. However, the Powhatans took the custom one step further. When important persons visited "their Townes, the Indians would not thinck they had expressed their welcome vnto them sufficiently ynough vntill they had shewed them a daunce."[97] The people who danced for visitors were probably representing both themselves and their towns in this honoring of guests.

CHAPTER 6

Social Distinctions

MEMBERS OF POWHATAN SOCIETY, with the exception of the Chicka-hominies, were not socially equal, but the English colonists did not fully record the precise nature of that inequality. Appearing in the records are the ordinary people, some of them actually "poor," who figure so largely in this volume;[1] a priesthood with very high standing; outstanding hunters and warriors who served as councillors to their rulers; and finally the ruling families (and probably also very prosperous councillors' families), whom English writers called the "better sort."[2]

Priests were men of great power, because they had tremendous influence over the rulers they served (see chap. 7).[3] In the early seventeenth century their status was so high that they were commonly believed, along with the rulers themselves, to be demigods and to be the only people permitted an afterlife.[4] Their ability to influence the gods and to foresee the future made them invaluable members of society. Indians of all classes "never [went] about any considerable Enterprize, without first consulting their Priests and Conjurers."[5] *Weroances* competed to attract to their territories priests who were more "beloved of their god." Priests of high standing were as-sured a place of honor in the *weroance*'s councils and a fine temple in which to work.[6]

Priests were distinguishable from other people even when they were not dressed up for a ritual performance. They retained a lock of hair near the ear on the shaved side of their head,[7] they had fewer holes in their ears for earrings,[8] and they carried rattles as their symbol of office.[9] When dressed in their regalia, they wore paint and a headdress; the chief priest also wore a medium-length feather cloak (see fig. 20, figure on left, though his cloak is not of feathers).[10] The only headdress the English recorded in detail was that of the chief priest at Pamunkey, who "conjured" John Smith while wearing a face-covering tassel of snake and weasel skins with a crown of feathers.[11] Robert Beverley indicated in the early 18th century that priests wore full regalia at all times in order to "terrif[y] the people into a venera-tion for [them]."[12]

Priests were arranged in some sort of hierarchy, but it was only vaguely recorded. Smith wrote of that "chief priest" at Pamunkey and of "inferiour

Priests" who dressed much like ordinary people,[13] and William Strachey's mention of priests more "beloved of their god" than others has already been alluded to. Beverley, who may have been overly influenced by de Bry's edition of Hariot's work[14] but who also saw Indians at first hand (see Prologue), distinguished between priests and conjurers. He described the conjurer as arriving on the scene with an "air of Haste, or else in some Convulsive posture, that seems to strain all the faculties" and as performing his rituals dressed in a small loincloth, a "Pocket at his Girdle," and "a black Bird with expanded Wings fasten'd to his Ear."[15]

The origins and training of Powhatan priests are poorly documented, primarily because of the priests' preference for secrecy among themselves. The English settlers found out only that they were "brought up to [their] functions" from boyhood[16] and that, later in the seventeenth century at least, the priesthood was confined to a certain family.[17] The enormous amount of time that they spent on duty, sequestered in the temples,[18] led Alexander Whitaker to describe them as celibate hermits whom no one dared approach.[19] It is true that priests lived in part off the offerings that people brought to them for their god,[20] but they were always capable of obtaining food as other men did.[21] Some priests, at least, were also permitted to marry. Uttamatomakin, who was interviewed at length by Samuel Purchas when he visited London in 1616–17, was married to Matachanna, a daughter of the *mamanatowick* himself.[22]

The Powhatans do not appear to have had a nobility analogous to that of England. However, there were commoners (only males are mentioned) whose valor in war earned them a position as consultants to their rulers. They are variously called *cronoccoes* or *cawcawwasoughs* in the early-seventeenth-century records;[23] the word was later anglicized to "cockarouse."[24] Strachey translates the term as "Elder,"[25] Smith equated it in 1624 with *weroance* or "captain,"[26] and John Banister understood that it meant "brave fellow."[27] Men so designated were councillors in time of need to their rulers (see chap. 7). Their position near the source of power enabled them to participate in chiefly feasts and receive *weroances*' castoff wives. They could even have been appointed by their superiors as lesser rulers in their own right (though there is no documentary evidence of it). Their abilities as hunters and fishers (Banister's account is of sturgeon fishing) made them desirable husbands, and they and their multiple wives together created wealthy households. However, there is no indication in the English records that their position was in any way hereditary or that it formed a definite stratum in Powhatan society.

The "better sort," or rulers and their families, were distinguished from ordinary people by the richness of their apparel, the refinement of their manners (at meals, at least), the labor that they did not have to perform (on ceremonial occasions) because they had servants, the real power they possessed, the deference which was paid to them, and the amount of ceremony in their way of life. The first three points have been described in previous chapters. Whereas ordinary folk ate whenever the food was ready or whenever they felt like raiding the "hominy pot," the "better sort" sat down in separate groups of men and women and ate organized meals in individual dishes brought by serving women. The "better sort" could afford many ornaments of copper and pearls, whereas their "inferiors" usually had only feathers, and they could cover themselves lavishly in deerskins and furs. A more detailed description of "better" female attire is in order here.

> The better sort of women cover them (for the most parte) all over with skyn mantells, fynely drest, shagged and fringed at the skirt, carved and coulored, with some pretty worke or the proportion of beasts, fowle, tortoyses, or other such like Imagery as shall best please or expresse the fancy of the wearer. . . . We haue seene some vse mantells, made both of Turkey feathers and other fowle so prettily wrought and woven with threeds that nothing could be discerned but the feathers, which were exceeding warme and very handsome.[28]

Powhatan rulers and their immediate families dressed richly with the help of their servants. This luxury is illustrated in the "toilet" of the favorite wife of Pipsco. Being the favorite wife of two rulers in succession (see chapter 5) had made the woman very proud and very insistent on her "royal" dignities. When visiting an English settlement, at least, she would not even disembark from her canoe under her own power; she insisted that two servants carry her ashore. Her "toilet" was correspondingly grand.

> I was once earely at her howse (yt being Sommer tyme) when she was layd without dores vnder the shadow of a broad leav'd tree, vpon a Pallett of Osiers [wickerwork made of willow] spredd over with 4. or 5. fyne grey matts, her self Covered with a faire white drest deare-skyn or towe, and when she rose, she had a Mayde who fetch't her a frontall of white Corrall, and pendants of great . . . pearles, which she putt into her eares, and a Chayne with long lynckes of Copper, . . . which came twice or thrice double about her neck, and they accompt a iolly Ornament, and sure, thus attyred with some variety of feathers, and flowers stuck in their hayres, they seeme as debonayre, quaynt, and well pleased, as (I wis [know]) a daughter of the howse of Austria behoung with all her Iewells. Likewise her Mayd fetch't her a Mantell . . . made of blew feathers, so arteficially and thick sowed togither, that yt showes like a deepe purple Satten, and is very smooth and sleek, and after she brought her water for her handes, and then a bunch or towe of fresh greene ashen leaues, as for a towell to wipe them.[29]

When the *mamanatowick* washed his hands before meals, the procedure was more ritualized: "When he dineth or suppeth, one of his women before and after meat, bringeth him water in a woden platter to wash his hands. Another waiteth with a bunch of feathers to wipe them instead of a Towell, and the feathers when he hath wiped are dryed again."[30]

Eiakintomino, shown walking in Saint James's Park, London, around 1614 (fig. 10), was apparently a man of wealth. He is clad in a long, fringed, deerskin garment that is knotted at the shoulder. He wears three necklaces and an armband apparently made of beads or pearls, and he carries a shoulder bag which is "possibly painted." [31]

Only two items exist today that may have been part of a *weroance*'s apparel, judging by the lavishness of their decoration in shell beads. These are the "Virginian purse" and "Powhatan's mantle," both of which are in the Ashmolean Museum, Oxford, and neither of which is properly documented before 1638. Their description and documentation are given in detail by Feest,[32] so a short account here will suffice.

The "purse" (fig. 22) was made by folding a long piece of buckskin lengthwise and sewing the edges together in the middle part of the length, after which the skin at each end was cut in strips. The result was a tube with long fringes at each end. A "wedge-shaped piece of skin" was added at one end of the tube to form the bottom of what now became a purse. The fringes were then divided into two groups at both the top and the bottom, and each group was made into an arrow-shaped, shell-decorated flap in which fringes formed the warps, sinew thread formed the wefts, and disk-shaped shell beads[33] were placed on the wefts as they were woven in. The finished purse is thus a leather bag with four heavy, arrow-shaped flaps, two at the top and two at the bottom, and the only way it could be worn would be to drape the top flaps over one's belt. Its overall dimensions are 77 centimeters long by 11 centimeters wide at its maximum (2 feet 6⅓ inches by 4⅓ inches).

The "mantle" (fig. 23) consists of four deer hides whipped together to form a fabric whose maximum dimensions are 2.35 meters by 1.6 meters (7 feet 8½ inches by 5 feet 3 inches). On this fabric, with the shorter sides serving as top and bottom, were sewn figures in *Marginella roscida* shells. The central figure, done in half-shells to give it a finer texture, is plainly human. The other figures consist of thirty-four "disks" or spirals and two quadrupeds, which Feest tentatively identifies as a deer and a cougar. Feest believes that the "mantle" was not a garment, even though it has a V-shaped opening at the "top." Powhatan "mantles" seem from Englishmen's descriptions of them to have been wraparound cloaks, whereas this piece, if worn at all, would have covered the wearer's shoulders and formed a long train in back. Such garments were worn on ceremonial occasions by European monarchs, but "to wear a skin this way would . . . be unique in native North America." [34] Later Virginia monarchs certainly had nothing like it: the embroidered garment taken from the Pamunkey temple during Bacon's Rebellion was said to be a "matchcoat," i.e., a cloak.[35] Feest postulates instead that the "mantle" was merely an object of value kept in a temple storehouse, analogous to the painted skin object that was observed in the Pamunkey chiefdom's temple later in the seventeenth century (see chap. 2).

The English writers give the impression that higher-ranking people were set far above the rest. Linguistically, however, the distinction was not so great. A ruler was called merely "commander," [36] or person in charge: *weroance,* in the case of males, and *weroansqua,* for females. Even the

Fig. 22. The "Virginia purse."
Courtesy Ashmolean Museum,
Oxford, England.

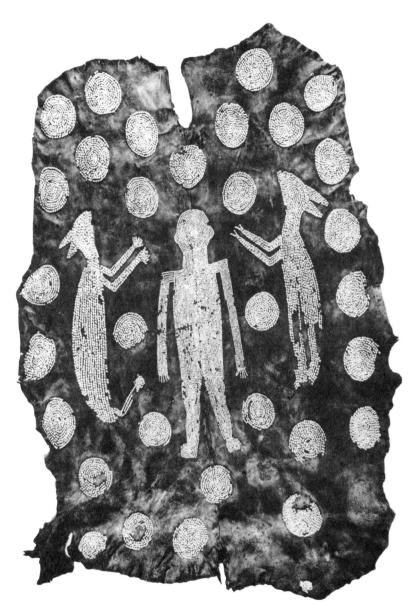

Fig. 23. "Powhatan's mantle" (front). Courtesy Ashmolean Museum.

mamanatowick was not addressed by a special title. Though he had taken his "throne name" from his natal town of Powhatan[37] and though he had the additional names of *ottaniack* (never translated) and *mamanatowick,* "his proper right [personal] name which they salute him with (himself in presence) is Wahunsenacawh."[38] This informality is reinforced by a statement Smith made in 1624, apparently referring to days on which Powhatan was not engaged in formal or ceremonial activities: "the King himselfe will make his owne robes, shooes, bowes, arrowes, pots; plant, hunt, or doe any things so well as the rest."[39] Henry Spelman went further in speaking of the "emperor": "The King is not know [*sic*] by any differenc[e] from other of yᵉ [better] chefe sort in yᵉ cuntry but only when he cums to any of ther howses they present w*ith* copper Beads or Vitall, and shew much reuerence to him."[40]

The buildings in which Powhatan rulers lived and entertained had a sapling framework up to "40 yardes long"[41] covered with bark.[42] These long dwellings had an entrance at one end and a hall at the other in which rulers and their wives, councillors, and bodyguards received visitors (see fig. 24). Powhatan understood well the mystique-building value of public appearances in elaborate quarters in the presence of many members of the opposite sex who were plainly "his." A visitor was conducted down the length of the house, with his suspense rising as he moved through "many darke windinges and turninges before any cum wher the Kinge is."[43] Finally he emerged in the chief's chamber, to find the ruler seated on the low bedstead built across the end of the room, his comfort increased by the "tenne or twelve Mattes"[44] on which he sat, as well as "his pillow of leather imbroydred (after their rude manner) with pearle and white beades."[45] When Powhatan first met Smith in 1608, he sat on such a bed in such a room, decked in "manie Chaynes of great Pearles about his necke, and couered with a great Couering of Rahaughcums [raccoon skins]" with the tails left on; he had a wife sitting on either side of him and more wives behind the two ranks of his councillors seated on mats on the floor in front of him.[46] Every wife wore red paint on her face and "a great Chaine of white Beades" around her neck.

The *mamanatowick* had one of these immensely long and extravagant houses in each of the chiefdoms he had inherited; every house was kept stocked with provisions for his visits.[47] In one of those chiefdoms, Pamunkey, he and his brothers kept "foure or five houses, each . . . fourescore or an hundred foot in length."[48] The house where Powhatan stayed was guarded by a body of "40 or 50 of the tallest men his Country doth afford." At night four sentinels were posted outside the house. Every half-hour one would "halloo" (by "shaking his lips with his finger betweene them"), and the others would answer. These sentinels were subject to a beating if they fell asleep.[49]

"Royal" hospitality, especially when practiced by Powhatan himself, was

Fig. 24. Detail of the John Smith map showing an English artist's rendering of Powhatan's court.

intended to be overwhelming. Important visitors were loudly welcomed by
the townspeople, who either put "their faces to the ground, scratching the
earth with their nailes,"[50] formed a lane for them to pass through and gave
a shout as they did so,[51] or "with loud tunes . . . made signes of great
ioy."[52] The visitors were seated opposite the town's ruler on a mat, with or
without local dignitaries on mats on either side. They were then formally
welcomed with protracted oratory by "2. or more of their chiefest men . . .
with such vehemency and so great passions, that they sweate till they drop,
and are so out of breath they can scarce speake. So that a man would take
them to be exceeding angry or starke mad."[53]

Then food was brought. In a feast given by the *mamanatowick* for visiting Englishmen in February 1608, one of the servants delegated especially
to Smith was "the Queene of Appomattoc, a comely yong Salvage."[54] Smith
was probably imputing to the Powhatans the English custom of having
royalty personally served by nobility. However, the "queen" was probably
only a wife of the Appamattuck *weroance*. The "queen of Appamattuck"
who appears in early English accounts as an antagonist of the English
was Opussonoquonuske, the chief's sister and *weroansqua* of a satellite
town. Gabriel Archer described her in April 1607 as a "fatt, lustie, manly
woman."[55] Nevertheless, the commanding of a *weroance*'s wife by his superior was significant as an index of Powhatan's power.

The feasting food consisted of high-prestige "dainties" such as venison,
powcohicora ("walnut milk"), and cornbread at any season of the year, as
well as other more seasonal foods, and the quantities were as large as the
people could manage. After the feast the central personages smoked tobacco together,[56] and the townspeople danced for both the entertainment
and the honor of the guest. When the evening ended, the (male) visitor was
escorted to a house, where he found a bed made and a female companion
"fresh painted red with Pocones and oile, to be his bedfellow."[57]

The quantities of food offered to guests were prodigious and were probably designed for recipients who had a retinue for whom they were responsible. Smith was once given several pounds of bread and a quarter of venison in an afternoon, followed by "meate for twenty men" at supper. He
gave most of it to his companions, "for this is a generall custome, that what
they give, not to take [back] againe, but you must either eate it, give it
away, or carry it with you."[58] Smith remembered in 1624 that when he was
first captured in 1607, he was given gargantuan portions and expected to
eat as much as he could by himself, the leftovers being "put in baskets" and
kept until Smith's next huge meal, at which time the old food in the baskets
was consumed by the people guarding him. He concluded that they were
fattening him for eating.[59] Later during that captivity Opitchapam welcomed him "with as many platters of bread, foule, and wild beasts, as
did environ him."[60] And still later, when he left Opitchapam's town for
Opechancanough's, the most recent leftovers went with him and were

eagerly claimed by Opechancanough's "women, and their children . . . as a due by Custome, to be merry with such fragments."[61]

In May 1614 Ralph Hamor paid an unexpected visit to Powhatan, arriving around midnight.[62] The household had eaten up all the food as supper, so all that could be produced, while the dignitaries talked, was "the quantity of a bushel" of boiled cornbread. Hamor and his interpreter, Thomas Savage, managed to eat several pieces and gave the rest to Powhatan's "hungrie guard." The next morning their breakfast was "a great bole" of boiled beans and "as much bread as might haue sufficed a dosen hungry men," followed an hour later by "boyled fresh fish" and soon after that by "roasted Oysters, Creuises and Crabbes." That night for supper, Powhatan's household had three does, a buck, and two cock turkeys, which were entirely eaten up. When Hamor left the next day, Powhatan sent with him the uneaten remnants of that morning's breakfast of boiled turkey, another whole turkey, and three baskets of bread.

Powhatan, and presumably his subordinates, could afford to live and entertain on such a lavish scale because of the tribute he collected, the large, relatively uninhabited territory between the Piankatank and York rivers that he could use as a hunting preserve, the fields that were planted especially for him, and the wives he possessed, who probably farmed for him when they were not on public show.

The records left by the English colonists do not mention authoritatively how often tribute was collected. A document of 1621 speaks in passing of the *mamanatowick* going on "his annuall progress through his petty provinces."[63] Powhatan either visited district chiefs, who presented him with it,[64] or sent his minions out in canoes to collect it[65] in "little Cades or Basketts which the great king appoints."[66] The things collected, according to Smith, were "skinnes, beades, copper, pearle, deare, turkies, wild beasts, and corne."[67] Strachey, who went to greater lengths to show Powhatan as a tyrant and got his information from Indians living voluntarily at Jamestown rather than from a *weroance,* characterized the tribute differently as "all the Commodityes growing in the [land], or of what ells his shiere brings forth apperteyning to the Land or Rivers, Corne, beasts, Pearle, Fowle, Fish, Hides, Furrs, Copper, beades, by what meanes soever obteyned" as well as "dying roots" for making pigments.[68] Smith's shorter list of commodities was based on more interviews with *weroance*s and is probably more reasonable.

The rate that Powhatan charged was supposed to be eight parts in ten.[69] That rate is far too high to be applied to all the commodities produced by a subject population that spent three-fourths of every year voluntarily living "from hand to mouth."[70] The fish and shellfish, the meats, and some of the plants would have to be dried, over fires in the humid climate, to prepare them for storage, and the cost in firewood would be excessive. There would also be a problem with storage space if everything were collected, whether in Strachey's "little . . . Basketts" or otherwise. Large amounts of seasonal goods would have to be stored at once, by Powhatan or by his chiefs, in central places. English writers indicate that tribute was stored in temples, one of which stood in every *weroance*'s territory, and three of which were at Uttamussak. These temples might be sixty feet long[71] (the one at Orapax in 1609 was longer; see below) and of an ordinary height, i.e., about ten feet. That does not make much room, after figuring in areas for worship and the bier for rulers' bodies, for the storage of tribute. Unless there were other buildings unknown to the English, the amount of tribute actually collected throughout Powhatan's domain cannot have been large.

Strachey felt sure that coercion was implied if not actually used: Powhatan "robs the poore in effect of all they haue even to the deares Skyn wherewith they cover them from Could, in so much that they dare not dresse yt and put yt on vntill he haue seene yt and refused yt."[72] That last passage indicates that Powhatan may not always have taken possession of the tribute he claimed. Of the things we know he collected, copper, pearls, and beads were inedible valuables; corn was the highest-status garden crop and was raised for him in specially cultivated fields (see below). Only the reference to "skinnes" and "wild beasts" indicates that more mundane things may have been tithable, and those probably only when Powhatan was actually present on a "progress." On the whole, I think it is most likely that Powhatan left his subjects free to consume the limited produce from their own gardens, the wild plant foods they gathered, and the seafood and lesser land animals they caught. If the *mamanatowick* really wanted 80 percent of the high-status things they acquired, it made sense for his subjects to spend much of the year living on low-status foods he did not want.

The planting of a field for Powhatan, and possibly also for his subordinate *weroance*s, was done with great ceremony, as befitted his rank.[73] When the day set for the planting arrived, the people (presumably men and women both) gathered and set out the plants in a large field in a single day. The size of the field and the inventory of plants can be inferred from the observation of the field belonging to the *weroance* of Weyanock near the Appomattox River in 1607. This field was estimated as being "some .100. acres, where are set beanes, wheate [corn], peaze, Tobacco, Gourdes, pompions, and other thinges."[74] After the planting of his field was finished, Powhatan made a circuit of the field, walking backwards and flinging beads to the people, who followed him and scrambled for them. (From 1609 onward, he did this while wearing the paste-jewel crown that James I of England sent him in the fall of 1608.) He showed some people special favor by giving them beads with his own hands. Later in the year, the corn was harvested by the same people, who then dried it and shelled it for him, and it was stored along with the rest of his treasure in his temple storehouse.[75] That building was located about a mile from his capital, which was then at Orapax on the upper Chickahominy River. It was "50 or 60 yards in length" and was closed to all but Powhatan and the priests who watched over it. In that building in 1609 were stored "skinnes, copper, pearle, and beades, which he storeth vp against the time of his death and buriall. Here also is his store of red paint for ointment, and bowes and arrowes." [76] There were also "all the Kings goods and presents *that* are sent him, as ye Cornne . . . [and] ye beades or Crowne or Bedd w*hich* ye Kinge of England sent him [in 1608]." [77]

Powhatan claimed all the copper traded into his dominions, reselling some of it to "neighbor Nations for 100. tymes the value" [78] and using more of it to "hire" warriors (see chap. 7). Once the English arrived, he received most of the tools and weapons that were stolen from the colonists. [79] Powhatan also traded regularly, with the Weyanock *weroance* acting as emissary, with Indians (probably Tuscaroras) to the southwest of his territories; the goods traded were not recorded but were described as "Presents to Powhatan." [80]

It is inaccurate to call Powhatan's organization a redistributive chiefdom. [81] That term implies regular and fairly frequent collection and distribution of food and valuables by a chief, with all members of his organization (often a ramage) participating. [82] Powhatan culture does not fit that model, as far as the surviving records show. There is little evidence of Powhatan or any other *weroance* collecting foodstuffs for later distribution, even in times when their subjects were in want. Only one statement that is even relevant has come down to us: "Powhatan . . . and some others that are provident, rost their fish and flesh vpon hurdles . . . and keepe it till scarce times." [83] The implication seems to be that they were making it themselves and saving it for their own households.

The tribute that Powhatan collected was "redistributed" to a limited number of people. Some of the goods either stayed with or went back to subject *weroance*s, for English accounts indicate that these people supported a way of life which imitated Powhatan's in dressing and in feasting of visitors. The food at feasts was distributed widely once it had been presented to its honored recipients. But we do not know how often feasts were held when Englishmen were not around. Powhatan and his *weroance*s competed for the services of the most able priests, by building them fine temples and helping support them by bringing offerings to the temple. Powhatan and his *weroance*s used their copper to "levy" warriors for expeditions against their enemies (see chap. 7). *Weroance*s gave copper and beads to warriors whose exploits they wished to reward. At the funeral of a *weroance,* his family flung beads to the "poorer people," who scrambled wildly for them; they feasted afterward, but Spelman is silent about how many people attended. [84] And lastly, Powhatan distributed beads to the people who planted cornfields especially for him, and if his petty *weroance*s had fields planted for themselves, they did the same. All of these practices do not fully add up to a redistributive chiefdom.

Men among the "better sort"—and perhaps women (there is no evidence)—could acquire and partially support many spouses. Powhatan him-self was said to have "many more than one hundred" wives when the En-glish colonists began dealing with him.[85] Most of these lived with their own people, not with him; he kept only "some dozen" with him, "in whose Company he takes more delight then in the rest, being for the most parte very young women, and these Commonly remoue with him from howse to howse." They were ranked among themselves, according to the favor they found with him. Any of whom he tired were given to his followers ("those that best deserve them at his handes") or else made free to dispose of them-selves. Wives he wanted to keep but not take along on trips were left be-hind guarded by "tow [sic] ould men." If Strachey heard aright, when Powhatan wanted to add to his collection of women, he visited one of his subject chiefdoms and had the weroance assemble the "fayrest and cumliest mayds." He then took his choice, paying whatever bride-wealth he pleased to the girl's (or girls') parents, and took his prize home for a time. When a wife had a child, however, his custom was to send her and the child back to her people, where they lived at his expense until he was ready to take the child from her and, presumably, continue its rearing in his household. Only a most favored wife, such as Winganuske, sister of one of Strachey's main informants, escaped being sent away when she became a mother.[86] The re-ported rapidity of turnover among Powhatan's wives is unequaled else-where in North America and is therefore a little suspect. When Strachey made his inquiries, there were twenty sons and ten daughters besides Win-ganuske's daughter living with Powhatan.

The English never recorded the family affiliations of Powhatan's wives, except for Winganuske, whose brother Machumps (apparently a com-moner) Powhatan allowed to visit the Jamestown fort.[87] No one ever re-corded who Powhatan's first wife was or whether her seniority had once given her higher status than other wives. Information about the origin of the spouses of other important Indian people is equally scanty. The minor weroance Iopassus had at least two wives, one of whom came from a town a day's walk away.[88] Among Powhatan's many children, we have data on only two marriages: Pocahontas's first husband was merely a "pryvate Cap-tayne,"[89] while her younger sister was married off to an unidentified rich weroance three days' journey away from Powhatan's 1614 capital near the mouth of the Pamunkey River.[90]

Because of the fluid nature of the mamanatowick's household, the only real "queens" among the Powhatans were those who were rulers them-selves by matrilineal inheritance. And because of the matrilineality of the ruling families, rulers' sons and daughters were "princes" or "princesses" only if they were children of a female in the line of succession or if their father, a ruler, was still alive. A mamanatowick's daughter, then, could not expect to be an important person indefinitely; eventually she would be the niece, and later the cousin, of a *mamanatowick*. It was probably for that reason that Pocahontas was married off as soon as she reached puberty in 1610 to that "pryvate Captayne called Kocoum."[91] And it was probably because of that less-than-stellar future that she was so amenable to conversion when the English captured her and treated her as a "princess" in the permanent, European sense.

Powhatan rulers were distinguished from lesser folk in death as in life. Whereas "common people" were buried in the ground, either individually or in groups (see chap. 8), a ruler's body eventually came to rest in a temple.[92] The body was first disemboweled and then placed on a scaffold (Smith called it a "hurdle") for decomposing, along with "tobacco and pipes, turkey and deer and other victualls and pocoon." Sometime afterward, if necessary, the rotting flesh was scraped away and dried "into asshes, which they put into little potts."[93] In the case of Powhatan's body, a three-year period seems to have been allowed for decomposing: in 1621 the English heard about a "Ceremony" for "the takinge vpp of Powhatans bones."[94] The dry bones were either made into a disarticulated bundle (Patawomeck informants) or else laid out properly articulated (James or York River informants);[95] they were then "hung" with jewelry and wrapped in skins and mats before being placed on a platform in the chiefdom's main temple. Whenever the temple was abandoned, in a migration of the people, the building and the bone bundles in it were left to disappear in the course of time.

CHAPTER 7

Law, Politics, and War

POWHATAN, AS *MAMANATOWICK*, was said by English writers to be an absolute ruler, but he was not so in the European sense. In fact, he seems to have exercised his powers most often in military matters. In 1607 his subordinate *weroances* had considerable autonomy, more than they had had when he was in his physical prime, and the common folk seem to have had some leeway, too. And at all times, Powhatan and his *weroances* had to abide by what was customary.

The Powhatans must have had a large body of customary law, but the English, who did not expect such a thing of "savages," asked few questions about it. A limited amount of family law was recorded by a few curious Englishmen (see chap. 5). But most of the rules of Powhatan society that the English recorded as "law" were those they saw enforced in the Indian towns by the political authorities, in modern terms, criminal laws. Reconstruction of the full spectrum of Powhatan law is impossible.

The land in Powhatan's dominions was held ultimately by him. (The Chickahominies probably considered their land as a common heritage.) The English assumed that Powhatan considered himself the "owner" of the land in the European sense, but he may have been merely the highest-ranking steward of the land. The evidence for this idea is indirect: later in the seventeenth century, when the paramount chiefdom had been broken up into smaller units, the *weroances* of those units supposedly held the title to the land as Powhatan had done, yet they "sold" land to Englishmen at a rate and with a willingness indicating that they had little understanding of European concepts of permanent, individual ownership.[1]

Weroances were observed to "knowe their severall [separate] landes, and habitations, and limits, to fish, fowle, or hunt in, but they hold [are granted] all of [by] their great Werowance Powhatan,"[2] and they paid to him part of what the land produced. The common people followed suit: "Each household knoweth their owne lands and gardens"[3] and presumably held them by permission of and paid tribute to their *weroances*. *Weroances* were apparently assigned their territories by Powhatan himself,[4] but unfortunately, nothing was recorded of how commoners claimed their garden plots. Unused plots reverted to common use, judging by Indian hunters' lack of understanding English buyers' cries of "trespass" later in the seventeenth century.[5]

Many of the rules of society in 1607 were enforced by Powhatan and his *weroances*, as the English understood the matter. Although the view of the English was biased by their cultural background, it does seem that many of the functions of finding and punishing miscreants had been taken over by the priests and *weroances*. The English observed at first hand on several occasions that what rulers decreed, was "right" and that what affronted them was "wrong." A spectacular example was observed in 1676, when a *weroance* from "New Kent" County (modern New Kent, King William, and King and Queen counties) was treating with the English. As he was speaking, one of his subjects interrupted him. The *weroance* promptly split the man's head with his tomahawk, killing him instantly, ordered the body carried away, and went on "where he left off, as unconcern'd as if nothing had happen'd."[6]

Nevertheless, Powhatan rulers were bound by custom:

> the only law whereby he ruleth is custome; yet when he pleaseth his will is lawe, and must be obeyed[;] not only as a king, but a half a god, his People esteeme him so. His inferiour kings are tyed likewise to rule by Customes, and haue permitted them power of life and death over their people as their Co-maund in that nature.[7]

On the other hand, the common folk retained some ability to wreak personal revenge. The father of a slain bowman attacked the newly captured John Smith in December 1608.[8] The fact that he did so while Smith was a detained guest of Opechancanough himself may indicate that clearly justified revenging of a wrong was still a personal matter among the Powhatans. Smith's writing that the Indians "seldome forget an iniury" also indicates that there may still have been some room for the common people to practice a system of personal revenge so long as it did not trespass on the rights of their rulers. In the late seventeenth century, after Powhatan's "empire" had been broken up, the system of personal revenge for all murders was observed to have become the norm again;[9] all other offenses required the payment of compensation.[10]

Weroances had life-and-death power over their subjects, as mentioned above. (The eight Chickahominy elders who ruled that tribe[11] may not have had such power.) Even minor offenses such as jostling an English visitor in the presence of a *weroance*[12] could bring orders for an immediate beating. Offenders might be beaten with "cudgels" until their skin was gory and they lost consciousness, but they "never cryed, complayned, nor seemed to aske pardon, for that they seldome doe."[13] The stoicism of the men was shown at such times, but even the most reckless warriors took pains not to bring punishment on themselves by offending their rulers. Gabriel Archer was impressed by even petty rulers who had "their Subiectes at so quick Comaund, as a beck bringes obedience."[14]

Like many other tribally oriented people, the Powhatans believed that stealing from one's own people was a serious crime but that stealing from outsiders (or non-"human" beings) was permissible. The English, being thus treated, concluded that Indians "are very thievish, and will as closely [surreptitiously] as they can convey any thing away from vs."[15] Indeed, the brazenness of the Powhatans when taking things from the English was cause for amazement: "The people steal any thing [that] comes neare them, yea are so practized in this art that lookeing in our face they would with their foot betwene their toes convey a chizell[,] knife . . . or any indifferent light thing: which having once conveyed they hold it an iniury to take from them."[16] Only the Pamunkey did not treat Englishmen that way.[17] Such "thefts" were considered "honorable" exploits in the Indian world, however, and it is significant that most of the loot was turned over to Powhatan,[18] on whose behalf the "thieving" was apparently being done.

On the other hand, the English heard that the Powhatans seldom stole among themselves, for fear of being found out by their "conjurers," according to the cynical Smith.[19] Theft from a compatriot was a capital offence on the Virginia mainland, as were murder (of a fellow Powhatan), infanticide, and even being an accessory to those offences.[20] Henry Spelman saw five people executed while he was living among the Patawomecks. One was a man who had robbed "a traueler of coper and beades," and the other four were a mother and two accomplices who had murdered her child and another Indian who had seen the offence but concealed it.[21] The means by which these persons had been convicted of their offenses were not recorded.

The people found guilty in the murder case were brought to the *weroance*'s (or *mamanatowick*'s) house, where a great fire had been built. An executioner first cut off the men's long lock of hair on the left side of their head and hung the hair on a "bowe" (bow or bough?) in front of the ruler's house. This act presumably deprived the men of their manhood in Powhatan society.[22] Then the criminals' bones were broken by beating them "with staues," and, still alive, they were thrown on the fire to die. Smith saw a similar execution at Werowocomoco in early 1608, though the victim was bound hand and foot rather than having his bones broken.[23] The robber's fate at Patawomeck was to be "knockt on ye heade and being deade his bodye was burnt."

Death by clubbing was a punishment for disobedient subjects, such as the man Amarice "who had his braynes knock't out for selling but a baskett of Corne, and lying in the English fort 2. or 3. daies without Powhatan's leave"; few people dared to visit the English without permission, for fear of meeting the same end.[24] The only details recorded for such executions come from Smith, who wrote that the heads of "them that offend him" were laid on "the altar or sacrificing stone" before being smashed.[25] The deaths of criminals were relatively quick; it was a "notorious enemy or Trespasser"[26] who was given a long, painful, and "honorable" death.

In at least one case, the executioner was a priest. Uttamatomakkin, a high-ranking priest and son-in-law of Powhatan, told Samuel Purchas in 1617 that he had personally executed by clubbing an Indian found guilty of stealing from the English. This particular theft from foreigners was punishable because there was a truce between the two peoples at the time, and the English had complained in person to Powhatan, who had the man caught and punished as they looked on.[27] That episode indicates that there could be religious as well as politico-judicial elements in punishing disobedience to "royalty."

Powhatan's organization was a paramount chiefdom, not a confederacy. Each chiefdom within the paramount chiefdom had a *weroance* (a district chief) answerable to Powhatan, and each town within a chiefdom had a ruler (also called a *weroance*) answerable to the district chief. (The passage of tribute among these people and the way of life that tribute supported were described in chapter 6.)

In this triple-tiered organization, some enlightened nepotism was practiced. Several people governing chiefdoms were close relatives of Powhatan: Pochins (a "son")[28] ruled Kecoughtan; Oholasc, mother of Tatahcoope (a reputed "son"), ruled Quiyoughcohannock as regent; Parahunt (a "son") ruled Powhatan; and Opitchapam, Opechancanough, and Kekataugh (brothers)[29] ruled Pamunkey,[30] a populous chiefdom that contained the region's most holy temple. On the Eastern Shore, Kiptopeke ruled Occohannock as a lieutenant under his brother, the *weroance* of Accomac.[31] At a lower level, the *weroansqua* Opossunoquonuske ruled a small town in her brother Coquonasum's chiefdom of Appamattuck,[32] and Iopassus ruled over Passapatanzy, a small town in the Patawomeck chiefdom ruled by his brother.[33] Assigning one's sibling to a subsidiary territory provided good training and gave him or her useful work to do.

There is no evidence in the English records of any chiefdom within Powhatan's "empire" being considered more important than others, except possibly for the chiefdom of Pamunkey, which had the honor of being ruled by Powhatan's three brothers. The English observed in 1607 that a brother of Powhatan's (probably Opitchapam) was more richly attired than any James River commander they had met.[34] However, his wealth probably stemmed less from the richness in "Copper and pearle" of his territory than from his position as the "emperor's" brother.

*Weroance*s who were siblings of their superiors presumably had their positions by matrilineal inheritance.[35] As we saw in chapter 5, ruling positions in a chiefdom passed through the children of the *weroansqua*, first the sons and then the daughters, in order of age, after which the children of the eldest daughter inherited. Those *weroance*s known to the English as sons of a male *weroance*—and only sons of the *mamanatowick* Powhatan are so recorded—had their positions by appointment. Some of the district chiefs who ruled directly under Powhatan were appointees, too, being unrelated loyalists whom he trusted. The evidence here is negative evidence: William Strachey knew a good deal about the lower James River chiefdoms, yet he says nothing about whether the *weroances* of Nansemond, Weyanock, or Warraskoyack (whose personal names he gives) were related in any way to Powhatan.[36] Powhatan's organization was relatively new in 1607, he having inherited the paramount chieftainship of Appamattuck, Arrohateck, and the town of Powhatan in the James River basin and that of Pamunkey, Mattaponi, and Youghtanund in the upper York River basin.[37] The rest of his dominions he had either conquered or intimidated into submission.[38] He therefore needed capable district chiefs whom he could trust.

*Weroance*s and *mamanatowick*s were not always on good terms with their successors. Force of personality still counted for enough in a ruler in the early seventeenth century that a charismatic younger sibling could make serious trouble. Among the Accomacs, the rightful *weroance* Esmy Shichans, known to the English as "the Laughing King"[39] because of his friendliness, was politically overshadowed by his younger brother, Kiptopeke.[40] Rather than fighting a battle he might lose, that easygoing man gave his brother the northern half of his territory (i.e., Occohannock) to rule, and Kiptopeke remained supportive of him.[41]

Relations were less warm between Opechancanough and the two brothers who preceded him as *mamanatowick,* once the English colony became well enough established to present a real military threat to the family's hegemony. By 1614 Opechancanough was known to have "the commaund of all the people," though he did not have the legal title.[42] In 1616 the English heard that Powhatan "was gone Southwards . . . some thought for feare of *Opochancanough* [and] . . . jealous lest He and the English should conspire against him."[43] In 1617 the English heard that Powhatan "had gone to" a chiefdom called "May—umps" on the Potomac River and had "left" the government in the charge of Opechancanough and "his other brother."[44] This may not have been a formal "abdication."[45] The next *mamanatowick,* Opitchapam, who was not charismatic but instead was "decrepit and lame,"[46] was continually overshadowed by Opechancanough in the eyes of the English, and in 1623 he approached the English with an offer (possibly sincere) to betray his brother.[47]

Powhatan had the power to move around whole tribal populations once he had conquered them, and he did so at times to strengthen his control of new territories. The case that the English heard about was that of the Kecoughtans.[48] That group had resisted Powhatan's blandishments and threats and remained independent until 1596 or 1597, when their *weroance* died. Powhatan then attacked them, killing their new *weroance* "and most of them, and the reserve, he transported over the [York] Riuer, craftely chaunging their seat, and quartering them amongest his owne people." In 1608 the Piankatank group's territory became vacant, and the Kecoughtan remnants were able to persuade Powhatan to let them occupy it. Meanwhile, Powhatan had settled loyalists under his son Pochins at Kecoughtan town, where they remained until the English pushed them out in 1610.

Powhatan was said to have been "Cruell . . . and quarrellous . . . with his own Weroances for trifles"[49] in the past, and he was still capable of all but wiping out whole chiefdoms of his own subjects when he was displeased. In 1608 he had a raiding party ambush the Piankatanks; the English never heard the reason for the attack.[50] The Piankatanks, who are described by Strachey as Powhatan's "neighbours, and subiectes," were removed from their territory and replaced by the Kecoughtan remnants mentioned above.

The resistance of the Chickahominies to Powhatan's domination is the more remarkable given his ability to conquer and control others. The Chickahominies managed to remain an autonomous group at Powhatan's back door only by being a populous, "warlick and free" people who nonetheless paid him "certayne dutyes" and allowed themselves to be hired for his wars "for Copper."[51]

On the other hand, in the early 1600s Powhatan sometimes took less interest in disputes between chiefdoms within his organization, perhaps because of advancing age. The English learned soon after they settled at Jamestown that the Paspaheghs and the Weyanocks were "at oddes," and the Paspaheghs showed them "their hurtes."[52] And when the English explored the Rappahannock River in 1608, they found the Rappahannocks and the Moraughtacunds in a state of enmity with each other, an enmity which Powhatan either chose to or had to ignore.[53] Powhatan frequently told the English that warriors sniping at them were "unruly" people of his whom he could not control, an assertion that Strachey did not believe.[54]

Despotic though rulers could be, custom decreed that they nonetheless had to listen to advice from councillors and priests before giving any orders. English accounts of the early seventeenth century say little about the procedure followed,[55] and it was left to John Clayton to describe it in the 1680s.[56] A council session (erroneously called a *matchacomoco* by later generations of Anglo-Virginians)[57] was held in the "wiochisan house that is their temple," and it was a grave and orderly affair. "The Junior [councillor] begins first & delivers his sentiment wthout interuption, the Second forbearing to speake till a good time after his sessation, or that he had ended his speech, and after that he speakes not a second time to the same thing, thus orderly they every one declare their judgemts, & advice, & after all the King tells them wt is his pleasure." The session sounds rather like an older-fashioned tribal-level meeting, in which consensus had been the goal, to which the greater power of a chief had now been added.

The most influential voices heard in council sessions were those of priests:

"commonly the Priests haue the resulting voice, and determine therefore their resolucions."[58] In matters of war and of discovering the culprits in covert crimes, the priests, with their ability as seers, were considered indispensable in decision making. Thus it is no surprise that *weroances* did their best to attract and keep the most able priests in their chiefdoms.

While the council session proceeded gravely on its way, the younger men who would actually do the fighting dressed themselves for war and fell "into an antique dance with their Tomohauks . . . in their hands threatening what they will do to their enemies."[59]

The Indian peoples who lived outside the Powhatan area were often considered enemies or, at best, neutral neighbors. A state of uneasy peace existed in 1607 between the Powhatan and their southern neighbors, the Algonquian-speaking Chowanocs and the Iroquoian-speaking Nottoways and Meherrins.[60] There was occasional raiding, however, between the Chowanocs and the town of Powhatan, at least in the reign of Opechancanough (ca. 1624–46).[61] The Siouan-speaking tribes to the west were actively hostile. These people, grouped into the Monacan alliance in the upper James River valley and the Mannahoacs in the upper Rappahannock valley, exchanged annual raids with the Powhatans, and only the greater threat presented by the English ever allowed them to make peace.[62] The Algonquian-speaking chiefdoms on the north bank of the Potomac River were generally friendly to Powhatan's organization in 1607, through an alliance with the Patawomecks, although the Moyaones/Piscataways had become enemies of the latter by 1624.[63] Very little is recorded of Powhatan relations with the groups north of the Occohannocks on the Eastern Shore. Finally, there were more distant but much feared enemies in people variously called "Massawomecks" and "Pocoughtaonacks,"[64] whose identity and homeland are uncertain. (They have been variously identified as the Erie or the Ottawa;[65] they were probably northern Iroquoians.) They came in canoes either down the Potomac River from the northwest or down the bay via the Susquehanna River to the north,[66] and they terrorized all the Powhatan groups within their reach.[67]

Lengthy council sessions were necessary before the Powhatans went to war, since they were fighting many enemies, and they themselves had limited manpower. The priests' reputed ability to see the outcome of a raid ahead of time therefore made their advice extremely weighty. On one recorded occasion, priestly advice to the *mamanatowick* set in train a massive attack that wiped out a whole enemy chiefdom.[68] The Chesapeakes, who occupied the modern cities of Norfolk, Chesapeake, and Virginia Beach, had never been drawn into Powhatan's organization by either threat or conquest. Sometime around the founding of the Jamestown Colony,[69] Powhatan's priests told him that "from the *Chesapeack* Bay a Nation should arise, which should dissolue and giue end to his Empier." He therefore "destroyed and put to sword, all such who might lye vnder any doubtfull construction of the said prophesie." Even if the English had arrived, Powhatan had not yet decided that they were enemies rather than potential allies. He therefore concluded that the prophecy referred to the Chesapeakes and it was they whom he exterminated. As "all the Inhabitants, the weroance and his Subiects" were killed, the obliteration of the Chesapeakes was complete, an unusual practice in Powhatan warfare (see below). The group's territory was then occupied by "new Inhabitants," who were probably loyalists from elsewhere in Powhatan's dominions.[70]

Powhatan men often went to war for reasons other than the European one of territorial acquisition: "they seldome make warrs for landes or goodes, but for women and Children, and principally for revendge, so vindicatiue and ielous they be, to be made a derision of, and to be insulted vpon by an enemy."[71] Abducting and adopting the enemy's women and children (i.e., their prime source of future warriors) was an extremely effective way of insulting them while boosting one's own population. It was also a deadly insult to capture an enemy's ruler and put him or her to work doing menial labor. For those reasons, it was normal in Powhatan warfare to kill male enemies, either in battle or later by torture, and to capture, bring home, and adopt enemy women, children, and rulers.[72] The Powhatans occasionally broke this rule, as in the case of the Chesapeakes, but they expected others to abide by it as a means of limiting warfare, and they were extremely insulted when enemies did not "play fair."[73]

No formal adoption procedure was ever described as such for the Powhatans. Whereas some other Woodland peoples introduced captives (some of them potential adoptees) to a town by making them run a gauntlet, the Powhatans had only the victory dance observed by Smith during his captivity (see chap. 5). Their only gauntletlike practice was part of the *huskanaw* for their own boys (see chap. 4) and may have had a different significance.

Some scholars[74] have suggested that Powhatan's attempt to have Smith clubbed to death on an altar stone and Pocahontas's saving of him[75] were all part of an adoption procedure. Aside from the serious problems raised by Smith's publishing the story for the first time seventeen years later,[76] I doubt on ethnographic grounds that a rescue took place. Clubbing was a punishment for disobedient subjects, not a treatment for foreigners, except during a battle. Priests were extremely influential in Powhatan decision making, as we have seen, and by Smith's own account they had already divined his purpose and declared him "friendly." The receptions he had been given, first as an honored guest of Powhatan's brothers and later from Powhatan himself, indicate that Powhatan believed his priests. It would make no sense for the *mamanatowick* suddenly to go against those priests' considered advice and have his honored guest killed. I think it unlikely that Smith needed rescuing in the first place.

The sequel that Smith described after his "rescue"[77] sounds a bit more like an adoption, though Smith did not call it that, and his late publication of the account raises the same problems as does the "rescue." Smith says that he was seated in the anteroom of a house "in the woods" (probably a temple). Powhatan and a body of men, all painted black, made a "most dolefullest noyse" in the inner room and then came to Smith and announced that "now they were friends." Further, Powhatan "gave" Smith the town of Capahosic to rule and said that he would consider Smith a son. This procedure comes closer to eastern Indian adoptions elsewhere, in which after a deliberation a captive would become a member of a specific family. We must remember, however, that neither Smith himself nor any contemporaries who talked to him ever wrote that he had been adopted by any Indians.

The Powhatan chiefdoms were capable of organizing their warriors for mass attacks, though the vast majority of their raids involved only a few men. Participation in a mass attack was not voluntary. The *mamanatowick* would appoint "a Weroance or some lusty fellow" to lead the forces and then send "an officer" to certain towns to "presse a number of Soldiers" by striking them on the back "a sound blow with a bastynado" and telling them to "be ready to serve the great king." The day and place of rendezvous were announced, and no man dared be absent once called on.[78] Warriors could also be hired for a raid. Powhatan monopolized the copper trade in his dominions specifically so that he would have the resources "to levy men withall."[79] The Chickahominies were one such group to be thus hired.[80] The only recorded fee for hirelings was paid by the ruler of Paspahegh, who wanted "14. or 15." other rulers to help him raid the English: each ruler got "one Copper-plate" for participating with his men.[81] Weapons may have been provided to warriors fighting for a ruler. Powhatan had "a great house . . . hung round with bowes and arrowes," where some visiting English dignitaries were quartered for the night in February 1608.[82] Strachey heard that bows and arrows were among the objects stored in temples.[83]

In large-scale attacks the Powhatans used either a "square order"[84] or else a "half-moon" formation to surround enemies.[85] In September 1607 an English party landed at Kecoughtan and was met by "sixtie or seaventie" men bedecked for war, charging "in a square order, singing and dauncing out of the woodes" with the image of their god Okeus borne before them. (The English dispersed them with musket fire.)

The only detailed account of the "half-moon" in use comes from a mock battle staged for English visitors at Mattaponi in 1607.[86] About two hundred men divided themselves into "Powhatans" and "Monacans," each side having a captain. The two companies lined up "a musket shot" (about six hundred feet) apart. The men arranged themselves in ranks fifteen abreast and "4 or 5 yards" apart and in diagonal files so that those at the rear "could shoot as conueniently as the Front." Messengers from the two sides then met in the middle to agree upon conditions: "that whosoever were vanquished, such as escape vpon their submission in 2 daies after should liue, but their wiues and children should be prize for the Conquerors." The two companies then moved closer in a series of leaps, while a sergeant "on each flanke, and in the Reare an officer for lievtenant" kept the men in formation. The leaping men, who were garishly painted and "singing" and screeching in falsetto, were a formidable spectacle.

The men shot off their arrows, after which they joined in hand-to-hand fighting, "charging and retiring, every ranke seconding [moving with the] other." Any man who could, flung an enemy to the ground by his hair and went through the motions of clubbing him to death. The "slain" man was then "out," and the "killer" retired to the rear of his company to give his fellows a chance. Soon the "Monacan" ranks had decreased enough that the "Powhatans" tried to outflank them by charging "in the forme of a halfe moone." The "Monacans" foiled the attempt by fleeing "all in a troop" to an area in the woods, where their confederates were lying in ambush. The "Powhatans" sensed the trap in time and promptly retired to the spot where their own ambush had been laid. Seeing them go, the "Monacans" took the opportunity to vanish into the woods. One suspects that the outcome was prearranged.

For large-scale assaults the Powhatans preferred to have the advantage of surprise. Part of their forces would present themselves as peaceful men, either guests or hosts, and then either during the welcoming feast or the night that followed it, these men would summon their fellows and attack their victims. This method was used with varying success against English visitors to Indian towns, and it was used with devastating effect in 1608 against the Piankatanks, all of whose men had been summoned into their capital town on the pretext of a communal hunt the next day. Twenty-four of that chiefdom's men were killed and scalped, the rest escaping, and the *weroance* and all the women and children were removed to Werowocomoco.[87]

The vast majority of Powhatan assaults on enemies were made in the form of small-scale ambushes, during which no particular order was kept. With the war captain leading the way,[88] each man tried to get within accurate shooting range of an enemy without unduly exposing himself to fire; thus he had to use whatever cover he could and move fast.[89] It was perfectly acceptable to dodge an enemy arrow by falling "downe, and after[ward] rvn[ning] away."[90] The war cries and body paint (and sometimes other decoration; see chaps. 3 and 4) were probably aimed at disconcerting the enemies so that they took a false step and exposed themselves. Staying alive while killing others was the object. Thus Spelman wrote that the Powhatan never fought in the open but always in wooded or reedy places;[91] high weeds in open fields were also useful,[92] as were well-grown corn stalks.[93]

Since the adversary was also using local cover to the full, outright kills were uncommon. It was more usual to disable an enemy, rush up to him, and "knock him on the heade" with a war club.[94]

Powhatan fighting gear consisted primarily of bows and arrows and war-clubs. The clubs took several forms, judging from English accounts. Some were stout wooden batons with one or two sharp edges, which the English called "swords";[95] others were batons with sharp stones or imported iron set into them.[96] The "sword" shown in Robert Beverley's account[97] is ta-pered and gently curving, with abstract engraving above the narrow, hand-held end and two long feathers and a turkey's beard at the wider, club end. A batonlike "sword" was known as a *monacock* or *monohacan*.[98] The other warclub was a tomahawk,[99] or hatchet with a socketed head made variously of deer antler or "a long stone sharpened at both endes."[100] There were also "cudgels" and "clubs"[101] and a "weapon like a hammer,"[102] all of which might have been ball-headed clubs.[103]

Some warriors in some Powhatan groups[104] used shields "made of the barkes of Trees[,] rownd and thick ynough to keepe out an arrowe."[105] These were "hanged on ther leaft shoulder to couer that side as they stand forth to shoote."[106] Often they were painted with bloodroot.[107] Later in the century some Northern Neck men were observed with bark shields which were painted in designs of both red and black (see chap. 4). No wickerwork armor like that of the North Carolina Algonquians[108] was observed among the Powhatans.

Trophies were taken from slain enemies for display later; the custom was a native Powhatan one.[109] The "hand of their enemy dryed" was sometimes worn in a man's knotted-up hair.[110] Scalps were also frequently taken. When most of the male population of Piankatank was killed in 1608, "the long haire of the one side of their heades with the skinne cased off with shells or reeds" was taken to Powhatan. He hung them "on a lyne vnto two trees, And thus he made ostentation of as great a triumph at Werowoco-moco, shewing them to the English men that then came vnto him [in Janu-ary 1609] . . . supposed to halfe conquer them by this spectacle of his terrible crueltie."[111] Later in the century, Clayton wrote of trophies which consisted of partial skulls and attached scalps, "the upper parts of mens heads they have Tom ahauked," which he also calls "skulls."[112] The normal disposal of such trophies was to "cary [them] as the Trophys of their victo-rys, & afterwards lay them up in the temples."[113]

Victory was celebrated on the spot as well as back in the towns. Warriors on a successful raid in 1611 displayed their joy immediately: "the Salvages did so Aclamate Showte and hallowe in Tryumphe of their gayned victory that the Ecchoe there of made both the Ayere and wood to Ringe."[114] Cap-tured Englishmen, at least, were brought home in a formal procession. Smith recorded the celebration that followed his own capture in 1607.[115] At the head of the procession was the leader of the party, Opechancanough, "well guarded" by four rows of five men each, a row on each side of him, one in front, and one behind him. Next came Smith, with a bowman preceding and one on each side of him. After that came the remaining warriors, walking in a long, snakelike file with a "sargeant" on each side running up and down the line in opposite directions to keep order. This file marched for "a good [long] time," apparently around the town, before the men "cast themselves in a ring with a [victory] daunce." Smith wrote much later[116] that the dance was actually three dances, in which they moved "in such severall [different] Postures, and singing and yelling out such hellish notes and screeches" that Smith's "stomacke at that time was not very good." On that occasion there were no scalps to be displayed or danced for.

The Powhatan ways of commemorating dead warriors and of making peace with former enemies went unrecorded by the English settlers. In the latter case, there was probably feasting and oratory. Beverley wrote in the early eighteenth century of peacemaking with a hatchet-burying ceremony,[117] but he may have been speaking of a non-Powhatan group's custom. The formal exchanging of strings and belts of wampum was a later development that spread from New England.[118] Gifts of clothing seem to have been the Powhatan norm instead, in the early years of the Jamestown Colony, in cementing alliances with the English.[119] The use of chains of pearls soon followed. The English demanded such a chain as a sign of peace from the Nansemonds in September 1608,[120] after which Indian "royalty" voluntarily used chains of pearls in appeasing angry English visitors.[121] In 1614 a chain of pearls was agreed upon as a badge of safe conduct for messengers between Powhatan and the English.[122]

Tobacco undoubtedly played a part in peacemaking. It was offered to important visitors (see chap. 6) and was also presented to visitors of dubious intentions. When the English first encountered the Appamattucks in 1607, one of the chiefdom's leading men came forward "with a bold vttering of his speech" and held an arrow nocked in his bow in one hand and a pipe of tobacco in the other.[123] The English were presumably expected to choose between them; they chose the pipe.

The Powhatans had strong feelings about oaths, which they took while lifting one hand toward the sun and laying the other hand on the heart. They also swore "by the life of the great king," Powhatan, and by their ancestors' spirits.[124] The gesture of hand toward sun and hand on heart was the more common one, and once they had made oaths in this manner, "no Christian will keep their Oath better vpon this promise."[125] The Powhatans also had a gesture of friendship, equivalent to the modern handshake, which was the interlocking of index fingers. Their sign for unity with someone was similar: the signer interlocked his own index fingers.[126]

CHAPTER 8

Medicine and Religion

THE POWHATANS PLACED MEDICINE and religion in one category of thought, since the same men were practitioners in both fields. The Indians and the English alike were prescientific people who looked to the supernatural as the cause of a very wide variety of phenomena and the means for controlling them.

Before seeking the aid of specific deities, the Powhatans applied herbal and other remedies. The English heard about some of these, but unfortunately they were not much interested in the cures used by an "inferior" culture. As time went on and English evangelism continued, Indian priests and laymen alike became more secretive.[1]

It is uncertain how much Indian laymen knew about herbal remedies in the early seventeenth century. A hundred years later the priests kept laymen almost totally ignorant,[2] possibly as a means of preserving their own high status. They sold medicines such as snakeroot to people who were about to engage away from home in activities in which they might be injured.[3] When an Indian found a drug that worked for him, he brought it to the temple for safekeeping. In that way "the remembrance of this herb & its virtue is not only preserved" by dedicating it to the temple's god, "But the Preist [sic] also becomes best instructed thereby & knowing in the art of medicine."[4] Thus the Powhatans had accumulated "Apothecary drugges of diverse sortes," some of which were known to work—the Indians claimed that they all worked wonders—and others which were a mystery to the English.[5]

The Powhatan term *wisakon* meant "medicine in general,"[6] though the early colonists assumed that it referred to one herb with a few specific uses. Merrill and Feest[7] point out that the Powhatan gave the name *wisakon* to unfamiliar tastes such as English spices[8] and liquors[9] and that the term is cognate with other Algonquian words for "bitter." Therefore, *wisakon* meant medicinal-tasting things, including real medicines.

Gabriel Archer was shown *wisakon* at Arrahateck in 1607 which looked like a liverwort or bloodwort and which was used for healing "poysoned woundes."[10] George Percy described a similar plant, adding that wounds had been cured within twenty-four hours. He also recorded how the plant was gathered: six persons (presumably men) went searching, arm-in-arm and singing. Upon discovering the herb, they sat down, still singing, "crossed" the plant for some time with their hands, and then gathered it in. This medicine was chewed and spat onto wounds.[11] The ceremonial behavior used in its gathering may have been typical of the way in which medicinal plants were gathered, though no other English writer touched on the subject.

Later in the seventeenth century John Clayton identified Powhatan wound-curing medicines as the following: "*Indian weed*," which may be a member of the *Valerianaceae* family; the "white plantain," which may have been *Gnafalium obtusifolium* L. (rabbit tobacco or sweet everlasting); and an herblike "self-heal" (*Prunella vulgaris*), which was shown him by an Appamattuck priest.[12] The wound to be healed was first cleaned, not by washing but by sucking and spitting. "Then they take the biting Persicary [*Polygonum hydropiper* L.] & chaw it in their mouths, & thence squirt the Juice thereof into the wound, . . . Then they apply their salve-herbs, either bruised or beaten into a salve with grease, binding it on with bark & silk grass."[13]

Roots and barks of "Herbs or Trees" were used in teas and poultices, much more commonly than were leaves. Poultices were applied around an afflicted spot rather than on it.[14] Not all wounds were successfully cured, however. John Smith noted that "old ulcers" or infected wounds were seldom cured among the Powhatans,[15] and William Strachey observed that although simple wounds were often cured quickly, multiple cuts or wounds with broken bones "such as our smale shott make amongst them" were beyond the powers of the priests to cure.[16] Fevers and sleeplessness during illnesses were ameliorated by applying the flowers of jimsonweed (*Datura stramonium*) to the temples as an opiate.[17]

Powhatan herbal cures often involved purging patients and making them vomit. Indian patients were never bled as European ones were.[18] According to Smith, the Powhatans drank a strong decoction of *wisakon* every spring; they drank so much of it that "it purgeth them in a very violent maner; so that in 3 or 4 daies after they can scarce recover their former health."[19] Since this practice has strong echoes of the widespread Southeastern custom of taking "black drink" in annual ceremonies, the plant used may have been *Ilex vomitoria* (yaupon holly), which grows as far north as southern coastal Virginia.[20] Clayton also learned that vomiting was induced by "a little sort of Squills" (possibly *Camassia scilloides*) or by warm water added to the sap of "lesser sassafras," which may have been spicebush (*Lindera benzoin* L.) or wild allspice.[21]

According to Clayton, purges were made from pokeweed, or American nightshade (*Phytolacca americana*), which can also be used as an emetic,[22] and a white-flowered variety of wild ipecac (*Euphorbia ipecacuanhae* L.) or a species related to it (possibly *Euphorbia corollata* L., or flowering spurge).[23] Clayton said the Powhatans also used the root of "Indian purge," which may have been the plant variously called feverwort or horse gentian (*Triosteum perfoliatum* L.), the bark of whose roots has emetic properties.[24] Other purges were made from "fleur-de-lis," or dwarf iris (*Iris verna*); one or more varieties of dogbane, or Indian hemp (*Apocynaceae*);[25] and a variant of angelica (possibly *Angelica atropurpurea* L.),[26] which was also used as an animal-attracting plant by Indian hunters (see chap. 2).

Traditionally the premier "Indian" herb in Virginia, for Powhatans and English alike, has been the snakeroot, which even the most secretive eighteenth-century priests let their people know about for use while foraging.[27] Curiously, no early English account mentions the Powhatans using it. In the 1680s Clayton was shown several plants by English friends and a different plant by an Indian; the Indian's exhibit resembled dogbane.[28] There are three varieties of herbs in Virginia today that go by the common name of snakeroot: white snakeroot (*Eupatorium rugosum*) and rattlesnake root (*Prenanthes alba*), which grow in rich soils in woods, and Virginia snakeroot (*Aristolochia serpentaria*), which grows in rich, limey soils. The last-named seems to have been most popular with English settlers in North America.[29] Interestingly enough, the one witness's account of an Indian person curing a snakebite says nothing of any herb; the cure was cauterization of the bite.[30]

Curing through cauterization was not uncommon among the Powhatans. They may have used the same procedure for cauterizing small areas as some Indians in the Carolinas did,[31] that is, heating a reed over the fire until it was almost hot enough to ignite and then applying it "upon a piece of thin wet Leather, to the place aggriev'd, which makes the Heat more pierceing."[32]

Though they did not bleed their patients, Powhatan doctor-priests were said to be "exquisite at Cupping,"[33] or drawing liquid out of a place by creating a vacuum over it. Smaller-scale swellings were handled either by cupping or by lancing. The lancing was done with "points of reeds," after which the liquid was sucked and spat out.[34] Smith reported that in the lancing process, small pieces of wood were inserted into the skin, after which they were burned down close to the flesh.[35] Sometimes scarification was used for swellings, the instrument being a fine, hafted piece of stone[36] or a rattlesnake's fang.[37] John Banister wrote that the incision seldom went below the epidermis.[38]

Dropsy, or larger-scale accumulation of water in the body, was cured by several methods, all of which involved sweating. Clayton observed that the Powhatans took the wood of the "Swamp-Plumb-tree" (species uncertain), burned it to charcoal, beat the charcoal to powder, and mixed the powder with grease to make an ointment. This ointment, smeared on the body, made the body "foment . . . very much, . . . For it opens the pores, to that degree, that the water runs down their leggs."[39] John Lederer noted that the Indians cured "sclerosis of the spleen with a poultice composed of a root [species unidentified] which has the effect of a vesicant and draws out plenty of water." He also wrote that dropsy was cured by preparing red-hot pebbles in a hollow in the ground, sprinkling them with "a decoction of three herbs one of which is an *Esula*," and having the patient bring his belly close to the heat.

> After the sick [person] has received the rather hot steam against the belly, the navel opens itself, and the doctor lets out a sufficient quantity of water, and as much as the sick [person] can bear; after which to close the opening again, he applies to it a certain kind of moss, and repeats this as often as he judges it necessary to dry up the belly.[40]

The sauna-like sweathouse was used by people who suffered from "dropsies, swellings, aches and such like diseases,"[41] by people who had fever or chills,[42] or just by healthy people who wished to be invigorated.[43] A sweathouse was attended by a "Doctor,"[44] who was in charge of heating up three or four stones until they were red hot. He then laid them on the hearth in the sweathouse and placed over them "the inner bark of white Oak beaten in a mortar." Then the people entered, as many as the building would hold,[45] and the attendant closed the door. After a time he opened the door and threw water on the stones, creating steam; he also sprinkled the people from time to time "to keep them from fainting." When the people had stayed in the heat for as long as they could stand (usually about 15 minutes),[46] they burst from the house and plunged into the stream that was always nearby. They then annointed themselves with a mixture of bear's oil and pulverized angelica and puccoon[47] to make their pores close even more tightly and to keep lice and fleas away.[48] This sort of "cure" was said to be very effective; at least one English gentleman had found it so.[49]

English writers of the early seventeenth century wrote nothing about the general state of health of the Powhatans, beyond giving an impression that they were strong and had sound constitutions. By the late seventeenth century, when European conquest and European diseases had probably taken their toll of the Indians' mental and physical health, two English observers took divergent stances. Robert Beverley wrote idealistically that "the Indians are not subject to many Diseases,"[50] which may have been true prior to the coming of the English. But a well-trained, anonymous botanist who wrote in the 1680s felt that "sad distempers" were "very common among them," and he gave specifics.[51] "Many are taken with the belly acke, which is a dreadful torment: many times it takes away the use of their limbs: after recovery, they seldome come to have the use of their hands and legs." That disease could be either polio or tabes dorsalis, one of the forms taken by the final stage of syphilis.[52] "There is another disease, they call the distemper, which consumes their throat and nose and other parts, as the French pox does, and they use the same remedies." This, again, sounds like the last stage of syphilis; however, unlike the optimistic Strachey,[53] the writer of the 1680s reported that "few or none are cured of it."

Syphilis is reported among the Powhatans by two of the earliest accounts in the English colony. Strachey said the disease was widespread (see chap. 5). Archer wrote after an expedition up the James River that "the great diseaze reignes in the men generally, full fraught with noodes botches and pulpade apparances in their forheades, we found aboue a hundred."[54] Where the Powhatans got syphilis is another matter. Osteological analysis of archaeological finds in Virginia is not far enough avanced at present to enlighten us. Syphilitic lesions have been found in prehistoric skeletons in other parts of North America. Syphilis appeared among Europeans very soon after Columbus's first voyage,[55] after which European explorers could have helped spread it further among native Americans.

When a disease was so serious that all other remedies failed, supernatural means had to be used, so a priest was called. The writer of the 1680s recorded that "some cubits of their money" were "hung" over the sick person's house, rather like an advertisement of illness within, and whoever cured the patient collected the money.[56]

Powhatan priests used several methods of curing, some of which resemble the shamanistic cures reported elsewhere in North America.[57] Smith wrote that a curer had sucked "blood and flegme" from the afflicted spot with "extreame howling, showting, singing, and . . . violent gestures, and Anticke actions over the patient."[58] The writer of the 1680s heard that priests also merely prayed over their patients, using repetitious words, howling, and violent gestures until they were in a sweat.[59] The priests' actions may have been designed to bring on a trance state, a frequent prerequisite for shamanistic curing.

Henry Spelman wrote in detail about a patient who was laid flat on a mat with a priest kneeling at his side. The priest spewed water on himself and then took his rattle in one hand and beat loudly on his chest with the other, after which he rose very gently and circled the patient, shaking the rattle softly over the sick one's entire body. Finally he sprinkled the patient with water while murmuring certain words, which concluded the ceremony.[60] The writer of the 1680s heard of priests sprinkling water infused with myrtle, holly, and herbs over patients and around their houses. He also heard of priests stretching themselves full-length on their patients, head to head, arm to arm, and so on, after which some patients rose "up on a sudden and [walked] about the house, as if nothing had ailed [them]."[61]

Powhatan priests knew more varied and more powerful cures than did the laity. They also had more intensely personal relationships with supernatural entities. However, ordinary citizens were still involved with these entities on a day-to-day basis. The use of omens in deciding where to hunt was described in chapter 2. People were also rewarded and punished directly by the deity Okeus. And there is one oblique reference in the English records to what may have been the well-known Native American "vision quest" or something similar, though the people involved in it seem to have been priests. Like "the Augurers in the old [i.e., Roman] tyme," "they" stood alone in some solitary place, either deep in the woods or "vpon some desolate promontory-Toppe." Here "they" called upon various deities in their pantheon "with impetious and intermynate Clamours, and howling and with such paines and strayned accions as the neighbour places eccoe agayne of the same, and themselues are all in a sweat and ouer wearyed." [62]

Priests had rituals for conjuring up gods, divining the future, raising or quelling storms, and disabling enemies with confusion. The English were skeptical about these "devilish" practices but thought that some of them seemed to work. Late in the seventeenth century priests were believed by the English to be able to find any lost article except a Bible! [63]

Priests summoned and conferred with Okeus, [64] the severe deity who was most important in the Powhatan pantheon. Later in the century the English thought that this god appeared to all initiated adult men in the form of a "handsome young Indian," [65] but a rare account from early in the century implies strongly that only priests met him face to face, and then perhaps only at Uttamussak. [66] Samuel Purchas interviewed the priest Uttamatoma-kin in the winter of 1616–17 while the latter was in England, [67] and he wrote about it in detail in the (now rare) 1617 edition of his *Pilgrimage*. Priests had not yet learned the necessity of secrecy in dealing with the English, and Uttamatomakin talked willingly of his religion and even demonstrated some of its rituals. Okeus was summoned and conferred with as follows:

> First, foure of their Priests or sacred Persons (of which he said he was one) goe into the House [temple], and by certaine words of a strange language (which he repeated very roundly in my hearing, but the Interpreter vnderstood not a word, nor doe the Common-people) call or coniure this *Okeeus*, who appeareth to them out of the aire, thence comming into the House; and walking vp and down with strange words and gestures, causeth eight more of the principall persons to be called in, all which twelue standing round about him, he prescribes to them what he would haue done. . . . His apparition is in forme of a personable Virginian, with a long blacke locke on the left side, hanging downe neere to the foote. This is the cause why the Virginians [Indians] weare these sinister [left-sided] locks; . . . After that he hath staied with his twelue so long as he thinks fit, he departeth vp into the air whence he came.

Banister also noted that the language used in Powhatan rituals was "not understood by the common people." [68] Beverley added that there was "a sort of general Language" which was perhaps "*Algonkine,* which is understood by the Chief men of many Nations" as a lingua franca; [69] he did not speculate about whether it may have been an archaic dialect, closer to the ancestors of other Algonquian languages.

Uttamatomakkin told Purchas in 1616–17 that Okeus had told his priests about the English before they ever arrived. He also informed Uttamatomakkin, before the latter's departure for England in the traveling party of Powhatan's daughter Pocahontas in 1616, when the party would return from England. The prophecy was coming true, at the time of the interview with Purchas, because of bad weather delaying the ship. Utta-matomakkin also said that, once home, he would not be able to go "into that house," meaning the temple where his duties lay, "till *Okeeus* shall call him."[70] Perhaps he would have been ritually unclean after a long sojourn with the English.

Only one Englishman witnessed a Powhatan divining ritual: Smith was put through such a ritual while he was a captive in the winter of 1607–8, the aim being to determine "if any more of his countrymen would arrive [*sic*] there, and what he there intended."[71] On "3 or 4" successive days, from about 10 A.M. to 6 P.M., the same ritual was held in the temporary house where Smith was being held prisoner.[72] He was seated beside the hearth and seven priests assembled (his 1624 account says the chief priest appeared first, after which two sets of three priests came "rushing in"). A circle of cornmeal was then laid around him, after which "the chief Priest" in full regalia led the others in a song accompanied with rattles. When the song ended, the chief priest laid "5 or 3 graines" of corn down on the ground, moved a little way around the circle of cornmeal, and commenced another song (the 1624 account says it was a short but vehement "ora-tion"), at the end of which he laid down more corn kernels and moved on again. Thus with songs and laying down of corn the chief priest circled Smith three times.

Next came a cycle of songs for dividing the piles of corn; at the end of each song a pile of kernels was divided "by certaine numbers" with a little stick. That was as much of the ritual as Smith remembered later, for each song was accompanied "with such strange stretching of their armes, & vio-lent passions and gestures" that he sat there in fear of his life. At the end of each day he and the priests feasted "with much mirth." Finally, somehow, the priests got their answer, and it was the wrong one: the English were friendly allies of the Indians. Much later in the century the Powhatans ad-mitted that their divining practices were useless against a people as utterly strange as the English: "They say that though their God can tell when their neighbouring Indians have any design upon them, yet he cannot acquaint them with the designs of the Inglish."[73]

Controlling the weather was a priestly function among the Powhatans, one of which the English remained extremely skeptical. Smith, who may have seen such things firsthand, wrote that during violent storms the "con-jurers" ran down to the shore, if they were not already in canoes, and after making "many hellish outcryes" threw tobacco, puccoon, or copper trin-kets into the water to appease the god causing the storm.[74] The English saw Powhatan rainmaking at least twice; on the later occasion, in the second half of the seventeenth century, the Indian rainmaker was hired by an En-glish planter.[75] The earlier occasion was at Nansemond in 1611, when the English were trying to explore the territory and its owners were trying to prevent them.[76] The Nansemonds saw their arrows merely ricocheting off the Englishmen's armor, and knowing that English guns used fire or sparks, they called on their priest to make rain that would neutralize those weapons. Accompanied by a "mad crew" of dancing warriors, the priest ran along the shoreline with his rattle, throwing fire into the air out of a censer and making "many dyabolicall gestures" and incantations.[77] An Indian accompanying the English expedition recognized the ritual and announced that there would soon be rain.[78] And so there was, "exceeding thunder and lighteninge and much raine," but it fell five miles away and did the Nansemonds no good.

The English were victims of "magic" that disoriented them on another occasion in 1611.[79] They had gone to the falls of the James against the express wishes of Powhatan, and one evening as they were sitting at prayer, safe behind their "trenches," they heard "a strange noise . . . comeinge out of the corne [planted nearby] towards . . . our men[,] like an Indian '*hup hup*' with an '*oho oho*.'" The English then fell into confusion, grabbing the wrong ends of their guns and falling over themselves, and they remained in that state for "half a quarter of an hower," after which "sudenly as men awaked out [of] a dream they began to search for their supposed enemies, but findeing none remained ever after very quiet." It is not surprising that English clergymen like Alexander Whitaker concluded that "there be great witches amongest [the Indians] and they [are] very familiar with the divill."

Powhatan priests' great power over the common people stemmed not only from their curing and magical abilities but also from their position as keepers of temples, which contained mysterious things and where ordinary folk could rarely go. Temples were constructed like ordinary houses except that they were larger and multiroomed. Some of them, at least, were also kept cleaner than ordinary houses, for George Percy noted that at Paspahegh in 1610 there was "amongst the reste [of the houses] a Spacyous Temple cleane and neattly keptt A thing strange and seldome sene amongste the Indyans in those partes."[80]

Temples doubled as royal storehouses and stood either in the towns or out in the woods. The greatest temple of all was at Uttamussak, in the woods near the mouth of the Pamunkey River, and near it was "a house Temple or place of Powhatans" and another building. These three structures were nearly sixty feet long and contained "the images of their kings and Divels and Tombes of their Predecessors." They were watched over by seven priests, whereas ordinary temples had but two or three. These temples could be entered only by priests and rulers, and even laymen passing by them in canoes on the river "solemnly cast some peece of copper[,] white [shell] beads or *Pocones* into the river, for feare their Oke should be offended and revenged of them."[81] When Powhatan received valuable presents, like the crown, bed, basin, and ewer the king of England sent him in 1608, they were stored in the temple nearest his residence, which is why Spelman saw King James's presents in the temple at Orapax.[82] Spelman's wording is interesting: "with him [the image of Okeus] are set all the Kings goods and presents that are sent him." The presents Powhatan received may have been offered, in turn, to the deity.

Ordinary temples were about twenty feet wide and one hundred feet long, with a door at the east end.[83] One first entered a large anteroom, with a hearth and a smoke hole over it; one priestly duty was to maintain "a contynuall Fire" in that hearth. The west end of the building was partitioned off into a sort of "chancel" by means of "hollow windynges and pillers," and on the pillars stood carved and painted busts, described as "divers black Images fashioned to the Showlders, with the faces looking [eastward] downe the Church."[84] In the west room was a platform on which rested the "bodies" of deceased rulers (see chap. 6). Under the platform was kept an image[85] of the vengeful god Okeus, painted black and with an "ill-favoured" expression; the image sat upright, hung with chains of pearls, and "vayled with a Matt."[86] There were also images of "wolves, foxes, ravens and other creatures stufft with straw, and glass or beads in their eye holes"; these were venerated in order to gain the useful traits of the animals represented.[87]

Temples were further ringed around with images which stood outside their walls. Powhatan's temple at Orapax had such a free-standing post at each corner, carved to resemble "a Dragon" [probably either a wolf or a mythological creature not described by the English], a bear, a "Leopard" [probably a cougar], and a huge man. All four were made "evillfavordly" and were intended to guard the temple.[88] A temple that Beverley violated was surrounded at a distance with posts "with Faces carved on them, and painted."[89]

The English knew, as Powhatan laymen did not, that Okeus' image was that and nothing more, for within five years of founding Jamestown, they raided several Indian towns and "Ransaked their Temples."[90] Smith saw an image carried in front of several dozen charging warriors at Kecoughtan in 1607; he described it as "made of skinnes, stuffed with mosse, all painted and hung with chaines and copper."[91] However, no Englishman made a careful examination of an image or the place in which it was stored until Beverley and some friends broke into the temple mentioned above late in the seventeenth century.[92] The image in that temple showed signs of having been "updated."

The temple was a small one, about eighteen feet by thirty. The western third of it was screened off with "very close Mats," and even the dismal light of the eastern anteroom did not penetrate it. Feeling about, Beverley and his friends found "some Posts in the middle; then reaching our hands up those Posts, we found large Shelves, and upon these shelves three Mats, each of which was roll'd up, and sow'd fast." All three bundles were then taken "down to the light" and carefully ripped open. (This act of desecration was not recognized as such by Beverley, although he knew to fear the

Indians' anger if they caught him in their temple.) One bundle contained "some vast Bones, which we judg'd to be the Bones of Men, particularly we measur'd one Thigh-bone, and found it two foot nine inches long." A second bundle contained some *monacocks*, one of which Beverley reproduced in his book (see chap. 7). The third bundle contained a small image of Okeus, in pieces which "wanted [needed] putting together."

The image's trunk consisted of "a Board three foot and a half long, with one indenture at the upper end, like a Fork, to fasten the Head upon." Extending from shoulder level halfway down the length of the board was a rib cage of "Half hoops nail'd to the edges of the Board, at about four Inches distance, which were bow'd out." About seven inches from the bottom of the board were two more boards, "fasten'd to it by Joynts or pieces of Wood," which jutted out at right angles for about fourteen inches on each side. This Beverley supposed would represent the splayed thighs of a squatting image. Packed with the three boards were "Rolls made up for Arms, Thighs and Legs, bent to at the Knees," as well as "red and blue pieces of Cotton [trade] Cloath" to clothe the image. No head or jewelry was found, though Beverley and his friends did not take much time looking for fear of the Indians' return. He wrote later that the image could give a convincing impression of life, when it was manipulated from behind by a priest and viewed at a distance by people standing in the dimness of the anteroom. Sometimes, for instance, a lighted pipe of tobacco would be put in the image's mouth, and a priest standing behind in the gloom would "drawe . . . the smoke."[93] Even some sophisticated Powhatan laymen were fooled, and when Beverley told one such Indian man about the image he had examined, the man was visibly upset.[94]

The English called the Powhatans devil worshipers, but only in a very limited sense were they right. More accurately, the Powhatans were appeasers of a severe deity who policed their actions. They also paid great respect to all things that could hurt them, "as the fire, water, lightning, thunder, our [English] ordinance [*sic*], pieces [guns], horses, &c."[95] For instance, the Indians who met the first English boar in the woods saw him bristle in hostility and, taking him for "the God of the Swine, which was offended with them," they reacted with "awfull feare."[96] The Powhatan term for each of these lesser but potentially harmful entities, as well as for their priests, was *kwiokos* (pl., *kwiokosuk*), or minor god.[97]

Both Strachey[98] and Beverley[99] discussed the Powhatan religion with willing and reasonably fluent informants, and their stories are the same. The Powhatans believed in a great god called Ahone, who had created the world and "the Moone and Starres his Companions, great powers, and which dwell with him," and who made the sun to shine.[100] Ahone was so beneficent that no offerings needed to be made to him. Okeus was another matter; he was a severe god whose relationship to Ahone was never made clear by Indian informants. Okeus kept a close watch on the doings of men, for he was always "present in the Air, in the Thunder, and in the Storms."[101] His was a "severe Scale of Iustice."[102] Anyone who displeased him even in minor things received punishment in the form of illness, loss of crops through storms, and infidelity on the part of wives. Okeus could reward a hunter by showing him where game was[103] or punish him by letting him be "shrewdly scratched," presumably by briars, as he went alone through the woods.[104] Not appeasing this god invited catastrophe. The Powhatans therefore venerated him by dedicating their temples to him.

Okeus's name was recorded with several variations in different parts of eastern Virginia: Oke,[105] Okee,[106] Okeus,[107] and Quioccos[108] in the James and York river region; Cakeres in Powhatan's household at Orapax;[109] and Quiquascacke at Patawomeck.[110] The Carolina Algonquians dedicated their temples to "Kiwasa,"[111] plainly a cognate word for the others. All versions are variants of an Algonquian word meaning "god."[112] The English accounts, as we have already seen, paint Okeus as the major deity to whom temples were dedicated, at the same time that they say that the Powhatans believed in other gods and called them *kwiokosuk*. The similarity between the words Okeus and *kwiokos* is intriguing. Until we learn more about Powhatan linguistics, especially what the various prefixes and suffixes meant, we cannot really be sure whether Okeus was a greater god than others or "he" was actually a collection of gods.

People sometimes made an offering after asking a priest to prescribe for a situation[113] or after a priest had demanded one,[114] but most often they made their offerings spontaneously whenever they were faced with difficulties or wanted to render thanks. The offerings consisted of "blood,[115] deare suet, and Tobacco,"[116] as well as other valuables such as dried tobacco and puccoon. Many offerings were made on altar stones, called *pawcorances*,[117] which stood either by people's dwellings, out in the woods,[118] or in any other spot that people felt they had "any remarkable occasion" to commemorate.[119] It was also on stones of this kind that criminals were executed by clubbing.[120] The connection, if any, with religious ritual is uncertain but likely, given the close connection between the priests' religious power and the *weroances*' political power.

The only altar stone that was recorded as being near a temple was the crystal one of Uttamussak, which is known only from Indian oral tradition recorded in the early eighteenth century.[121] This stone, the most sacred of its kind, was "a solid Chrystal, of between Three and Four Foot Cube," and "was so clear, that the Grain of a Man's Skin might be seen through it." The stone was also so heavy that when the site was abandoned and the Indians "remov'd their Gods and Kings, not being able to carry it away, they buried it thereabouts." No such stone has been found to this day on Pamunkey Neck.

There was a "rock by the path side" on the south side of James River near the falls which bore several "footprints" five feet apart. These "the

Indians" said had been made by "their god" (no record was made of which god).[122]

In the early seventeenth century, at least, the Powhatans showed a special reverence for the sun.[123] After bathing in the river each morning, people made a circle on the ground with dried tobacco, sat down within it, and lifting their hands and eyes toward the sun, they prayed with much noise and many emphatic gestures. A similar ritual was performed at sunset.

The Powhatans had no rigid schedule for rituals; instead, they made offerings as needed or as the seasons arrived, particularly the harvest. In times of military triumph and at the first "gathering togither [of] their fruits," everyone in a chiefdom gathered to give thanks and dance for several hours before feasting.[124] People offered part of the first fruits of all plants and animals to the gods and part to their rulers before they partook themselves. People also made offerings at the full moon and before great undertakings such as raids and hunts.[125]

The celebration of first gathering of corn was the Powhatans' most elaborate festival, "at which they revel several days together." They engaged in "pastimes" (games?) and "more especially their War-Dances, and Heroick Songs; in which they boast, that their Corn being now gather'd, they have store enough for their Women and Children; and have nothing to do, but to go to War, Travel, and to seek out for New Adventures."[126] The god or gods to whom the offerings were made were not recorded, but Okeus probably figured prominently.[127]

As polytheists, the Powhatans appear to have allowed for individual choice in what gods to emphasize. John Rolfe reported that Indians were "very inconstant . . . in all that they speake of their religion: one denying that which another affirmeth."[128] They were also willing to add gods to their pantheon. Our best source for these attitudes is the priest Uttamatomakkin, who told Purchas about Okeus as an alternative creator god, and said that he himself was too old to learn the worship of the Christian God, recommending they teach the young people in Pocahontas's retinue instead. It was not until the English clergymen wore out his patience with evangelizing that he understood something of the monotheism of Christianity and became rabidly opposed to it.[129] The *weroance* Pipsco asked the English in the summer of 1607 or 1608 to pray to their god for rain, "for his Gods would not send him any."[130]

Three accounts of the creation of the world were collected from various Powhatan informants, two of them regrettably sketchy. It seems that a considerable variety in beliefs was tolerated among the Powhatans. From people in the James-York area the English heard of the "great god" Ahone, who created the moon and stars and possibly other entities as well.[131] Uttamatomakkin told Purchas that it was Okeus who had "made Heauen and Earth; had taught them to plant so many kindes of Corne; [and] was the Auhour of their good."[132] Unless Purchas's interpreter garbled things, Uttamatomakkin's Okeus sounds rather like Ahone; his "Okeus" may have been several gods, one of whom created the world.

The creation story recorded among the Patawomecks is much more detailed.[133] Five gods were involved. The chief god, who often appeared to human beings as "a mightie great Hare," created men and women and kept them for a time in a great bag in his dwelling place, which was in the direction of the rising sun. Then the other four gods, who were the winds of the four directions and "like great Giants," only without substance, paid the hare a visit and wanted to eat the men and women. The Hare "reproved" them and drove them away, after which he created "the water and the fish therein and the land and a great deare, which should feed vpon the land." This made the four winds jealous, so they returned, killed the deer "with hunting poles" or spears, dressed and ate the carcass, and departed again. The Hare, seeing this done, took the hairs of the slain deer and "spredd them vpon the earth with many powerful wordes and charmes whereby every haire became a deare." He then opened the bag and released the men and women, assigning, "a man and a woman in one Country and a man and a woman in another Country, and so the world tooke his first beynning of mankynd." No flood story was recorded among the Powhatans until late in the seventeenth century,[134] which suggests that this myth was a later borrowing from the English.

Powhatan funeral customs and beliefs about an afterlife reflected the stratified society in which the people lived. The burial of rulers has been described in chapter 6. Ordinary people and probably also councillors were treated less elaborately in death. Archaeology has shown both primary (one-stage) and secondary (two-stage) burials, as well as occasional cremations, throughout the Powhatan region.[135] Historical accounts describe the first two kinds,[136] and the burning to death of criminals may explain the third. In a primary burial, which was given to most ordinary people, the corpse was wrapped with its jewelry in skins and mats and laid in a stake-lined grave. Though English writers says graves were deep, excavations have shown them to be shallow, which accords with the digging tools the Powhatans had;[137] corpses might be flexed or extended, lying on their backs, faces, or sides. After a primary burial, female relatives remained at home, mourning loudly and with their faces painted black. Wailing for the dead could also be done by men, as the English found out in 1609 when a captured Chickahominy nearly smothered and his brother, also a captive, thought him dead and immediately "broke forth in . . . bitter agonies."[138]

In a secondary burial, accorded to high-status people and sometimes to commoners, the corpse was wrapped in a mat and laid on a scaffold "about 3 or 4 yards" high, while relatives mourned loudly. If the deceased came of a well-to-do family, the relatives threw beads to the poor, and a jolly feast followed. When the corpse was laid on the scaffold, other corpses lying there were examined, and any that had been reduced to bones were taken down, wrapped in a new mat, and hung in the houses of their relatives, where they remained, according to Spelman, until the houses were abandoned. In practical reality, the bone bundles were probably kept until the next periodic burial of all corpses in a nearby ossuary, an event that seems to have occurred every five years or so.[139]

The English collected varying accounts of afterlife beliefs from the Powhatans. The few writers who got to know nonrulers reported that only rulers and priests were thought to live after death;[140] those who interviewed rulers got their opinions on their afterlife.[141] Beyond apparent agreement that the afterlife was reserved for high-status people, stories differed. Smith's and Strachey's James River informants told them that souls traveled westward until they reached the setting sun. There they found

> most pleasant feildes, growndes and pastures, where yt shall doe no labour, but stuck fynely with feathers and paynted with oyle and Pocones rest in all quiet and peace, and eate delicious fruicts, and haue store of Copper, beades, and hatchetts, sing, daunce and haue all variety of delights and merryments till that [soul] waxe ould there as the body did on earth, and then yt shall dissolue and dye, and come into a womans womb againe, and so be a new borne vnto the world.[142]

Archer understood from other James River people that souls traveled eastward to an undisclosed destination,[143] while Uttamatokmakkin, when asked by Purchas what happened to the dead, "pointed vp to Heauen; but [souls] of wicked men . . . hung betweene Heauen and earth?"[144]

Iopassus, a lesser ruler in Patawomeck, told Spelman that a soul first went treetop high, where it saw a broad, flat, easily traveled path with many edible berries and fruits growing on either side. The soul ran along this path toward the home of the Hare god in the rising sun, stopping in mid-journey at the house of "a woman goddesse" to refresh itself with hominy, hickory-nut milk, and other delicacies. Arriving at the Hare's house, the soul found its forefathers there, "living in great pleasure in a goodly feild, where they doe nothing but daunce and sing, and feed on delicious fruicts with that great Hare." The souls living with the Hare aged, however, and when they became "starke old men" they died and reentered the Powhatan world.[145]

The Powhatans did not believe in separate afterlives for the good and the wicked, and they were confused by "leading" English questions about such things, as Uttamatomakin's response to Purchas's question indicates. They apparently felt that Okeus punished the wicked sufficiently in this world. It was only late in the seventeenth century that reports were heard of a Powhatan version of heaven and hell.[146] Before that time, afterlives were officially for people of very high standing, and other folk bent their efforts toward being "successful" men and women while they lived.

The Powhatans as a Chiefdom of Coastal Algonquians

WE TURN NOW to an analysis of Powhatan culture as a whole, as revealed by the early-seventeenth-century English writers, so that it can hereafter be compared more readily and accurately with other chiefdoms. I shall be emphasizing, of course, the organization existing under the man Powhatan[1] and excluding the independent Chickahominies.

I shall analyze Powhatan culture in terms of the following indices: the duration of the chiefdom as of 1607; the amount of consolidation of new or geographically peripheral groups; the possible exterior causes of the chiefdom's development; the extent of hierarchy and bureaucracy; the amount of social separation between governing officials and those governed; the size and density of the population governed; the amount of ecological variation in the land base; the amount and nature of domestic trade; the evidence for collection of tribute and redistribution of goods; the evidence for government monopolies of both domestic and foreign goods and services; the evidence for governmental alliance with religious powers; and, as a summary, the nature of Powhatan's power over those he governed.

All of the English writers who mentioned the matter agreed that Powhatan's "empire" had been a recent development and was, to some extent, still forming. Powhatan originally inherited chiefdoms in the upper James and York river basins; from there he either conquered other groups or intimidated them into joining his organization (see chap. 7). Kecoughtan was added through conquest around 1597. The Chesapeakes were known—or remembered, since their conquest date is uncertain—as enemies. Powhatan was also willing to attack the Piankatanks, one of his own chiefdoms whose loyalty he doubted.

The territories that Powhatan governed had already achieved a name, Tsenacomoco,[2] at least among their occupants. However, the organization was still adding parts and integrating existing parts along several fronts in 1607. The next fall Powhatan had the Piankatanks attacked. The Chickahominies, near the empire's heartland, had steadfastly resisted Powhatan's efforts to incorporate them, but by late 1607 they were paying "certayne dutyes to Powhatan, and for Copper wilbe waged [can be hired] to serve and helpe him in his Warrs."[3] In that fall they also participated in a communal hunt with the Paspaheghs, Youghtanunds, Pamunkeys, Mattaponis, and Chiskiacks,[4] although they may have joined it late in order to announce that John Smith was in the area and could be captured. Both the Chickahominy and the Piankatank cases testify to the relative newness of Powhatan's domination over even the central part of his dominions.

The groups on the periphery of the empire always retained considerable autonomy, despite Powhatan's confident statements to the English. The Eastern Shore Accomacs and Occohannocks admitted Powhatan as their ultimate ruler.[5] Yet in their geographical isolation from the mainland they were more effectively ruled by a single *weroance* of their own (called an "emperor" in later English documents), and they exhibited certain cultural differences from the mainland people in living primarily by horticulture and fishing and in their lack of a *huskanaw* ritual.[6] The Potomac River groups also retained real autonomy, in that they were generally but not wholly loyal to Powhatan, at least after the English arrived.[7] However, incomplete integration of peripheral groups is a normal condition in chiefdoms and states through history, and less-than-perfect loyalty from Eastern Shore and Potomac River people does not in itself indicate that Powhatan's paramount chiefdom was new.

Many scholars believe that complex societies arise primarily because of internal factors, but external factors should not be ignored. Therefore, before we continue our examination of Virginia Algonquian society, it is relevant to consider the outside pressures on that society during Powhatan's lifetime.

Disastrous epidemics occurred in many parts of the New World after Europeans began visiting and settling there.[8] The Roanoke colonists reported that dreadful diseases causing high mortality afflicted any Indian groups who had offended the English (i.e., most Indian groups) a few days after the English left.[9] That some groups in Virginia experienced epidemics is indicated by Powhatan's statement to Smith that he had "seene the death of all [his] people thrice"[10] and by Smith's hearing of mass deaths after the exhumation of two children's bodies at Accomac.[11] Turner is hesitant to accept the idea of epidemics in the region, suspecting that Powhatan's statement may merely reflect his being an old man who had outlived his contemporaries.[12] Turner also notes that there are very few accounts (only the two cited above) of mass Indian deaths in the Virginia English records, and no mass burials like those necessary in an epidemic have been found on the Virginia coastal plain. I reply that since archaeology is in its infancy in the area, such mass burials may yet be found.

Although I hesitate to endorse Dobyns's scenario of pandemics spreading over thousands of miles,[13] it seems to me that the chance of the Powhatans escaping epidemics in the late sixteenth century is very slim. Certainly there were epidemics in Virginia in 1617 and 1619,[14] though the diseases cannot be identified. Severe epidemics with high mortality can cause social disruption, as Europeans discovered at the first outbreak of the Black Death.[15] Such disruption may well have helped Powhatan expand his dominions, if it did not cause him to do so.

The Virginia Algonquians experienced pressure from foreign nations, both European and Native American, in the late sixteenth century. They received several visits and one colonization attempt from the Spanish. They heard of the English settlement attempts on Roanoke Island and of the party of Englishmen who wintered with the Chesapeake group in 1585– 86. And they saw a brief English visit in 1603 and another by an un-identified ship at about the same time.[16] They must have been aware that European interest in their area was increasing.

Simultaneously, Iroquoian-speaking groups called Massawomecks and Pocoughtaonacks (or Bocootawwanaukes) were moving in from the north and northwest, with the aim of expanding their fur-hunting territories. The latter were said to be cannibals, a reputation which may have come from the Iroquois practice of ritually eating part of captives who had been tor-tured to death; the practice of torture itself may have been a late develop-ment among the Iroquoians in an effort to terrorize their enemies.[17] The English heard about both groups from Powhatan himself;[18] Smith met Massawomecks in his second expedition up Chesapeake Bay in 1608;[19] and Henry Spelman witnessed a Massawomeck attack on Patawomeck in 1610.[20] The foreign pressure from Europeans and Indians alike may have encouraged Powhatan to expand his dominions in order to ward off the danger to his original territories.

Powhatan's organization, as we have seen, was run by a hierarchy of rul-ers, called *weroances* (feminine: *weroansquas*), or "commanders." Every hamlet had a *weroance* who was subject to the district *weroance,* based in the major town ("kings howse," in Smith's terms) of the district, who in turn was subject to the *mamanatowick,* Powhatan. Each of these *weroances* was "potent as a prince in his owne territory."[21] Though the statements about these three levels of rulers are clear, there is no evidence of ranking among the village *weroances* or among the district *weroances.* Sometimes a *weroance* or *mamanatowick* placed his children or siblings in command-ing positions on lower levels. We know of Powhatan's "sons" ruling over Kecoughtan, Powhatan (town), and Quiyoughcohannock; of Coquona-sum's "sister" ruling over a minor town of Appamattuck; and of the Patawo-meck *weroance*'s "brother" Iopassus ruling over the minor town of Pas-sapatanzy. However, there is no evidence of these people outranking other rulers on their own levels because of the relationship with their superior.

Priests, outstanding warriors and/or elders (called "cawcawwasoughs" or "cockarouses"), and probably subordinate *weroances* were all called into council when an important *weroance* wanted advice. Yet there is no evidence of a politico-military bureaucracy among the Powhatans. The term "bureaucracy" implies a hierarchy of positions with well-defined duties, filled ideally by long-term occupants chosen according to ability and at-tached to the organization by a contract in which the duties are specified. None of the relationships among Powhatan *weroance*s and their priests and councillors (William Strachey called them "Freindes") were as formal as that, as far as the documents show, except possibly the *mamanatowick*'s bodyguard. (It is a pity that we know so little about councillors.) And when Powhatan decided to make war, he appointed a war captain (*weroance* or commoner) on an ad hoc basis and sent out an "officer" (presumably also an ad hoc appointment) to "press" men to fight under the captain.

Powhatan *weroance*s and their immediate families were set off from other folk by etiquette, clothing, housing, the possession of bodyguards and servants, burial practices, and so on. All of these distinctions impressed the English, who came from a highly stratified society themselves. How-ever, English references to a Powhatan "better sort" are few (see chap. 6) and are made only in discussing dress and eating habits, with the implica-tion that *weroance*s and their families are meant. There seems not to have been a group whose social standing and way of life were truly intermediate between the rulers and the ruled, which could be called non-"royal" "no-bility" and from which the beginnings of a bureaucracy could be drawn. It is true that councillors could share in feasts with their rulers and receive cast-off wives from them, both of which would increase their wealth. In some degree they were a peripheral kind of "better sort." But the English writers, who would have been alive to such matters, say nothing whatever about a real Powhatan "aristocracy."

Among the *weroance*s themselves, some trappings of "royalty" were missing. For one thing, even Powhatan himself was addressed to his face by his personal name, Wahunsenacawh, rather than by a title. Secondly, even the "emperor" Powhatan is specifically said to have been adept at perform-ing all the tasks normal to ordinary men. Thirdly, the evidence is very poor for politically based marriages, so typical of the rulers of states and chief-doms alike; surely the English would have mentioned such things had they heard of them from the Indians.

The land over which Powhatan ruled was not densely populated by Eu-ropean standards of the time: there were a minimum of 0.79 persons per square kilometer (2.2 per square mile; see chap. 1). Most Powhatan settle-ments were small (see chap. 3), and the existing contemporary maps of the region show a denser population in the brackish and freshwater reaches of the rivers. Some archaeologists have made much of these data.

Lewis Binford, apparently basing his measurements on Smith's map (he shows neither his source nor his computations), has estimated the mean distances between Powhatan settlements as 10 miles in the saltwater zone, 3.12 miles in the freshwater zone, and 1.56 miles in the transitional zone between the two.[22] This estimate, plus the apparently very dense population in Pamunkey Neck, supposedly proves his hypothesis that Powhatan's paramount chiefdom arose in the transitional zone, where there is greater ecological variety (freshwater marshes and springtime anadromous fish runs), and that it probably arose specifically in Pamunkey Neck (which is in the transitional zone). I am skeptical about his conclusions. First of all, Powhatan inherited more territories in the freshwater zone (i.e., Powhatan, Arrohateck, Appamattuck, Youghtanund, and the upper part of Mattaponi) than in the transitional zone (Pamunkey and the lower part of Mattaponi), although the carrying capacities of the two zones are not very different.[23] Secondly, Strachey's population estimates for Pamunkey Neck cannot be trusted (see chap. 3). Thirdly, Smith's map was based upon spotty information gathered in 1607–8. Some guides on English expeditions were more informative than others, and a later writer like Strachey was able to learn, with better interpreters, of additional towns of whatever size. It simply does not do to take Smith's map literally to the point of calculating the spacing between settlements. Only after much more archaeological investigation of the coastal plain is done shall we be able to make such calculations and then talk more confidently about the causes of the rise of the paramount chiefdom.

The ecological variety to be found in eastern Virginia is tremendous, as shown in chapter 1. That variety is spread more or less evenly over the region, thanks to the gentle tilt of the coastal plain and the presence of four major rivers crossing it within a north-south distance of seventy miles as the crow flies. There was little reason for Powhatan settlements to specialize and then trade with one another, when they could each produce practically the whole list of Indian foodstuffs, building materials, and utensils within their own territories. And the English writers mentioned no specialization at all. The goods traded around eastern Virginia (see chap. 2) appear to have included inedible luxury goods like copper, iron, antimony, puccoon, shell beads, and pearls; probably a few nonluxury goods on a small scale like saltwater mollusks for eating and bark sheathing for houses; and possibly basic foodstuffs like venison and suet, fish, and horticultural produce in times of need (there is no record of it).

Powhatan collected tribute from his subject peoples at unrecorded intervals and laid claim to much more; one estimate, probably exaggerated, is eight parts in ten of his subjects' goods (see chap. 6). He probably had his subordinate *weroances* amass tribute for him first, but no English record says so. The tribute actually collected was primarily luxury goods, which took up a limited amount of storage space; there is no record of foodstuffs being stored by *weroances* for the benefit of common folk during the lean times of the year or of specialized foods being gathered centrally for dispersal later. Powhatan had large cornfields planted especially for him, and he had what seems to have been a large hunting preserve near his capital. He also claimed all of the copper imported into his dominions from European sources. "Redistribution" took place when he entertained subordinate *weroance*s or important visitors, fed councillors and priests called for conferences, rewarded outstanding warriors or the people who planted cornfields for him, "hired" warriors from time to time, and contributed to the support of priests. However, English observers say nothing about how frequently he did these things or how widely throughout the population he spread this "bounty." In the absence of data of that sort, scholars should not call Powhatan's organization a redistributive chiefdom.

Powhatan, and to a lesser extent his subject *weroance*s, had a monopoly over several kinds of goods and services, both domestic and foreign. Powhatan had an advantage, if not a monopoly, in manpower for certain purposes such as planting his cornfields and fighting his wars. His monopoly over English copper has already been mentioned. Powhatan had fewer monopolies over the goods available from "foreign" Indians. There is no record that he tried to appropriate all the copper flowing into his domain from the west and northwest, except through the collection of tribute from his people who may have bought it; he did, however deal regularly with Indians to the southwest called Anoegs (probably Tuscaroras).

There were probably other ties between Powhatan and "foreign" Indians, either direct or indirect, but the English recorded only vague references to his claims to rule all peoples from the Chowanocs to the Tockwoghs (on Maryland's Eastern Shore) and westward to the Monahassonughs (in the foothills of the Appalachians).[24] As for relations with the English, Powhatan made no effort to monopolize these. He usually left his subject *weroance*s to make their own way with the English, except when he had some particular plan in mind.[25]

Powhatan rulers and priests were firm allies, who lived in a state of symbiosis. Priests were supported in large part by the rulers they served, through offerings and probably also by being invited to feasts. Rulers derived much of their authority from the supernatural forces for which priests were intermediaries. They relied on priests to foretell the outcome of military campaigns, detect and sometimes execute the culprits in covert crimes, and act as agents of the god Okeus, the other major source of social control besides rulers in the Powhatan world.

The close association between priests and rulers is shown by several concrete observations made by the English. The holiest temple in Powhatan's domain, at Uttamussak, could be entered only by priests and rulers. Rulers' most prized possessions, as well as their collected tribute and stocks of "bowes and arrowes" (i.e., their armories),[26] were kept in temples, which doubled as storehouses; at such sites, the goods were practically sure to be safe from pilfering hands. Rulers' bodies were kept in temples after death, and rulers and priests alone were thought to have an afterlife, because they were considered to be demigods. Their souls did not remain in this afterlife indefinitely, however, forming a collection of ancestral spirits with whom the living could communicate. Instead, the souls "aged," "died," and were reborn on earth.

The nature of Powhatan's power over his subjects can be reconstructed from early English observations with reasonable assurance of accuracy, even allowing for the writers' bias as citizens of a fully developed nation-state. In attempting this reconstruction, I find Haas's list of indices most useful and will therefore follow it.[27]

Truly powerful rulers control the subsistence and other resources within their territories. They exercise this control either through heavy taxation (legal means) or forcible confiscation (violent means). Powhatan may have been able to wield such extreme power, but there is no historical evidence that he did so, unless the attack on the Piankatanks was retaliation for non-payment of tribute. He claimed ultimate ownership of his domain, and as far as we know his people acquiesced. He may also have been able to discourage many people from living within twenty miles of his capital in order to have a large hunting preserve. However, his actual tribute collection from his people appears to have been limited primarily to luxury goods and gardens planted for him, as shown in chapter 6. Had he wanted to demand a large share of his people's other resources (i.e., seafood, waterfowl, small land animals, wild plants), his demands would have been hard to meet because of the perishability of those resources and the extra labor and firewood required to process them so that they would keep.

Powerful rulers have a variety of means of exercising their power, for they can bring strong sanctions, positive and negative, to bear on their subjects. Powhatan used a number of sanctions. He rewarded cooperative subjects with beads, copper, or cast-off wives, all of which were highly valuable. He gave public recognition and new personal names to hunter-warriors whose deeds deserved it. He may have rewarded some great warriors by making them *weroances*, though the records only mention his doing it for a few of his "sons." Yet his society did not have a small collection of permanent titles (hereditary or not), demarcating membership in a stratum called "nobility," to make his men compete the harder for his favor. Powhatan and his *weroances* had strong negative sanctions to exercise toward individual subjects. They could punish disobedience or even disrespect with instant death. They also supervised the punishment (and perhaps the trials) of thieves and murderers, cases in which they themselves had been only indirectly wronged. *Weroances* who angered Powhatan were deposed, as Pipsco was. Whole populations, like the Piankatanks, might be attacked and dispersed or deported if they incurred his wrath. There may also have been negative economic sanctions at Powhatan's command, but the English wrote nothing about them.

Powerful rulers have great scope in their power; that is, they can get their subjects to do a great many things, some of them distasteful. Powhatan was able to get his people to pay him tribute and spend time planting corn espe-cially for him. He awed even the fiercest and proudest warriors into grovel-ing submission. And he could order men to go to war whether they wanted to or not. But he could not quite keep all his subjects from sniping at the English (or so he said), nor did he get Pipsco to give that stolen wife back to Opechancanough.

Powerful rulers have a great amount of power; that is, it is highly prob-able that their subjects will obey whatever orders they give, however unrea-sonable. The English received the distinct impression that such was the case among Powhatan's chiefdoms, although to be fair, the English had most of their experiences with people in the loyal heartland. Among more periph-eral groups, the amount of Powhatan's power is questionable, and the amount of local *weroances*' power is largely unrecorded. The extension of Powhatan's power (the number of people he actually controlled) was proba-bly not as great as he himself told the English it was. The problem here is one of definition: "power," as Haas uses it, implies thorough control, and in the real world, as we have already seen, peripheral groups are always hard to control thoroughly.

The costs of holding and exercising power are outweighed, for a power-ful ruler, by the benefits to be derived. Very powerful rulers must support strong police or military machines to quell disobedience, and they must be able to afford the sometimes great expenses of rewarding obedience. Powhatan did both of these things on a relatively small, informal scale; the evidence indicates that he found the price well worth it.

A populace that obeys a ruler's orders instead of going about its own business bears the costs of this compliance. The costs of complying with Powhatan's orders appear to have been only moderately heavy, in spite of what Strachey heard from his Indian friends at Jamestown. The tribute pay-ments that Powhatan demanded were probably not as onerous as Strachey said they were, although in the matter of deerskins for clothing some people did feel the pinch: "the common sort have scarce to cover their nakednesse but with grasse, the leaves of trees, or such like."[28] The time taken by planting, weeding, and harvesting Powhatan's cornfield may not have been very onerous, either, since large numbers of people assembled for these tasks and executed them quickly. There may have been psychological costs involved in obeying Powhatan's order to make a raid on a group of fellow Algonquians, such as the Piankatanks, but the seventeenth-century English took little interest in psychological matters and recorded nothing that helps us here.

The costs to a populace if it disobeys a ruler's orders play a large role in determining whether that populace decides to submit. The English writers agreed that Powhatan did not hesitate to send warriors against recalcitrant peoples and that the costs of disobedience were very high: death or dispersal for the men and captivity for the *weroance,* women, and children. Military sanctions, however, were all that Powhatan is known to have used. If a group was far enough away and had enough bowmen, as the Patawomecks did, then in practice Powhatan hesitated to try to bring it to heel. Thus in 1610 the Patawomecks were able to help Spelman escape death at Powhatan's hands and harbor him with impunity thereafter.[29]

The opposite side of the coin of refusal costs is the gains a populace may expect if it obeys a ruler; a powerful ruler will be able to make obedience advantageous. The peoples Powhatan ruled may have received some benefits through redistribution of tribute goods, and their *weroances* certainly did. The people may have been helped during famines by the corn stored in their *weroances*' temples, though there is no concrete evidence for it. However, the primary gains that Powhatan's subjects perceived seem to have been military; we know this from reading between the lines of documents written by Englishmen who hoped to subjugate Powhatan. The people in the paramount chiefdom felt themselves surrounded by enemies: the Monacans and Mannahoacks to the west, the Pocoughtaonacks to the northwest, the Massawomecks and later the Piscataways to the north, and, before long, the English colony planted in their midst. In spite of the raids on individual towns that the Monacans and Massawomecks and the English carried out, the Powhatans probably felt less vulnerable for having strong allies in their *mamanatowick*'s organization. Proof of this assertion comes from the fact that within months of the arrival of the English, the formerly hostile Chickahominies had made a truce with Powhatan; by 1611 the Monacans had done the same; and by 1616 the Chickahominies had actually joined his organization.[30]

In summary, Powhatan's "empire" was a paramount chiefdom, although only an incipient one. He ruled over other leaders who were powerful enough that we can label them "chiefs" rather than headmen, the latter term implying rule by influence and arbitration. And Powhatan's government was neither powerful enough nor formally enough organized that we can call it a "state" by anyone's definition. Powhatan society still lacked many of the traits of more complex chiefdoms elsewhere in the world.[31] Occupational specialization was limited to rulers and priests. Hereditary statuses were limited to rulers themselves and possibly also to priests. The amount and kind of goods in the tribute-redistribution system was limited and probably not crucial to the economic well-being of most Powhatan families. Evidence is weak for the existence of an organized network for long-distance trade. And public works consisted of "kings howses" and temples which were merely elongated longhouses sheathed with bark instead of mats.

A problem remains: the Powhatans had developed a paramount chief who by 1607 ruled thirty-odd chiefdoms. Why did such a large, triple-layered political organization develop? The answer may lie in the location of Powhatan's original inheritance. The seventeenth-century English sources wrote that Powhatan had started his career in the freshwater zones of the James, Pamunkey, and Mattaponi rivers and spread his dominions outward. Two reasons for the "empire's" origin in that location can be advanced.

Firstly, Powhatan's organization may have been a "natural" development within an area of rich resources. His original inheritance may have been similar to others existing in the brackish and freshwater zones of Virginia's rivers (the inner coastal plain), where the deer hunting was good, the marshes produced seafood and attracted migratory fowl, and the rivers filled with anadromous fish coming to spawn in the leanest months of the year. The human population of the region may have been growing steadily for centuries, resulting first in chiefdoms and, with subsequent competition among them, in a paramount chiefdom; Powhatan happened to be the "winner." This view is favored by archaeologists such as E. Randolph Turner,[32] but it has yet to be proved conclusively. Proof will require, first, detailed botanical and zoological surveys of coastal and piedmont Virginia[33] to demonstrate conclusively and, we hope, quantifiably that the inner coastal plain is richer than the other zones for supporting human populations utilizing a mixed economy. Second, archaeological excavation will have to demonstrate conclusively not only that human populations on the inner coastal plain were larger and denser (and became still more so over the centuries) but also that they actually utilized the large quantities of the foods supposed to be more readily available there than elsewhere (e.g., anadromous fish, migratory fowl). That utilization will be difficult to prove, given the delicate nature of fish and bird bones and the less-than-stellar preservation in eastern Virginia as a whole. Finally, public structures (chiefs' houses and temples) and status burials (particularly adult ones) that indicate social differentiation between "chiefs" and others[34] will have to be found in the region and dated to many parts of the Woodland period and perhaps even earlier. At present, the archaeological evidence for these things is almost nonexistent.[35]

Alternatively, the paramount chiefdom may have originated near the fall line because of its being a boundary with non-Algonquian peoples. Proponents of this hypothesis fall into two categories. Archaeologists such as Stephen Potter see the Algonquians living near the fall line as middlemen in a long-term lucrative trade between the coastal plain and the piedmont.[36] Proof of that will have to come, as with the first hypothesis, from detailed study of the natural resources, showing different tradable commodities on each side of the fall line, and from archaeological excavations, showing that such trade did in fact take place over long periods of time and that some people became wealthy from it (status burials, again).

On the other hand, ethnohistorians like me are prone to see the same Algonquians as more exposed than others to the movements of "foreign" Indians coming down the larger rivers from the northwest, so that as a means of defense, chiefdoms and eventually a paramount chiefdom would form near the fall line on the rivers. The arrival of Europeans on the coast would present an additional threat and spur the development of the paramount chiefdom toward the east. If the movements of Indians west of the fall line accelerated only during the protohistoric period, then the paramount chiefdom (i.e., Powhatan's inheritance) and perhaps even the lesser chiefdoms may have existed for only a relatively short time before 1607. The visits, friendly and hostile, of "foreigners" to eastern Virginia have been discussed above and in chapter 7; some external pressure was definitely there, though European records do not tell us how long or how intensively it had existed between Indian peoples. Archaeological proof, which is inadequate at present, would have to consist, firstly, in showing a preponderance of fortified sites near the fall line and a paucity of them to the east and, secondly, in showing how shallow the time depth is for really rich status burials (indicating a paramount chief) and possibly for fortified sites as well.

In the meantime, it is worthwhile to examine chiefdoms among the peoples on the New England coast, who were similar to the Powhatans in culture[37] and related in language and were also impinged upon early by European settlers. The historical evidence from New England is sparse but indicative. The early accounts of that region, which stem from short-term visits to coastal Massachusetts without adequate interpreters,[38] show small aggregations of groups,[39] which may barely qualify as chiefdoms, whose leaders were not especially powerful. Champlain, for example, wrote in 1606 of people in what was later the Massachusett territory: "They have chiefs, whom they obey in matters of war, but not otherwise, and who engage in labor and hold no higher rank than their companions."[40]

Later accounts from New England, which stem from longer-term European settlement throughout the region following severe and well-documented epidemics (one was in 1616),[41] show fewer aggregations with more powerful chiefs. In 1620 the Pokanocket sachem Massasoit was observed to eat a meal provided for him by the English before any of his companions did, and he subsequently allied himself with the English on behalf of "at least thirty places."[42] He was one of the few sachems the Pilgrims felt qualified as a "king," and even then his power seems primarily to have been military.[43] Daniel Gookin wrote of New England of the 1630s as having four "chief sachems," those of Pequot, Narragansett, Pokanocket, and Massachusett, whose subjects (in Gookin's time, at least, the 1670s) were free to leave and ally themselves with other sachems.[44] In 1636 William Wood wrote of the Massachusett and possibly of other New England groups that though sachems did not receive "revenues" or have bodyguards, they exercised great control over their people, and some of them were the overlords of other sachems.[45] Chiefs in what is now southern New York (and probably Long Island) were observed to have bodyguards and receive great respect.[46]

Among the Narragansetts the paramount chief had absolute power[47] and sometimes acted as executioner as well.[48] Chieftainship throughout New England was hereditary in the patrilineal line,[49] and chiefs among the Pokanockets and others married only members of other chiefly families.[50] As Salwen points out,[51] the difference may lie in the areas covered by the narratives: the most hierarchical area after 1620, what is now Rhode Island, was not visited before that date. On the other hand, as he says, there may really have been a change in New England Algonquian political organization in the wake of the epidemics. Such change within a very few years, in the presence of documented outside influences, would be a strong argument that paramount chiefdoms, at least, among other coastal Algonquians were due in large part to historical events rather than to geographical and ecological factors.

Powhatan's organization probably arose out of a combination of geographical, ecological, and historical influences. Unless further manuscript sources are discovered, archaeology will have to tell us which influences played the major role in the development of the paramount chiefdom. The only question is whether adequate excavations can be carried out as eastern Virginia becomes increasingly urbanized and suburbanized.

Anthropologists interested in "culture areas" and scholars needing to divide North America into regions in order to cover the continent systematically have always had difficulty in placing the Powhatans. Euro-American scholars show their culture's penchant for dichotomizing by splitting the native culture areas of eastern North America into "Northeast" and "Southeast." Biased by modern political and social geography, they usually draw the line near where the Yankees and the Confederates did, that is, Virginia. The Powhatans have thus been placed on either side of that line: in the Southeast (by Speck,[52] Swanton,[53] Murdock and O'Leary,[54] and Spencer and Jennings[55]) or in the Northeast (by Kroeber[56] and by the Smithsonian's *Handbook of North American Indians* [vol. 15]). The only anthropologist to state clearly the reasons for his placement was Frank Speck, who saw "Southeastern" cultural traits in the early-seventeenth-century accounts and among the twentieth-century Virginia Indian people he visited.[57] Unfortunately, most of those "Southeastern" traits cannot in fact be documented for the Powhatans. Kroeber placed the Powhatans in the "Northeast" precisely because they lacked "Southeastern" traits!

Flannery's trait list and tabulation of distribution of traits[56] shows that the Powhatans had somewhat more traits in common with "Southeastern" Indians than with the New England Algonquians. My own retabulation, after eliminating some of Flannery's traits because of "late" and therefore too-inclusive sources (such as Beverley), shows approximately the same thing. However, that is only a quantification; qualitatively, the picture is different. Many of the "diagnostic" traits (Flannery's term) that the

Powhatans got but the "Southeastern" Indians did not get through the New England Algonquians (e.g., considering beaver tails a delicacy, use of dogs in hunting [fowl only among the Powhatan], painted animal skins, concept of a supreme being) were customs that had just as great an effect on Indian daily life as the "diagnostic" traits that the Powhatans acquired but the New England Algonquians did not acquire from the "Southeastern" Indians (e.g., stalking in disguise, fish poisoning, daily bathing, matrilineal chieftaincy). Most importantly, the traits that the Powhatans shared with both the New England Algonquians and the "Southeastern" Indians (e.g., agriculture and its related crops, implements, and festivals; women as farmers; storage pits; wearing breechclouts instead of tailored clothes; rigorous training of youth; bride-wealth; tendency toward despotic rulers; priesthood; solar worship) had the most pervasive influence of all on Indian daily life.

I suggest here that the dichotomy itself, between "Northeastern" and "Southeastern," is forced and misleading when applied too stringently to native cultures of eastern North America. An examination of several truly basic culture traits (my list differs from Flannery's) shows a continuum from New England and the Great Lakes down to Florida and the Gulf States. The traits are horticulture; annual cycles involving scattering to forage at certain seasons and then regrouping for planting and ceremonials; settlements of limited size at any time of year; incipient or full social stratification; prestigious leaders, with or without great power; at least some specialization of occupation in the medico-religious area; and, frequently, polygyny and bride-wealth because the women who did the farming were economically valuable.

In short, the Powhatans formed a middle group in a broad north-south continuum of essentially similar cultures, just as their natural environment was a "middle" ground in a north-south continuum of coastal environments. Their culture was a Woodland culture, a term that archaeologists use for horticultural, ceramic-making people in eastern North America. I would suggest that cultural anthropologists and ethnohistorians adopt the same term.[59]

Powhatan culture had much in common with other Indian cultures of the eastern woodlands, though it lacked the mound-building that some prehistoric and early Contact Period Woodland peoples had. Without drastic alteration to the basic Woodland lifeway, protohistoric Powhatan culture also possessed other things unique to its place and time: a heavy reliance on the region's waterways for food and communications and a burgeoning political development. The coming of the English cut short the latter but did not greatly alter the other basic cultural elements for over a century,[60] so well adapted to the land were they. It was only when the Powhatans had lost nearly all of their land that their centuries-old culture became obsolete.

Notes

Prologue: English Observers and the Indian Groups They Saw

1. For a brief discussion of what archaeology has to contribute to ethnohistory, see Feest 1987.

2. Smith 1986a [1608], 1986b [1612], 1986c [1624]; for evaluations of his writings, see Barbour 1964 and 1986, Emerson 1967, Glenn 1944, and Rozwenc 1959.

3. Culliford (1965) has pieced Strachey's biography together admirably.

4. Internal evidence in his book (Strachey 1953 [1612], pp. 65 and 125).

5. Strachey 1953 [1612], p. 61.

6. Barbour 1986, p. xlix.

7. Spelman 1910 [1613?].

8. It was the Piscataway north of the Potomac River who were blamed, at any rate. See Rountree forthcoming.

9. Brown 1964 [1890], p. 964. Percy's two accounts are 1969a [1608?] and 1969b [1608?]. His "Trewe Relacyon" (1921–22 [1612]) contains more bits of information. For another brief biography of Percy, see Barbour 1986, p. xlv.

10. Barbour 1986, p. xxix.

11. Brown 1964 [1890], p. 814.

12. Archer 1969a–c [1607]. The ascription to Archer is Philip Barbour's (1969, pp. 80, 98, 102), although a previously published version of the latter two accounts (*Virginia Magazine* 14 : 374–78) ascribes them to Christopher Newport, who endorsed them.

13. Barbour 1986, p. xlvii.

14. Brown 1964 [1890], pp. 974–75.

15. Smith: Barbour 1986, p. xlvi; latter two: internal evidence in his works.

16. Purchas 1617 and 1904–6 [1625].

17. Clayton 1965 [1687] and 1968 [1687].

18. Pargellis 1959.

19. Banister 1970.

20. Beverley 1947 [1705].

21. Sainsbury 1860, 20 : 547.

22. Rountree forthcoming.

23. The original pronunciation seems to have been Pow-*hah*-tan, to judge from the near-universal insertion of the *H* by seventeenth-century writers and also by the position of the accent in the only English source that includes an accented version ("Powa'htan," in Spelman 1910 [1613?], p. cii). Only one English author indicates the accent: Spelman 1910 [1613?], p. cii. Unfortunately, that edition of Spelman's work is imperfect, and his manuscript has since been lost from view (Christian F. Feest, personal communication 1984). Today, however, native Virginians—including Indians—pronounce the name *Pow*-a-tan.

24. 1978; personal communication 1984.

25. Smith 1986b [1612], p. 173 (almost exactly copied in Smith 1986c [1624], p. 126); more explicitly stated in Strachey 1953 [1612], p. 56.

26. Smith 1986b [1612], pp. 150, 225 (copied in Smith 1986c [1624], pp. 107, 163); copied by Strachey 1953 [1612], p. 49.

27. Quoted in Lewis and Loomie 1953, p. 161.

28. Siebert 1975, pp. 288, 292–94.

29. Fausz (1977, p. 64) states clearly that "the Chickahominies spoke a language different from Powhatan (Pamunkey) Algonquian." On p. 65 he follows Binford in postulating an independent Nansemond chiefdom (see my discussion below) and then cites Siebert as further evidence, saying that the Nansemond "spoke a language that was virtually unintelligible to the Powhatans." There is no linguistic evidence for either of these statements.

30. Strachey (1953 [1612], p. 40) recorded an Indian oral tradition that the Powhatan had not been in Virginia "much more in 300. years."

31. Archaeological evidence, especially in ceramics, does not indicate an intrusion of new people at any time in the last millennium.

32. Smith 1986b [1612], pp. 146–48, 150 (almost exactly copied in Smith 1986c [1624], pp. 103–5, 107); Strachey 1953 [1612], pp. 63–69. "Men" in the list of ethnic groups therefore refers to men able to fight.

33. Smith n.d. [1608]; see Rountree MS A, sec. 2.

34. John Pory, in Smith 1986c [1624], pp. 289, 291.

35. Williams 1973 [1643], p. 94 (Narragansett); Huden 1962, p. 16 (Natick). Barbour agrees (1971, p. 285), calling it "other-side town."

36. For the controversy about the timing, see Rountree forthcoming.

37. Huden 1962, p. 53, citing *chisapeak*, Abnaki for "big salt bay" or "at the large part of the river"; the former makes better sense, given the location of the people. Barbour (1971, p. 287) says "people on the great river."

38. The ending *-emond*, occasionally recorded as *-amung*, may be cognate with New England Algonquian languages' *-amaug*, "a fishing place" (Trumbull 1870, p. 18, and 1974 [1881], p. ix), which was sometimes anglicized to *-amond*. The capital "town" was actually a dispersed collection of houses and gardens on the three points adjacent to the junction of Exchange Branch and the Nansemond River. What would look like three towns to us was one "town" to the Nansemonds.

39. Early anglicization of the name: Warwicksquick.

40. Several of my colleagues prefer "Weanock," the name that appears on Smith's map. The early English settlers actually pronounced the first syllable as either *wye* or *way*, to judge from the variant spellings in seventeenth-century documents. Even those who met the Weyanock themselves heard both sounds, indicating that the real Indian pronunciation may have been somewhere between as indicated by the spellings "Weanock" (Smith and Strachey and an anonymous contemporary annotator of Smith [Smith 1986b (1612), p. 31n.]) and "Winauh," "Winauk," "Wynauk," or "Wynauh" (Gabriel Archer). Because of these variations, Ives Goddard suggests (personal communication 1985) that the Indians accented the middle syllable (weh-*yan*-ock). However, the *wye* pronunciation (with a first-syllable accent) has lasted in Virginia. The last remnants of the tribe merged with the Nottoway and took a surname variously spelled "Wineoak" and "Wynoak" (Rountree 1987), and that is the modern pronunciation of the name in Charles City County, the territory they had left behind. I therefore spell the name Weyanock in this book.

41. Huden (1962, pp. 277, 286), citing Eastern Niantic *wayanitoke*, "waves around the bend"? and Nipmuck *wayunkeke*, "at the bend" or "land at the bend." The Virginia Weyanock is at a spectacular bend in the James, so I feel this translation fits better than Barbour's (1971, p. 301) "either 'fine, pleasant place' or 'sassafras.'"

42. *Apé*, Narragansett for "trap" (Williams 1973 [1643], p. 225); *appaum*, Wampanoag for "trap" or "possibly" "waiting place" (Huden 1962, p. 27); *apimetek*, Abnaki or Pennacook for "'bower'[?]" (Huden 1962, p. 27). Barbour (1971, p. 286) says "trap-fishing river."

43. Barbour 1979, p. 291, citing *powwaw*, "priest," and either Abnaki *udaine*, "town," or Abnaki *-adene*, "hill." Narragansett, more closely related than Abnaki to Powhatan, has *otan*, "town," (Williams 1973 [1643], p. 94), so I prefer "town." *Pau-* is a New England Algonquian stem for "falls" (Trumbull 1870, p. 9). Trumbull (ibid., pp. 9–10) saw "Powhatan" as *pau*, "falls," + *at*, a locative, + *hanne*, "rapid stream"—a construction that I find cumbersome.

44. Strachey 1953 [1612], p. 33. He is quite definite that the name is for the falls but does not relate it to the town's name.

45. McCary and Barka 1977, which is a survey rather than a full report on any one site in that area.

46. From *usketehamun*, "a . . . thick pottage" made by boiling the last, hard remnants of cōrn left after pounding it into meal in a mortar (Strachey 1953 [1612], p. 81).

47. *Pespataug*, Eastern Niantic for "at the small inlet" and Narragansett for "where the stream flows out" (Huden 1962, p. 183); Barbour (1971, p. 296) agrees.

48. McCary 1958.

49. Maps show no capital town, but the ethnic group was in the heart of Powhatan's "empire" and was therefore probably a chiefdom.

50. Strachey (1953 [1612], p. 69) lists more ethnic groups along the Pamunkey and York rivers, but since neither Smith's map nor his texts identify them as capitals of chiefdoms—and Smith was an eyewitness, while Strachey was not—I have omitted them from my text. The groups are as follows: Cantaunkack (100 men), Mummapacun (village of Menapacunt on Smith map; 100 men), Pataunck (Potauncak; 100 men), Ochahannauke (presumably not the Eastern Shore group; 40 men), Cassapecock (100 men), Caposepock (300 men), Pamareke (400 men), Shamapa (Shamapint; 100 men), Chepeco (300 men), and Baraconos (Parokonoso; 10 men). For locations of these places see Smith n.d. [1608] or the Zúñiga map (Anonymous 1969 [1608]).

51. For the problem with the location of the capital town, see n. 50 above.

52. Barbour 1971, p. 291; based on Penobscot *madapena'n*. Trumbull (1870, p. 34) translates *mattapan* as "end of portage" or a temporary "sitting down place."

53. Local tradition favors other sites, but scholarly opinion prefers this one. See Rountree MS A. and McCary 1981.

54. Smith 1986b [1612], p. 173 (paraphrased in Smith 1986c [1624], p. 126).

55. Strachey 1953 [1612], p. 57. Barbour (1971, p. 302) says "rich, royal place."

56. Smith n.d. [1608].

57. 1953 [1612], p. 45.

58. Feest (1978, p. 255) spells it "Nansatico"; seventeenth- and early-eighteenth-century spellings varied, but the most common was "Nansiatico." The modern place-name is spelled with a *z*.

59. MacCord 1965.

60. Bushnell 1937, pp. 16–35; the trade beads found at this site have been recently identified as of Dutch manufacture (Robinson 1984).

61. Smith n.d. [1608].

62. Anonymous 1969 [1608].

63. *-comico* is "town"—cf. *werowocomoco*, "king's town," and *matchacomico*, "great house" (Strachey 1953 [1612], p. 188), where councils were held (Beverley 1947 [1705], p. 192). The syllable *wick-* or *weck-* or *wequ-* or *waqu-* (Narragansett, Mohegan, Natick, Nipmuck, Eastern Niantic, Wampanoag) means "end" (Huden 1962, pp. 270, 278–79, 281, 283, 286–87, and Trumbull 1974 [1881], p. x). Barbour (1971, p. 302) disagrees, hesitantly translating Wiccocomico as "Pleasantville."

64. Potter 1982.

65. Schmitt 1965.

66. Barbour 1971, p. 296; Huden (1962, pp. 197–98) cites Narragansett *potowomut* but says that the Indians may have meant what was done there, not the name of the place.

67. 1953 [1612], pp. 37, 56.

68. It is always to be understood that the Chickahominy, who lived well within these boundaries, were not part of the "empire."

69. Feest 1978, p. 255, and personal communications 1984 and 1986.

70. 1985, p. 238.

71. Turner 1982, p. 49, and 1985, p. 214.

72. For incidents of obedience and disobedience among peripheral groups, see Rountree forthcoming.

73. Kingsbury 1906–35, 3:73.

74. Spelman 1910 [1613?], p. cviii.

75. Smith 1986a [1608], p. 51 (Rappahannock); Smith 1986c [1624], p. 149 (Piankatank, Nandtanghtacund, and Onawmanient on the "rivers of *Rapahanock, and Patawomek*"). The later list may be an exaggeration.

76. 1986b [1612], p. 150 (copied in 1986c [1624], p. 107); copied by Strachey (1953 [1612], p. 49).

77. Smith 1986c [1624], p. 291.

78. For a detailed discussion of this phenomenon in relation to the Virginia Indians of the nineteenth and twentieth centuries, see Rountree 1986; for a more general treatment of ethnic "cores" and "fringes" through time, see Rountree MS B. The phenomenon also figures strongly throughout Powhatan history; see Rountree, forthcoming.

79. Binford 1961, p. 102.

80. Fausz 1977, p. 65, and 1985, p. 266.

81. Strachey 1953 [1612], p. 66.

82. Ibid., p. 64.

83. Ibid., p. 108.

84. Turner 1982 and 1986, p. 22.

85. Feest 1973.

86. See Spencer and Jennings 1975, chap. 2, and Dobyns 1983 for recent thinking on Amerindian population estimates and the epidemics which assaulted them. The likelihood of protohistoric epidemics among the Powhatan is discussed in Rountree forthcoming.

87. Smith n.d. [1608].

88. Siebert 1975.

89. Rountree MS A.

90. Strachey 1953 [1612], p. 56.

91. Smith 1986b [1612], p. 174 (almost exactly copied in Smith 1986c [1624], p. 127); almost exactly copied in Strachey 1953 [1612], p. 59.

Chapter 1: The Land and Its People

1. The data for this paragraph come from my personal experience of a lifetime spent in the region. For precise figures, see Turner 1976, chap. 2, and U.S. Weather Service statistics.

2. Lamb 1963.

3. Cedarstrom 1945.

4. Oaks and Coch 1963; there was so much variation in sea levels during the Pleistocene and earlier times that geologists hesitate to speak of a "normal" sea level.

5. McIntyre 1976.

6. Campbell 1927.

7. River widths and depths from Alexandria Drafting Company, n.d.

8. The three streams that become the Mattaponi are crossed today by Interstate Route 95; signs have been placed on the bridges across those streams, naming them the Matta (and, upstream, the Ma and the Ta), the Po, and the Ni. This division of the name appears on Virginia maps as early as 1731 (Hoffman 1964a), but no such names appear in the land patents of the late seventeenth and early eighteenth centuries (Nugent 1977 and 1979), when that area was being settled by the English. Additionally, "Mattaponi" is an anglicization of

the original Indian name (see Prologue). The division into Ma, Ta, Po, and Ni is therefore English, not Powhatan.

9. See John White's map in Hulton 1984, p. 86.

10. Harshberger 1958 [1911], pp. 427–43; plant names in this source are Latin, translated here with the use of Harvill 1970.

11. Klimas and Cunningham 1974, p. 141. Early English accounts of Indian use of plants in Virginia are very skimpy.

12. "Quahog" and "maninose" are Indian words (for the latter, see Lippson and Lippson 1984, p. 68) but apparently not Powhatan words. The Strachey dictionary (1953 [1612], p. 196) gives *caiuwaih* as the word for "oysters," and no word is listed for "clams."

13. English sources are poor; data are from Klimas and Cunningham 1974.

14. For documentation of this disease among the Powhatan, see chap. 8.

15. Modern Virginians do not name their junipers and cedars precisely. The "juniper" spoken of here is really *Chamaecyparis thyoides*, while the "red cedar" is really *Juniperus virginiana*.

16. For mammals see Palmer 1954; for birds see Pough 1953; for fish see Lippson and Lippson 1984.

17. Smith 1986b [1612], p. 155 (copied in Smith 1986c [1624], p. 111).

18. Common house mice and house rats are Old World imports.

19. Swanton 1964 [1946], p. 325; Dunbar 1964; Barbour 1972.

20. E. Randolph Turner, personal communication 1985.

21. The first European animals adopted by the Powhatans were pigs; see Rountree forthcoming. As far as the records show, the first two Powhatans who kept horses were one "Captain Pipsco" in 1670 (McIlwaine 1924, p. 320) and a "king" of Pamunkey in the 1680s (Clayton 1965 [1694], pp. 105–106). These were exceptions for many decades thereafter; see Rountree forthcoming.

22. Wynne 1969 [1608], p. 246. According to the *Oxford English Dictionary*, a warrener was an employee in charge of a park or, more specifically, a rabbit-warren, while a hay was either a hedge enclosing a park or the park that was enclosed by the hedge.

23. Smith 1986b [1612], p. 155 (copied in Smith 1986c [1624], p. 111).

24. In the absence of early English accounts of species taken, I list here the species caught for food today; the Powhatan list may well have differed.

25. Lippson and Lippson 1984, p. 197.

26. Strachey 1953 [1612], p. 127.

27. Ibid., p. 128.

28. That development is discussed in Rountree forthcoming.

29. Snow 1978, p. 58; see also major ethnographies of those Algonquian tribes (e.g., Speck 1950, pp. 7, 9), as well as the following *Handbook* references: Salwen 1978, p. 164, and Brasser 1978, p. 200.

30. There are two kinds of evidence for this statement. First, Smith's map (Smith n.d. [1608] shows rough alternations of villages in stretches of major rivers lacking large tributaries, which may indicate use of both sides of rivers by those groups. Second, there are records of capital towns on each side of a major river among the Weyanock (Smith n.d. [1608]; Tindall n.d. [1608]; Nugent 1934, passim) and the Rappahannock (Smith n.d. [1608]; Smith 1986a [1608], pp. 52–53; Anonymous 1969 [1608]).

31. Strachey 1953 [1612], p. 45.

Chapter 2: Subsistence

1. Strachey 1953 [1612], p. 131; he calls the quartz "crystal."

2. Ibid., p. 109.

3. The reeds were not the soft reeds common in Virginia today (*Phragmites australis*) but a stiffer cane (*Arundinaria*); cane knives had limited usefulness in cutting tougher materials such as hide (Callahan 1981, pp. 232–34, 236).

4. Smith 1986b [1612], pp. 163 and passim (copied in Smith 1986c [1624], p. 117 and passim); closely paraphrased by Strachey 1953 [1612], p. 108 and passim.

5. McCary 1964. This canoe was subsequently reworked by English hands so that its walls were thinner and lighter and its bottom was flat instead of rounded. Nonetheless, it closely resembles the canoe pictured in the White painting from the Pamlico region (Hulton 1984, p. 73).

6. Smith 1986c [1612], p. 163 (almost exactly copied in Smith 1986c [1624], p. 117); closely paraphrased by Strachey 1953 [1612], pp. 81–82.

Strachey recorded their Powhatan name: "Quintan." See the de Bry engraving of canoe making (Harriot 1972 [1590], p. 55), which has no prototype in the surviving White paintings.

7. 1910 [1613?], p. cxiv.

8. Strachey 1953 [1612], p. 82 ("40. or 50. foote in length"). George Percy saw one of forty-five feet (1969a [1608?], p. 134).

9. Strachey 1953 [1612], pp. 81–82; copied, with additions, from Smith 1986b [1612], p. 163 (copied in Smith 1986c [1624], p. 117).

10. Strachey 1953 [1612], p. 82.

11. For example, in 1623 an English party was ambushed in the upper reaches of Potomac River. The members lost their pinnace to the Indians and barely made it to their ship. But once they were aboard, a favorable wind allowed the ship to outdistance the Indians' canoes (Kingsbury 1906–35, IV: 58).

12. Smith 1986a [1608], p. 73.

13. Purchas 1617, p. 957.

14. Pargellis 1959, p. 243.

15. Glover 1904 [1676], p. 23. He is not very specific: "At the head of their *Canoes* they fixed a Hearth . . . [in which they made] a blaze with fire put to the shivers of *Pine tree*." The "hearth" was probably a pot or earth-lined wooden container analogous to the sand-lined birch-bark container that in the Great Lakes region was suspended out in front of a canoe's bow by a framework of sticks (based on Nancy O. Lurie, personal communication 1985; see illustration by Kane in Spindler 1978, p. 710).

16. 1947 [1705], p. 149; the hearth was raised to "within Two Inches of the Edge," or gunwales, of the canoe. This account agrees with, and may have been drawn from, the White painting (Hulton 1984, p. 73).

17. Clayton 1968 [1687], p. 418.

18. Quote from Smith 1986b [1612], p. 164 (copied in Smith 1986c [1624], p. 117); explanation from Strachey 1953 [1612], p. 82.

19. Smith 1986b [1612] (copied in Smith 1986c [1624], p. 117); copied by Strachey 1953 [1612], p. 82.

20. Pargellis 1959, p. 243; Banister 1970, p. 354. Banister could be writing about either the Appamattucks or the Siouan-speaking Monacans; his saying that a man who landed a particularly big sturgeon "with swimming wading & diving" was "accounted a Cockkarous" (an Algonquian term for "great man") may indicate that he was writing of Appamattuck practices. William Byrd also wrote an account of having seen an Occonneechee fisherman being pulled overboard (1966, pp. 316–17).

21. Smith 1986b [1612], pp. 163–64 (copied in Smith 1986c [1624], p. 117); closely paraphrased by Strachey 1953 [1612], pp. 75, 82.

22. Strachey 1953 [1612], p. 75.

23. Smith 1986b [1612], p. 164 (copied in Smith 1986c [1624], p. 117); copied by Strachey 1953 [1612], p. 82.

24. Smith 1986b [1612], p. 164 (copied in Smith 1986c [1624], pp. 116–17); copied by Strachey 1953 [1612], pp. 81–82.

25. The best examples come from Siouan-speaking territory to the west. For a popularized treatment of such traps, with photographs, see Peck 1984.

26. Banister 1970, p. 354 (copied by Beverley 1947 [1705], p. 148); he could have been writing about either Appamattuck or Monacan practices here.

27. Strachey 1953 [1612], p. 75.

28. Hulton 1984, p. 73.

29. Robert Beverley (1947 [1705], p. 148) explained the fence with trap midway along it as sometimes stretching "quite a-cross a Creek," which might work on the upper Mattaponi River, where he lived, but which would not work at all in the lower Tidewater. Beverley also used an engraved illustration (p. 150) borrowed from de Bry's, explaining that the position of the fisherman was wrong but necessary to show the weir to full advantage (p. 151). Placing the canoe at the "head" end of the weir would have served the same purpose and been more accurate. I doubt Beverley's firsthand knowledge of fish weirs (much less his illustrator's).

30. See Rountree forthcoming. So far as I know, no maritime historian has traced the history of fish weirs in Virginia. They seem to have passed out of favor in the Chesapeake by the nineteenth century and were revived again after 1870; today the poles and nets are so expensive and so vulnerable to storms that weir making is dying again (Charles F. Elliott, personal communication 1984).

31. "Weir" (pronounced "ware") and "pound" are used interchangeably by modern Tidewater Virginia fishermen (Robert Elliott and Charles F. Elliott [a waterman and a local historian, respectively, both of Fox Hill, Hampton, Virginia], personal communications 1984). In my own family (from the town of Hampton, not a fishing village), "pound" is the more common term.

32. Elliott 1976, p. 47, and personal communication 1984.

33. Charles F. Elliott, personal communication; he has, however, had a weir maker record the procedure on audio tape.

34. Archer 1969a [1607], p. 92.

35. Strachey 1953 [1612], p. 128.

36. Archaeologists have recovered tiny projectile points and small round-headed points, which were probably used in hunting birds. Strachey (1953 [1612], pp. 187, 204) gives separate words for "arrow" and "head of an arrow that is round," but Siebert (1975, p. 313) translates the latter term as "fletched arrow with a head." The evidence, then, for a Powhatan term for "bird point" is poor at present. The practice of hunting the sora (rail) by using "sora-horses" or fire pots in the bows of canoes is not attested before the late nineteenth century, when a Pamunkey leader sent a "horse" to the Smithsonian Institution (Smithsonian Institution 1893, p. 224; illustrated in Twentieth Annual Report of Bureau of American Ethnology, pl. cxxxvi). The use of them has been described for Virginia Indians by Pollard (1894, p. 15) and Speck (1928, pp. 340–42).

37. Indian "wealth" consisted of deerskins, agricultural produce, puccoon roots, copper pieces, pearls, shell beads, etc., and most of these things, once acquired, had to be shared with Powhatan. There is evidence, however, that agricultural produce was grown specially for him in separate fields. See chap. 6.

38. 1953 [1612], p. 87.

39. Smith 1986b [1612], p. 164 (copied in Smith 1986c [1624], p. 118); Strachey 1953 [1612], pp. 83–84. The "enjoyable" part may show some bias by observers who considered hunting a sport.

40. Smith 1986c [1612], p. 164 (copied in Smith 1986c [1624], p. 118); Strachey 1953 [1612], p. 82.

41. Purchas 1617, p. 954 margin.

42. Smith 1986b [1612], p. 155 (copied in Smith 1986c [1624], p. 110); copied by Strachey 1953 [1612], p. 125.

43. Banister 1970, p. 386.

44. Kingsbury 1906–35, 3: 438.

45. Strachey 1953 [1612], p. 125.

46. Smith 1986b [1612], pp. 164–65 (copied in Smith 1986c [1624], pp. 118–19); closely copied by Strachey 1953 [1612], p. 83.

47. See Rountree forthcoming.

48. Frank Speck (1928, pp. 312–30) was convinced that the individual territories he

found among the early-twentieth-century Pamunkeys and various Northeastern groups were an aboriginal Algonquian survival. This idea was disproved for the Northeastern tribes by Leacock (1954).

49. Smith 1986b [1612], p. 164 (copied in Smith 1986c [1624], p. 118); closely copied, with minor additions and deletions, by Strachey 1953 [1612], p. 83. The latter term first appears in a Banister letter of 1679 (1970, p. 43).

50. 1970, pp. 42−43.

51. Smith 1986b [1612], p. 164 (copied in Smith 1986c [1624], p. 118); copied by Strachey 1953 [1612], p. 83. This kind of hunting was used by Indians and non-Indians until fairly recently, but it is now illegal in Virginia.

52. Kingsbury 1906−35, 3: 557.

53. Strachey 1953 [1612], pp. 82, 83; copied, with additions, from Smith 1986b [1612], p. 165 (copied in Smith 1986c [1624], p. 118).

54. 1978.

55. 1978. For other criticisms of his thesis, see Krech 1981.

56. See the account of the Indians' seasonal round below. Late in the century, Banister (1970, p. 42) wrote that the main hunting time of the year was fall through spring.

57. Turner 1978.

58. Smith 1986a [1608], p. 59.

59. Butchering techniques and personnel went unrecorded by the English, except for one passage in which Strachey (1953 [1612], p. 114) said that women "dresse the meat brought home."

60. Smith 1986b [1612], p. 164 (copied in Smith 1986c [1624], p. 118); closely paraphrased by Strachey 1953 [1612], p. 83.

61. Smith 1986a [1608], p. 91. Fausz (1981, p. 24) says that that particular hunt was organized by Powhatan in order to intercept Smith, who was exploring the Chickahominy River. He seems to imply that a multitribal party that big would not merely have been hunting. I disagree. First, a party bent on capturing a waterborne explorer would not set all the surrounding woods on fire, as this party did (Smith 1986a [1608], p. 47). Second, once such a party had captured its prey, it would return home; instead this one went on hunting, while calling the conjurers out into the woods to deal with Smith (ibid., p. 59).

62. Wynne 1969 [1608], p. 246.

63. Schmitt 1965, p. 19; he says it is identical to the modern Pamunkey and Mattaponi callers illustrated in Speck 1950, p. 357.

64. For a detailed discussion of hunting-related rituals among other Algonquians, see Tanner 1979, chaps. 7−8.

65. Clayton 1965 [1687], pp. 34−35. When Clayton acquired some of the root himself, he attracted only a large rat, which ran across his face one night as he was sleeping.

66. See also the White painting of a warrior (Hulton 1984, p. 78).

67. Strachey 1953 [1612], p. 108; Percy 1969a [1608?], p. 140.

68. Smith 1986b [1612], p. 163 (copied in Smith 1986c [1624], p. 117); copied by Strachey 1953 [1612], p. 108.

69. Strachey 1953 [1612], p. 108; Percy 1969 [1608?], p. 140.

70. 1986b [1612], p. 163 (copied in Smith 1986c [1624], p. 117; copied, with additions (birds as targets), by Strachey 1953 [1612], p. 108.

71. 1969a [1608?], p. 140.

72. 1986b [1612], p. 163 (copied in Smith 1986c [1624], p. 117); copied by Strachey 1953 [1612], p. 108.

73. Smith 1986b [1612], p. 163 (copied in Smith 1986c [1624], p. 117); copied by Strachey 1953 [1612], p. 108; Percy 1969a [1608?], p. 140.

74. 1953 [1612], p. 108; partly copied from Smith 1986b [1612], p. 163 (copied in Smith 1986c [1624], p. 117). Later in the century, Banister described the stone as "a sort of white transparent stone" (1970, p. 382), probably quartz or quartzite, a common material for the stone projectile points found by archaeologists in the Tidewater.

75. Schmitt 1965, p. 18; Mary Ellen Hodges, personal communication 1985.

76. Smith 1986b [1612], p. 163 (copied in Smith 1986c [1624], p. 117); copied by Strachey 1953 [1612], p. 108. Banister wrote (1970, p. 382) that this glue was made of the "velvet horns of Deer; but it has not the quality, it is said to have, of holding all weathers."

77. Percy 1969a [1608?], p. 140.

78. Strachey 1953 [1612], p. 108; copied, with additions, from Smith 1986b [1612], p. 163 (copied in Smith 1986c [1624], p. 117, who does not identify the species of bird).

79. Smith 1986b [1612], p. 163 (copied in Smith 1986c [1624], p. 117); copied by Strachey 1953 [1612], pp. 108-9.

80. Archer 1969a [1607], p. 90. Clayton (1965 [1687], pp. 36-37) said he had found no evidence of such poison in his researches; the technique may have been lost by then.

81. Smith 1986b [1612], p. 164 (copied in Smith 1986c [1624], p. 118); copied by Strachey 1953 [1612], p. 109.

82. That was determined in a shooting contest; see Rountree forthcoming.

83. Fausz 1977, p. 222.

84. Hamor 1957 [1615], p. 39. Smith also mentions them in passing when describing a women's dance and a victory dance (see chap. 5).

85. White painting, in Hulton 1984, p. 78.

86. Hariot 1972 [1590], p. 46.

87. Strachey 1953 [1612], p. 109 (skins used, one of which was "badger," an animal not found on the coastal plain), 124 (raccoon likened to English badger).

88. Spelman 1910 [1613?], p. cxii; he lived with both groups but does not differentiate between them in his ethnographic account.

89. Banister 1970, pp. 376, 382.

90. Strachey might have been interested enough to search out such data, but he lived in Jamestown during a period of unrest which confined him primarily to the English fort and to the male Indian visitors who came there.

91. Strachey 1953 [1612], p. 80; copied with additions from Smith 1986b [1612], p. 162 (copied in Smith 1986c [1624], p. 116).

92. Banister 1970, p. 374; corroborated in the matter of snakes in general by Pargellis 1959, p. 231. Both authors may not have been speaking of the Powhatans.

93. 1979, p. 107.

94. Ibid, p. 102.

95. 1953 [1612], p. 77: "Theire habitations or Townes, are for the most parte by the Rivers; or not far distant from fresh Spings comonly vpon the Rice [rise] of a hill."

96. 1979, p. 107.

97. Smith 1986b [1612], pp. 162-63 (copied in Smith 1986c [1624], pp. 116-17); Strachey 1953 [1612], p. 80.

98. 1976, pp. 182-87.

99. Feasts were put on for English visitors in February (Smith 1986a [1608], pp. 65, 67), April (Percy 1969a [1608?], pp. 135-36), and May (Archer 1969a [1607], p. 84; Hamor 1957 [1615], p. 43).

100. See Rountree forthcoming.

101. Strachey 1953 [1612], p. 79; Spelman 1910 [1613?], p. cvi.

102. Smith 1986b [1612], p. 162 (copied in Smith 1986c [1624], p. 116). Smith's text in 1612 reads, "their fields or gardens which are smal plots of ground. Some 20, some 40. some 100. some more, some lesse."

103. Archer 1969a [1607], p. 93.

104. 1976, pp. 192-94.

105. Snow 1978, p. 58.

106. Day 1953, p. 44.

107. 1910 [1613?], p. cxi. Both methods of felling trees were practiced by coastal Algonquians. The New England Pawtuckets chopped their trees three feet above the ground (Salwen 1978, p. 163), and burning was the Pamlico method shown in de Bry's engraving

(Hariot 1972 [1590], p. 55). (There is no prototype of the de Bry engraving among White's paintings.)

108. Percy 1969a [1608?], p. 134.

109. Smith 1986b [1612], p. 157 (copied in Smith 1986c [1624], p. 112); closely para- phrased by Strachey 1953 [1612], p. 118.

110. English records say nothing of any fertilizer being used. The Plymouth colonists were instructed by the Indian Squanto to put small fish into the holes in which they planted corn and beans, but there is evidence that Squanto himself learned the practice from Europeans during an earlier period of captivity (Ceci 1975a and b).

111. Smith 1986b [1612], pp. 157–58 (copied in Smith 1986c [1624], pp. 112–13); Strachey 1953 [1612], pp. 114, 118.

112. Percy 1969a [1608?], p. 140.

113. Strachey 1953 [1612], p. 123.

114. English writers differ on numbers of each: four corn to two beans (Smith 1986b [1612], p. 157 [copied in Smith 1986c (1624), p. 112]), three or five corn to one or three beans (Strachey 1953 [1612], p. 118), four or five corn to two beans (Spelman 1910 [1613?], p. cxi), and five corn to two beans (Anonymous 1947 [1610], p. 12).

115. Spelman 1910 [1613?], p. cxi; he goes on to note that Indian women acquired iron "scauels [shovels?] and spades" from the English at the first opportunity.

116. Smith 1986b [1612], p. 157 (copied in Smith 1986c [1624], p. 112); Strachey (1953 [1612], p. 118) says "4. or 5. foote."

117. Spelman 1910 [1613?], p. cxii.

118. Beverley 1947 [1705], pp. 143–44; copied, with additions, from Banister 1970, p. 357. Beverley added that the smaller of the early corn (Banister called it "Rathe-ripe," a term later colloquialized into "rarep" [Feest 1972, p. 1]) matured in mid-May and the other did so in late May.

119. Smith 1986b [1612], p. 157 (copied in Smith 1986c [1624], p. 112); closely para- phrased by Strachey 1953 [1612], p. 119. The Roanoke colonists used the same distinction between large and small varieties of beans, and Thomas Hariot (1972 [1590], p. 14) noted that both kinds matured in ten weeks after planting. Ewan and Ewan, editors of Banister, suggest that *assentamens* were "probably varieties of *Phaseolus*" (Banister 1970, p. 265). Beverley added (1947 [1705], p. 144) that while "beans" were planted with corn, "pease" were usually planted in a separate patch.

120. Smith 1986b [1612], p. 158 (copied in Smith 1986c [1624], p. 113); Strachey omits mention of intercropping in describing the planting of squash and passionflowers (1953) [1612], p. 79).

121. 1947 [1705], p. 144.

122. Smith 1986b [1612], p. 157 (copied in Smith 1986c [1624], p. 112; copied by Strachey (1953 [1612], p. 119), who says "300. and 600."

123. Strachey 1953 [1612], p. 79.

124. Ibid., p. 114.

125. Hariot 1972 [1590], p. 68; there is no record of the practice in Virginia, but children played a major part in farming.

126. Banister 1970, p. 382.

127. Smith 1986b [1612], p. 157 (copied in Smith 1986c [1624], p. 112); copied by Strachey 1953 [1612], p. 119.

128. Spelman 1910 [1613?], p. cxii.

129. Strachey 1953 [1612], p. 115.

130. Smith 1986b [1612], p. 138 (copied in Smith 1986c [1624], pp. 130–31). An En- glish exploring party met an Indian man in 1607 who was said to be 110 years old; testing him, they had their interpreter count out the man's years, first with 11 beans, each signifying ten years, and then with 110 beans (Archer 1969a [1607], p. 94). Thus a Powhatan inter- preter, at least, could count and multiply to over one hundred.

131. Purchas 1617, p. 954; Purchas's source was the priest Uttamatomakin; see Rountree forthcoming.

132. Beverley 1947 [1705], p. 211.

133. Pargellis 1959, p. 241; the reason is that the word resembled "the sound, the geese seem to make."

134. Smith 1986b [1612], pp. 156–57 (copied in Smith 1986c [1624], p. 112); copied by Strachey 1953 [1612], p. 124.

135. Strachey 1953 [1612], p. 72; Pargellis 1959, p. 241.

136. Strachey 1953 [1612], p. 72; presumably learned in interviews with Indian visitors to Jamestown.

137. Purchas 1617, p. 957. See also Purchas 1906 [1625], 19:118–19.

138. Purchas 1617, p. 957.

139. Kingsbury 1906–35, 3:584.

140. Pargellis 1959, p. 241.

141. Beverley 1947 [1705], p. 211.

142. Smith 1986c [1624], p. 150. Fausz (1985, p. 240) has diagrammed the Powhatans' view of their homeland, the seas, and England, based on the foregoing account. There is a series of concentric bands: Tsenacomaco is in the center, a sea is around it, England surrounds the sea, and another sea surrounds England.

143. The latter idea comes from Feest, personal communication 1984.

144. Feest 1975, pp. 157–59. Feest feels that the name is actually two Powhatan words, the first being (approximately) *sakahocan*, or writing, and the second being *quiacosough*, or lesser deities.

145. Smith 1986c [1624], p. 261, partially contradicted by Purchas (1617, p. 954), who indicates that Uttamatomakin merely tried mentally to count the Englishmen he saw in England.

146. Smith 1986c [1624], p. 291.

147. Banister 1970, p. 384; he is probably talking about the Powhatans in that passage.

148. Smith 1986b [1612], p. 171 (copied, with additions, in Smith 1986c [1624], pp. 123–24); copied by Strachey 1953 [1612], p. 97.

149. Quotation and use of stones: Smith 1986c [1624], pp. 123–24.

150. Banister 1970, p. 376 (closely paraphrased in Beverley 1947 [1705], p. 185); he calls the process of drying "barbecuing," unlike Clayton (see below).

151. Beverley 1947 [1705], pp. 181, 185.

152. Smith 1986b [1612], p. 157 (copied in Smith 1986c [1624], p. 112); copied by Strachey 1953 [1612], p. 119.

153. Beverley 1947 [1705], p. 178.

154. One is shown in a White painting (Hulton 1984, p. 75).

155. Smith 1986b [1612], p. 158 (copied in Smith 1986c [1624], p. 113); copied by Strachey 1953 [1612], p. 80.

156. Strachey 1953 [1612], p. 128.

157. Ibid., pp. 80, 128; copied with additions from Smith 1986b [1612], p. 158 (copied in Smith 1986c [1624], p. 113).

158. Archer 1969a [1607], pp. 84–89; that must have been tough meat to start with!

159. Clayton 1965 [1687], p. 37.

160. Banister 1970, p. 376.

161. Smith 1986b [1612], p. 157 (copied in Smith 1986c [1624], p. 112); closely paraphrased by Strachey 1953 [1612], p. 113.

162. Smith 1986b [1612], pp. 157–58 (copied in Smith 1986c [1624], p. 112); closely paraphrased by Strachey 1953 [1612], p. 80.

163. Spelman 1910 [1613?], p. cxii.

164. Smith 1986b [1612], p. 158 (copied in Smith 1986c [1624], p. 112); copied by Strachey 1953 [1612], p. 80.

165. Strachey 1953 [1612], p. 115.

166. Banister 1970, pp. 156–57 (paraphrased by Beverley 1947 [1705], p. 178), 376. Beverley added (p. 178) that hominy and meat were sometimes boiled together.

167. English accounts give no descriptions of these mortars.

168. Smith 1986b [1612], p. 158 (copied in Smith 1986c [1624], p. 113); closely paraphrased by Strachey 1953 [1612], p. 80.

169. Translation: "he crushes it by tool or instrument" (Siebert 1975, p. 331). The Chickahominies took their name from this word.

170. Strachey 1953 [1612], p. 81; footnote by editors of that volume: "Frumenty, a dish made by boiling wheat in milk."

171. The Powhatan word for "bread," variously spelled as "apones" or "ponap" (Strachey 1953 [1612], p. 81, and Smith 1986b [1612], p. 158 [also Smith 1986c (1624), p. 113]), has been borrowed into English as "pone."

172. Smith 1986b [1612], p. 158 (copied in Smith 1986c [1624], p. 113); copied by Strachey 1953 [1612], p. 81; Englishmen who sampled the result were not impressed.

173. Strachey 1953 [1612], pp. 80–81; copied, with additions, from Smith 1986b [1612], p. 158 (copied in Smith 1986c [1624], p. 113).

174. Percy 1969a [1608?], p. 142; less complete account in Smith 1986b [1612], p. 158 (copied in Smith 1986c [1624], p. 113), copied by Strachey 1953 [1612], p. 81.

175. Hamor 1957 [1615], p. 43.

176. Strachey 1953 [1612], pp. 120, 185, 199; p. 120 copied from Smith 1986b [1612], p. 153 (copied in Smith 1986c [1624], p. 109).

177. Pargellis 1959, p. 243 (only roots of trees in general); Banister 1970, p. 376 (stickweed only, to salt meat or make lye for soaking corn); Beverley 1947 [1705], p. 180 (whole list, for general "seasoning").

178. Archer 1969b [1607], p. 103.

179. Smith 1986b [1612], p. 158 (copied in Smith 1986c [1624], p. 112); copied by Strachey 1953 [1612], p. 80.

180. Clayton 1965 [1687], p. 37; he actually called the kettle the "hominy pot."

181. Strachey 1953 [1612], p. 121.

182. Banister 1970, p. 376. Ewan and Ewan, his editors, suggest that the "stickweed" could be either a *Helianthus* species or *Parthenium integrifolium* (p. 392, n. 26).

183. Klimas and Cunningham (1974) list several possibilities.

184. 1953 [1612], p. 123.

185. Archer 1969b, p. 101. The editor, Philip Barbour, identifies "sigilla Christi" as probably a species of trillium.

186. Smith 1986b [1612], p. 151 (copied in Smith 1986c [1624], p. 108); closely paraphrased by Strachey 1953 [1612], p. 119.

187. Archer 1969a [1607], p. 83.

188. Smith 1986b [1612], p. 152 (copied in Smith 1986c [1624], p. 109); closely paraphrased by Strachey 1953 [1612], p. 120. Ewan and Ewan, Banister's editors, tentatively identify this plant as *Vaccinium stamineum* L. (Banister 1970, p. 262).

189. The name has been borrowed into English from the Powhatan *pushemins* or *putchamins*.

190. Smith 1986 [1612], pp. 151–52 (copied in Smith 1986c [1624], p. 109). Strachey (1953 [1612], p. 120) describes only the fruit.

191. Banister identified it as an arum that grows in marshes (1970, p. 377).

192. Strachey 1953 [1612], p. 120; copied, with additions, from Smith 1986b [1612], p. 153 (copied in Smith 1986c [1624], p. 109).

193. Ewan and Ewan, Banister's editors, identify it as the same species (p. 392, n. 30). They also suggest in the same note that *Arisaema triphyllum* could have been called "tuckahoe."

194. Smith 1986b [1612], p. 153 (copied in Smith 1986c [1624], pp. 109–10); copied by Strachey 1953 [1612], p. 122, who also spells it Taccaho (p. 178).

195. Smith 1986b [1612], pp. 153−54 (almost exactly copied in Smith 1986c [1624], pp. 109−10); Strachey 1953 [1612], p. 122.

196. Archer 1969c [1607], p. 101; Strachey 1953 [1612], p. 80; Banister 1970, p. 377 ("earthnuts"; identification by Banister's editors).

197. Smith 1986b [1612], p. 151 (copied in Smith 1986c [1624], p. 108); Strachey 1953 [1612], p. 129. Banister wrote later in the century that "the Indians" rarely ate acorns (1970, p. 377); paraphrased in Beverley 1947 [1705], p. 181.

198. Banister 1970, p. 376; closely paraphrased in Beverley 1947 [1705], p. 185. Banister specifies maple wood for the ashes in the lye, though maple is uncommon even on the inner coastal plain.

199. Another name borrowed from the Powhatans; the original name was "chechinquamin."

200. Smith 1986b [1612], p. 152 (copied in Smith 1986c [1624], p. 109; Strachey 1953 [1612], p. 119. Banister wrote later (1970, p. 376) that they were first scalded "to kill the worm."

201. Smith 1986c [1612], pp. 152−53 (almost exactly copied in Smith 1986c [1624], p. 109); Strachey 1953 [1612], p. 119.

202. Banister 1970, p. 377; paraphrased by Beverley 1947 [1705], p. 181.

203. The English word "hickory" is an anglicization of this word.

204. This is the sole reference in English documents to the shallow, bowl-shaped grinding stones and stone pestles found archaeologically in the region.

205. Clayton 1968 [1687], pp. 424−25.

206. Smith 1986b [1612], p. 152 (almost exactly copied in Smith 1986c [1624], p. 109, where the term is spelled "pawcohiccora"); Strachey 1953 [1612], p. 129.

207. Strachey 1953 [1612], p. 121.

208. Smith 1986b [1612], p. 153 (almost exactly copied in Smith 1986c [1624], p. 109); Strachey 1953 [1612], p. 120. The word is a cognate with northern Algonquian words for "wild rice" (Siebert 1975; pp. 414−15). Ewan and Ewan suggest that it may have been "a Manna grass, *Glyceria*; Barnyard grass, *Echinochloa walteri*; and . . . *Panicum virgatum*, *Paspalum*, and *Elymus virginicus*" (Banister 1970, p. 264).

209. Clayton 1968 [1687], p. 431.

210. Archer 1969a [1607], pp. 84, 90−91.

211. Strachey 1953 [1612], p. 81.

212. Beverley 1947 [1705], p. 182; he wrote, "tho they have [water] in cool and pleasant Springs every where, yet they will not drink that, if they can get Pond Water, or such as has been warm'd by the Sun and Weather."

213. 1976, pp. 182−88, and personal communication (1954).

214. Banister 1970, p. 377; paraphrased by Beverley 1947 [1705], p. 181.

215. In England at that time, forks were a new importation from the Continent.

216. Or onto the ground, the anonymous writer of the 1680s adds (Pargellis 1959, p. 235).

217. 1953 [1612], p. 98.

218. 1910 [1613?], p. cxiii.

219. Archer 1969a [1607], pp. 84, 85; Percy 1969a [1608?], pp. 135−36.

220. The source for this statement and the rest of the paragraph is Spelman 1910 [1613?], p. cxiii.

221. Beverley wrote, concerning unidentified "Indians," that "they never serve up different sorts of Victuals in one Dish; as Roast and Boyl'd, Fish and Flesh; but always serve them up in several Vessels" (1947 [1705], p. 178). Beverley may have been writing about non-Algonquians, or he and Spelman may have been writing about different parts of the coastal plain at different times.

222. Strachey 1953 [1612], p. 84.

223. Archer 1969a [1607], p. 89.

224. Strachey 1953 [1612], pp. 35, 132.

225. Ibid., pp. 57, 132.

226. Percy 1969 [1608?], p. 138.

227. For a discussion of ideas, David Quinn's and mine, about possible refugees to the Chesapeakes, see Rountree forthcoming.

228. See, for example, Smith 1986a [1608], p. 81.

229. Ibid.

230. Strachey 1953 [1612], p. 75.

231. Ibid., p. 115.

232. Archer 1969a [1608], p. 87.

233. Smith 1986c [1624], p. 173.

234. Percy 1969a [1608?], p. 137.

235. Harvill 1970, p. 194.

236. Source for provenance of both shellfish: Lippson and Lippson 1984, pp. 35, 41, coordinated with map on p. 6.

237. Lippson and Lippson 1984, p. 39, coordinated with map on p. 6.

238. Archer 1969a [1607], p. 83.

239. Lippson and Lippson 1984, p. 36, coordinated with map on p. 6.

240. Strachey 1953 [1612], p. 78.

241. They form part of a high understory of the forest (Harshberger 1958 [1911]).

242. Strachey (1953 [1612], p. 34) wrote that the highlands had more "Beasts," and the lowlands, more "Fish and Fowle."

243. Strachey 1953 [1612], p. 115.

244. Smith 1986c [1624], pp. 290–91. E. Randolph Turner (personal communication 1985) is skeptical of the reported difference in maize production between the Eastern Shore and the mainland. His reason is a good one: the mainland people, under trading pressure from the English, had good reason to minimize their harvests when talking to Englishmen, while the Eastern Shore people, under no pressure at all at that time, felt free to speak accurately about what they gathered in.

245. Strachey 1953 [1612], p. 125.

Chapter 3: Towns and Their Inhabitants

1. Smith 1986b [1612], p. 161 (copied in Smith 1986c [1624], p. 116; paraphrased by Strachey 1953 [1612], p. 77.

2. Hariot 1972 [1590], p. 66, illus. p. 67.

3. Strachey 1953 [1612], p. 77.

4. Early English records mention no palisaded Powhatan towns unambiguously. In 1609 the English bought Powhatan town and then either reinforced its existing fortifications (Smith 1986b [1612], p. 271; Smith [1986c (1624), p. 221] calls it a "Fort" at the time of purchase) or fortified it for the first time (Strachey 1953 [1612], p. 56). Archaeological excavations have turned up Woodland sites with palisades, but those may or may not be dated to the Early Contact Period. The sites presently known to have been fortified are Patawomeck (Schmitt 1965; Historic Period; palisade), a town at the junction of Lamb's Creek and Rappahannock River (Bushnell 1937, pp. 61–62; date uncertain; a ditch and an embankment which may once have held a palisade), an unpublished site in Charles City County (mentioned in Turner 1976, p. 258; palisade), Flowerdew Hundred in Prince George County (Edwards 1978; date uncertain; palisade), and the Great Neck site in Virginia Beach (E. Randolph Turner, personal communication 1985; protohistoric; palisade).

5. Clayton 1968 [1687], pp. 434–35.

6. Strachey 1953 [1612], p. 78.

7. Smith 1986b [1612], p. 162 (copied in Smith 1986c [1624], p. 116); Strachey 1953 [1612], p. 78.

8. Strachey 1953 [1612], p. 78.

9. Archer 1969a [1607], p. 91; Smith 1986b [1612], p. 151 (copied in Smith 1986c [1624], p. 108); Strachey 1953 [1612], p. 119.

10. Smith 1986b [1612], p. 162 (copied in Smith 1986c [1624], p. 116). Others have exaggerated the situation. Fr. Andrew White wrote of the Potomac River banks that the woods were so clear that "a coach and fower horses may travale without molestation" (1910 [1634], p. 40). L. G. Tyler wrote: "The frequent fires made by the Indians in hunting had cleared away the underbrush in Virginia so that it is said a coach with four horses could be driven through the thickest group of trees" (1907, p. 64n.). Edmund S. Morgan (1975, p. 55) described Virginia's forest as a "veritable park," replaced with "second-growth pine forests."

11. Smith 1986b [1612], p. 162 ("2 to 50" in Smith 1986c [1624], p. 116).

12. Actual recorded sizes of towns: Kecoughtan, 18 houses on three acres (Smith 1986a [1608], p. 37); Pamunkey, 100 houses (Smith 1986a [1608], p. 51); Powhatan town, "some 12 houses" (Smith 1986b [1612], p. 206); Manosquosick (in Chickahominy territory), "thirtie or fortie houses" (Smith 1986a [1608], p. 39); an islet in James River near Powhatan town, 6 to 7 families (Archer 1969a [1607], p. 86); and a village on the lower Pamunkey River, at least 40 houses (Hamor 1957 [1615], p. 8).

13. 1986b [1612], p. 162 (copied in Smith 1986c [1624], p. 116); copied by Strachey (1953 [1612], p. 79).

14. 1910 [1613?], p. cvi.

15. 1969b [1607], p. 103. Lewis Binford (1961, pp. 87–89) went further, envisaging three settlement patterns on the coastal plain: separated village-hamlet clusters in the saltwater zone, a village-hamlet continuum (with no gaps) in the brackish and freshwater zones, and "consolidated village-hamlet complex[es]"—large villages with hamlets "widely dispersed" around them—in the Mattaponi-Pamunkey River area. His evidence for these patterns is apparently Smith's map (Smith n.d. [1608]).

16. 1964 [1610], p. 89.

17. 1953 [1612], p. 67.

18. 1986a [1608], p. 37.

19. 1953 [1612], p. 69. These are Caposepock and Chepeco, possibly towns within Pamunkey territory, as well as "Opechancanough," which was probably in fact part of all of the territory of Youghanund, with 300 bowmen each; Pamareke, which is perhaps the same as the whole Pamunkey territory, had 400 bowmen. It seems likely that Strachey's high population estimates and the great number of villages he lists on the Pamunkey River (most not on Smith's map [n.d. (1608)] and some appearing on the "Zúñiga" map [Anonymous 1969 (1608)] but not as "king's howses" and therefore not as whole territories) reflect both English ignorance of that region in 1607–11 and the intense interest the English felt in the region that Powhatan's brothers and successors ruled.

20. Siebert 1975, p. 352. "Wigwam," borrowed from the New England tribes, was not used by the Virginia colonists until the eighteenth century (in Beverley 1947 [1705], p. 174); "cabin" was the usual term in the seventeenth century.

21. At the time of this writing, only two sites have yielded direct evidence of house patterns. One was the De Shazo site (MacCord 1965), where a rectangular house of twelve by eighteen feet was found, oriented north and south. The other site was one on Long Island, Virginia Beach, where part of a house was excavated and found to be rectangular with an apsidal end (Clarence Geier, personal communication 1985); Martha McCartney feels (personal communication 1985) that this house may have been built by visiting Tuscaroras later in the seventeenth century.

22. The following account, unless otherwise noted, comes from Smith 1986b [1612], pp. 161–62 (copied in Smith 1986c [1624], p. 116; Strachey 1953 [1612], p. 78. For detailed house-building procedures, see Callahan 1981, pp. 378–92 and illustrations on pp. 401–25. Callahan's experiments showed that tools used in making houses included stone knives and flakes and celts; bone awls; shell scrapers and saws; wooden mallets; and wooden pounders for preparing cordage.

168 NOTES TO PAGES 60–62

23. Clayton 1968 [1687], p. 435.
24. 1981, pp. 313–15.
25. Beverley 1947 [1705], p. 174.
26. 1981, pp. 321–24.
27. Durand de Dauphine 1934 [1687], p. 152.
28. 1981, pp. 338–40; tools needed were needles, awls, and knives of stone or mussel shells (1981, passim).
29. Strachey 1953 [1612], p. 78. Banister wrote later that all houses were covered with bark (1970, p. 383), an unlikely situation in the late seventeenth century when most traditional Indian people were struggling to acquire enough food for their families.
30. 1969b [1607], p. 103; all later writers noted the same thing, at a time when the remaining Indian settlements were far up the rivers.
31. Fenton 1978, p. 303.
32. Hudson journal of 1609, in de Laet 1909 [1625, 1630], p. 49.
33. 1981, pp. 333–38.
34. Strachey 1953 [1612], p. 78. Smith also mentions a smoke hole (1986b [1612], pp. 161–62 (copied in Smith 1986c [1624], p. 116).
35. Banister 1970, p. 372; Beverley 1947 [1705], p. 176. Lightwood is the dry but resinous knots from dead pine trees.
36. Strachey 1953 [1612], p. 115; he calls them "candles" of pine splints.
37. Beverley 1947 [1705], p. 176.
38. Hulton 1984, pp. 62, 66.
39. Spelman 1910 [1613?], p. cvi.
40. Beverley 1947 [1705], p. 176.
41. Strachey 1953 [1612], p. 78.
42. 1986b [1612], p. 161 (copied in Smith 1986c [1624], p. 116); see also Strachey (1953 [1612], p. 78).
43. 1986b [1612], p. 245 (copied in Smith 1986c [1624], p. 194; the England of Smith's time was enduring a fuel shortage (Bridenbaugh 1968, pp. 98–101), so that the Jamestown colonists had a hearty appreciation for warm houses. Callahan (1981, pp. 434–39) has made an estimate for heating of longhouses (at ca. 70° F.) during the winter: two to three cords per small settlement. From this he concludes that firewood availability was a factor in locating new housing. I agree with his conclusion but feel that his estimate of wood needed is too low. A new, well-insulated, two-story passive solar house of 954 square feet of floor space and 267 square feet of south-facing glazing in Portland, Oregon, needed a whole cord of wood in one winter in the early 1980s (Wright and Adrejko 1982, pp. 64–69). My assumption, which could be wrong, is that the heating needs of such a house roughly equalize those of a no-window, mat- or thatch-insulated longhouse of one-quarter the floor area in eastern Virginia. Callahan's "small settlement" would have had to be small, indeed.
44. See the incident of January 1609 at Pamunkey in Rountree forthcoming.
45. Simmons 1978, p. 191.
46. Nugent 1934, pp. 76, 259, 437, 528.
47. Strachey 1953 [1612], p. 83; partially copied from Smith (1986b [1612], p. 164 [see also Smith 1986c (1624), p. 118]).
48. Pargellis 1959, p. 232; less direct statement in Spelman 1910 [1613?], pp. cvi–cvii.
49. The following account, unless otherwise noted, comes from Strachey 1953 [1612], p. 79; copied, with additions, from Smith 1986b [1612], p. 162 (copied in Smith 1986c [1624], p. 116). The *mamanatowick*'s own bedstead-throne was no higher than the beds of commoners (Smith 1986a [1608], p. 53).
50. Clayton 1968 [1687], p. 435; he also says the bedsteads were only six inches off the ground.
51. Beverley 1947 [1705], pp. 176–77.
52. Hamor 1957 [1615], p. 43.

53. Clayton 1968 [1687], p. 435.

54. Banister 1970, p. 380; closely paraphrased by Beverley (1947 [1705], p. 220).

55. Strachey 1953 [1612], p. 115.

56. Ibid., pp. 78—79.

57. Banister 1970, p. 379; Clayton (1965 [1687], p. 27) also states that sweathouses were always on a river bank. Banister indicates that they were dug into the bank, which is feasible away from the bay, where the water table is lower.

58. Smith 1986b [1612], p. 168 (copied in Smith 1986c [1624], p. 121); copied by Strachey 1953 [1612], p. 111.

59. Smith 1986c [1624], p. 155; also Smith 1986a [1608], p. 63.

60. See Rountree forthcoming.

61. Banister 1970, pp. 186, 360, 383. Beverley wrote in 1705 (1947, p. 182) that Indian "spoons" held a pint; he was probably referring to ladles.

62. Hulton 1984, p. 63.

63. Banister 1970, p. 321 (mussel shells); Beverley 1947 [1705], p. 184 (clam shells).

64. Hoes made of these materials have been found archaeologically throughout the eastern woodlands.

65. 1953 [1612], p. 115.

66. Hulton 1984, p. 74.

67. A Pamunkey maker of such pots told me in 1982 that food boiled about half again as fast when the heat source surrounded the container in this way.

68. The evidence here is archaeological, from a wide variety of sites (Mary Ellen Hodges, personal communication 1985). Such pipes contrast with the rusty color of ordinary ceramics. But tobacco was not an ordinary plant to the Powhatans.

69. Copper: Percy 1969a [1608?], p. 136; Strachey 1953 [1612], p. 123. Clayton said Indian pipes were shorter (1965 [1687], p. 38). Punctate designs made with long, serrated edges of sharks' teeth (Stephen R. Potter, personal communication 1988). The teeth are miocene fossils; one was found in a midden at upper Cuttatawomen (MacCord 1965).

70. Smith 1986b [1612], p. 164 (copied in Smith 1986c [1624], p. 117); copied by Strachey 1953 [1612], p. 83.

71. Strachey 1953 [1612], p. 129.

72. Ibid.

73. 1970, p. 326.

74. See especially the illustrations of textiles reconstructed from impressions on ceramics in Bushnell 1937, pp. 23, 46—47, and 52 and in Winfree 1969, pp. 188, 190—91, 200, 202.

75. Spelman 1910 [1613?], p. cxii.

76. Smith 1986b [1612], p. 163 (copied in Smith 1986c [1624], p. 117); copied by Strachey 1953 [1612], p. 82; Spelman (1910 [1613?] p. cxii) mentions tree "bark" and "heampe."

77. Siebert 1975, pp. 373—74.

78. Strachey 1953 [1612], p. 75.

79. Banister 1970, p. 40. Banister's editors identify the plant as *Apocynum cannabinum*. The Indians in question could have been either the Algonquian-speaking Appamattucks or the Siouan-speaking Monacans.

80. Smith 1986b [1612], pp. 154, 255 (copied in Smith 1986c [1624], pp. 110, 204); for identification of pigments see below.

81. Archer 1969c [1607], p. 103; Smith 1986b [1612], p. 160 (copied in Smith 1986c [1624], p. 114); copied by Strachey 1953 [1612], 71. The English of the time were smaller than modern Europeans, and their diet made many of them suffer from rickets (Bridenbaugh 1968, pp. 26—27, 101—2).

82. Pargellis 1959, p. 230.

83. There is no record of Powhatan young children's loins being covered with moss (probably until they became continent), as is shown in White's painting from the Pamlico

region (Hulton 1984, p. 63). Durand de Dauphine noticed that at Portobacco, children went naked even in winter (1934 [1687], p. 153).

84. Strachey 1964 [1610], p. 89. The White paintings show many of these aprons, but on both sexes (Hulton 1984).

85. Smith 1986b [1612], pp. 160–61 (copied in Smith 1986c [1624], p. 115); copied, with additions, by Strachey 1953 [1612], p. 71. This custom differs from the North Carolina Algonquian norm, which, according to the White paintings, was aprons for both sexes.

86. Percy 1969a [1608?], p. 136.

87. Smith 1986b [1612], p. 154 (copied in Smith 1986c [1624], p. 110); copied by Strachey 1953 [1612], p. 122.

88. Smith 1986b [1612], p. 160 (almost exactly copied in Smith 1986c [1624], p. 115; copied by Strachey 1953 [1612], p. 71.

89. Strachey 1953 [1612], p. 72.

90. Archer 1969c [1607], p. 102 ("sandalls"); Strachey 1953 [1612], p. 73 ("leggings"), 108 ("sandalls, Buskins" [boots]); Smith 1986b [1612], p. 163 (copied in Smith 1986c [1624], p. 116) ("shooes, buskins").

91. Banister 1970, p. 374; paraphrased by Beverley (1947 [1705], p. 164), who contradicts Banister's statement that moccasins were "without feet [soles]" by saying that the makers sometimes "sow a piece to the bottom, to thicken the Soal."

92. 1986a [1608], p. 73. I suspect that Indian men's endurance in those extremely cold early-seventeenth-century winters was heightened whenever Englishmen were present.

93. The original word was *meskote-*, coat or robe of fur (Siebert 1975, p. 325).

94. Percy 1969a [1608?], p. 142; Strachey 1953 [1612], p. 114.

95. Archer 1969a [1607], p. 92.

96. Percy 1969a [1608?], p. 142.

97. Archer 1969c [1607], p. 103.

98. Strachey 1953 [1612], p. 114.

99. Beverley 1947 [1705], p. 159.

100. Percy 1969a [1608?], p. 136; Smith 1986b [1612], p. 160; Spelman 1910 [1613?], p. cxiii. Strachey 1953 [1612], p. 73. For the original painting of Eiakintonomo, see Feest 1972, pp. 3–5, illus. facing p. 4; and Feest 1978, illus. p. 260.

101. Smith 1986b [1612], p. 160 (copied in Smith 1986c [1624], p. 114); Strachey 1953 [1612], p. 73.

102. Spelman 1910 [1613?], p. cxiii.

103. Purchas 1617, p. 954; corroborated by Strachey (1953 [1612], p. 88), who said men would "fashion themselves . . . as neere to his shape as they ymagyne." Purchas's informant, a priest, was therefore so insistent upon the "rightness" of this "god-given" hairstyle that he "obiected to our GOD this defect, that he had not taught vs so to weare our haire." Margaret Williamson (1979) has theorized that Powhatan male hairstyles symbolized the men's position halfway between the sacred (gods, rulers and priests) and the secular (women). Her idea is interesting but difficult to prove, especially since her argument that priests' position was very close to that of gods' because of their celibacy does not hold up. Purchas (1617, p. 955), whom she does not cite, learned that his priestly informant Uttamatomakkin was in fact a married man. See chap. 7.

104. A very few decorated bone combs have been found archaeologically (Mary Ellen Hodges, personal communication 1985; broken specimen in collection of Virginia Research Center for Archaeology).

105. See the knots on Carolina Algonquian men in the White paintings, in Hulton 1984, pp. 71, 76, 78.

106. Strachey 1953 [1612], pp. 73–74; copied with additions from Smith 1986b [1612], p. 161 (see also Smith 1986c [1624], p. 115).

107. Archer 1969c [1607], p. 103.

108. No writer describes a general rule; examples of bearded men can be found in Percy

1969a [1608?], p. 142; Smith 1986b [1612], p. 173 (copied in Smith 1986c [1624], p. 126); Strachey 1953 [1612], p. 57; and Spelman 1910 [1613?], p. cxiii.

109. Strachey 1953 [1612], p. 57; Smith (1986b [1612], p. 173 [copied in Smith 1986c (1624), p. 126]) speaks only of a very thin beard.

110. Archer 1969a [1607], p. 84, and 1969c [1607], pp. 102–103.

111. Percy 1969a [1608?], p. 137.

112. Percy 1969b [1608?], p. 147; Cope 1969 [1607], p. 110; White 1969 [1608?], p. 147; Smith 1986b [1612], p. 413.

113. Strachey 1953 [1612], p. 74; copied, with many additions, from Smith 1986b [1612], p. 161 (see also Smith 1986c [1624], p. 115).

114. 1969a [1607], p. 137.

115. 1953 [1612], p. 125.

116. Lippson and Lippson 1984, p. 39.

117. Archer 1969a [1607], p. 93. Banister noted (1970, p. 321) that pearls could be found in the dens of muskrats because the muskrats ate mussels. He did not say, however, whether the Powhatan used this situation to collect more pearls.

118. Strachey 1953 [1612], p. 132; he said these pearls came from "oysters."

119. Lewis and Loomie 1953, p. 198n.

120. Cope 1969 [1607], p. 109.

121. Banister 1970, p. 321.

122. Strachey 1953 [1612], p. 65.

123. Collection of Virginia Research Center for Archaeology.

124. Floyd Painter, personal communication 1985.

125. Smith 1986a [1608], p. 69.

126. 1953 [1612], pp. 65, 75.

127. Banister 1970, pp. 322–23, 373; copied, with additions, by Beverley 1947 [1705], pp. 227–28.

128. Smith 1986a [1608], p. 71; Smith 1986b [1612], p. 217 (copied in Smith 1986c [1624], p. 156). In the mid-seventeenth century the Indian trade featured both colors of shell beads, as well as glass ones; blue or black shell beads were legally valued by the English at twice the price of white ones. By the time Banister wrote, three kinds of shell beads were known to the colonists and, presumably, to the Indians.

129. Smith 1986c [1624], p. 157.

130. Banister 1970, p. 373; Beverley 1947 [1705], pp. 162 (illus.), 167 (illus.), 228.

131. Lippson and Lippson 1984, p. 41.

132. 1947 [1705], pp. 227–28.

133. Beverley 1947 [1705], pp. 168–69 (illus., and labeled "runtees").

134. Banister 1970, p. 373.

135. Ibid.

136. Ibid.

137. Percy 1969a [1608?], p. 136; Smith 1986b [1612], p. 216 (copied in Smith 1986c [1624], p. 155).

138. 1969a [1608?], p. 142.

139. Strachey 1953 [1612], p. 73; copied with additions from Smith (1986b [1612], p. 161 [see also Smith 1986c (1624), p. 115]), who speaks of the tattooing as "black spots." Late in the seventeenth century Durand de Dauphine reported that people (only women?) at Portobacco had facial tattoos "in the shape of snail shells" (1934 [1687], p. 152).

140. Percy 1969a [1608?], p. 142. The designs on women in the White paintings seem most often to be geometrical (Hulton 1984, pp. 63, 65, 67, 77).

141. The portrait engraving of Pocahontas, taken in life, shows no facial tattooing; either she had not had any yet at her capture, or else the artist omitted it.

142. Strachey 1953 [1612], p. 70; copied with additions from Smith (1986b [1612], p. 161 [see also Smith 1986c (1624), p. 115]).

143. Strachey 1953 [1612], pp. 70–71.
144. Ibid., p. 71.
145. Siebert 1975, p. 369, and Ewan and Ewan in Banister 1970, p. 263; the plant's common name is still puccoon.
146. Harvill 1970, p. 194.
147. Siebert 1975, p. 413, and Ewan and Ewan in Banister 1970, p. 263.
148. Klimas and Cunningham 1974, p. 36.
149. Smith 1986b [1612], p. 154 (copied in Smith 1986c [1624], p. 110).
150. Banister 1970, p. 383; the identification of the inkberry is his editors'.
151. Smith 1986c [1624], p. 167.
152. Percy 1969a [1608?], p. 137.
153. Smith 1986b [1612], p. 169 (copied in Smith 1986c [1624], p. 122); copied by Strachey 1953 [1612], p. 95.
154. Percy 1969b [1608?], p. 147.
155. White 1969 [1608?], p. 147.
156. Smith 1986b [1612], p. 171 (copied in Smith 1986c [1624], p. 124); Strachey 1953 [1612], p. 98.
157. Percy 1969a [1608?], p. 137.
158. Strachey 1953 [1612], p. 73.
159. Smith 1986b [1612], p. 236 (copied in Smith 1986c [1624], p. 183).
160. The one White painting showing body paint depicts a man armed for hunting or war. He is wearing a rather delicate set of designs, rather than having whole sections of his body covered (Hulton 1984, p. 78).
161. Strachey 1953 [1612], p. 73. Use of *terra sigillata* is corroborated in a 1608 incident in which Smith was surrounded by cudgel-wielding warriors painted with the substance (Smith 1986a [1608], p. 87).
162. Gibbon's notes on Indians, published in his book *Introductio ad Latinam Blasonam* (1682), quoted in Feest 1967b, pp. 5–7. Banister (1970, p. 381) corroborates the colors red and black for war. By 1659 all three chiefdoms had grouped together on a reservation near Dividing Creek, where Gibbon's host, Richard Lee, lived; see Rountree forthcoming.
163. Beverley 1947 [1705], p. 192; see also chap. 4 in the description of Nemattanew.
164. Strachey 1953 [1612], p. 73; brackets based on editors' note. Corroborated by Banister (1970, p. 381 (he calls it "swans down"). Strachey does not mention on what occasions the down was worn.
165. Beverley 1947 [1705], p. 192.
166. Percy 1921–22 [1612], pp. 279–80.
167. 1977, pp. 348–49; 1981, p. 30; 1985, p. 244–45. Sheehan (1980, pp. 170–71) has followed him, erroneously describing Nemattanew's feathers as a cloak.
168. In Rountree forthcoming, I also deal with the Powhatans' probably not needing a religious movement in order to attack the English, as Fausz postulates.
169. Barolome Martinez, in Lewis and Loomie 1953, p. 161.
170. Purchas 1617, pp. 954–55. This edition of Purchas was not consulted by Fausz, as far as his bibliographies show. The only connection between a bird and a religious item was recorded in the matter of altar-stones; see chap. 8, note 117.
171. Fausz goes on in his dissertation to draw an analogy between the Powhatans' "religious" use of feathers and the appearance of feathers in the mortuary-related Southeastern Ceremonial Complex (1977, pp. 82, 345; illus. IV.2). He adds as further evidence that "some" items from the latter complex have been found in Virginia. The only possible candidate at present from Virginia is the "Bruff maskette" (Fig. 19 of this volume) found near the site of Patawomeck. It does not match at all well with Southeastern Ceremonial Complex motifs. Altogether, I find Fausz's connections among Nemattanew's feathers and any Powhatan religious movement and the Southeastern Ceremonial Complex to be rather farfetched.

172. 1986c [1624], p. 149. Beverley's description of men's war paint (1947 [1705], p. 192) appears to be drawn from this account of Smith's; no one else mentions circles around the eye as designs in war paint, so that that design may well have been for priests.

173. Bridenbaugh 1968, pp. 103–4.

174. Wingfield 1969 [1608], p. 216; Archer 1969c [1607], p. 104; Percy 1969a [1608?], p. 145; Smith 1986b [1612], p. 162 (copied in Smith 1986c [1624], p. 116); Strachey 1953 [1612], p. 113.

175. Strachey 1953 [1612], p. 65; see also Smith 1986c [1624], p. 151.

176. Smith 1986b [1612], p. 174 (copied in Smith 1986c [1624], p. 127); closely paraphrased by Strachey (1953 [1612], p. 62), who adds that the feathers were washed before drying.

Chapter 4: Manliness

1. Feest (1966b, p. 76) was the first scholar to make this point: "The two chief values of Powhatan Algonkian Indians were power through coercive command and wealth. The two were closely related to each other."

2. Strachey 1953 [1612], p. 113.

3. Spelman 1910 [1613?], p. cix; no more details were ever recorded.

4. Its first appearances in the historical record are in the border inscription of the engraved portrait made of her in 1617 and in Purchas 1617, p. 943.

5. Purchas 1617, p. 943; paraphrased in Stith 1969 [1747], p. 136; her "release" may rather have been a case of syncretism, in which she believed that receiving a new and more powerful Christian name (Rebecca) made her able to disclose the old personal name.

6. Strachey 1953 [1612], p. 113.

7. Or, in the case of the Chickahominy, probably by his town's member of the tribal council, though evidence is lacking.

8. Strachey 1953 [1612], pp. 113–14.

9. In the winter of 1621–22 the *mamanatowick* and his brother took new names, which should have warned the English of a great movement in Indian country. See Rountree forthcoming.

10. 1953 [1612], p. 56.

11. Purchas 1617, p. 955; Banister 1970, p. 380.

12. Smith 1986b [1612], p. 171 (copied in Smith 1986b [1624], p. 124); copied by Strachey 1953 [1612], p. 98; Beverley writes (1947 [1705], p. 207) as though less-accomplished youths were initiated late, after they had finally qualified.

13. By this term I mean councillors, called "cockarouses" or great men (the Powhatan term here has been anglicized). I am not certain that the early-seventeenth-century English writers used the term in the same way, for they said very little about them at all.

14. Pargellis 1959, p. 234; Banister 1970, p. 381; Beverley 1947 [1705], p. 209. Early-seventeenth-century writers spoke only of candidates becoming priests; in this they had been misled.

15. Purchas 1617, p. 955.

16. This term and the mosaic of fragmentary accounts of the early, public part of the ritual described in the next four paragraphs come from White 1969 [1608?], pp. 147–49; Smith 1986b [1612], pp. 171–72 (copied in Smith 1986c [1624], pp. 124–25); Strachey 1953 [1612], pp. 89, 96, 98–99; and Spelman 1910 [1613?], pp. cv–cvi. White, or his editor, Purchas, says the public festivities took two days; Smith and Strachey say they took one day and give a more specific chronology.

17. Banister (1970, p. 381) was the first English writer to use the term.

18. The term is found in Purchas 1617, p. 955, and Smith 1986c [1624], pp. 124, 291. Barbour once felt that "black" was an error for "blake," northern English dialect for "pale,"

reflecting the white color the candidates were painted (1969, p. 367n and Smith 1986b [1612], p. 171, n. 5). However, he later changed his mind and accepted "black" as an accurate recording which he could not explain (1980).

19. Purchas 1617, p. 957.

20. Strachey 1953 [1612], p. 98.

21. White 1969 [1608?], p. 149.

22. Purchas 1617, p. 955; his source is John Rolfe, husband of Pocahontas.

23. English writers are very vague at this point.

24. Spelman wrote that two or three of the initiates were designated by an omen from the Indians' vengeful deity and that these were immediately bound hand and foot and thrown on the fire. However, his account does not state clearly whether he actually witnessed such a thing. John Rolfe heard from Pocahontas (or his in-laws) that no one was killed and that the women had been mourning because of the coming separation from their sons for a few months (Purchas 1617, p. 953).

25. Beverley (1947 [1705], p. 209); he expanded Banister's passage (1970, p. 381) on deaths during the *huskanaw* not being the rule. My next paragraph is taken primarily from Beverely (pp. 209–10), as well as from Banister and from Pargellis (1959, pp. 234–35).

26. Purchas (1617, p. 955) heard from John Rolfe that it was four months; Smith, based on White, says nine months.

27. No Virginia English author attempted to identify the plants in any way. However, the *huskanaw* was also practiced in late-seventeenth-century North Carolina, where pellitory and other intoxicating plants were used (Lawson 1967 [1709], p. 241; paraphrased, with additions, in Brickell 1968 [1737], p. 405). Merrill and Feest (1975, p. 179) identify the pellitory as either *Zanthoxylum americana* or *parietaria floridana*.

28. Only the anonymous writer of the 1680s (Pargellis 1959, p. 234) mentions beatings. He says the "madness" lasted "several weeks."

29. Beverley actually saw one belonging to the Pamunkeys in 1694, a week after thirteen boys had been released from it. He had it added to the illustration of the priest and the conjurer (Beverley 1947 [1705], p. 164 and fig. 20 of this book).

30. Or, probably, councillor-rulers among the Chickahominies.

31. Beverley (p. 209) received the distinct impression that the candidates were "such as were generally reputed rich."

32. "The Observations of Master John Pory," quoted in Smith 1986c [1624], p. 291.

33. Lawson 1967 [1709], p. 241; copied by Brickell 1968 [1737], pp. 405–6.

34. See, for instance, Driver 1961, pp. 374–75, and various accounts in Thwaites 1897–1901.

35. Percy 1921–22 [1612], p. 263; White 1969 [1608?], p. 150; Smith 1986b [1612], p. 175 (copied in Smith 1986c [1624], p. 127); almost exactly copied by Strachey 1953 [1612], p. 60.

36. White 1969 [1608?], p. 150.

37. Strachey 1953 [1612], pp. 85–86.

38. Spelman 1910 [1613?], p. cxiv.

39. Smith 1986c [1624], p. 293; Fausz and Kukla 1977, p. 117. The other documents on Nemattanew's death (Anonymous 1900–1901, p. 213; Kingsbury 1906–35, 4: 11) say nothing of any bravado shown at his death, or, as Smith describes, of any deliberate courting of death by openly wearing a murder victim's cap in front of the victim's friends (who then shot him).

40. Kingsbury 1906–35, 3: 438.

41. Creating such an impression was desirable for a "fringe" group wishing to keep some autonomy.

42. Glover 1904 [1676], p. 26.

43. Smith 1986b [1612], p. 174 (copied in Smith 1986c [1624], p. 127); almost exactly copied by Strachey 1953 [1612], pp. 59–60.

44. There are two other accounts of a *weroance* killing a disobedient subject on the spot, but one comes from Maryland and the other comes from the year 1676 (see chap. 7). In 1623 Spelman and his companions saw a *weroance*, probably Piscataway, have a subject's head cut off and thrown into the fire for having warned the English visitors not to trust their hosts (Kingsbury 1906–35, 4: 83).
45. Spelman 1910 [1613?], p. cviii.
46. For less detailed summaries of several periods of uneasy peace, see Rountree forthcoming.
47. 1986b [1612], p. 160 (copied in Smith 1986c [1624], p. 115).
48. 1953 [1612], p. 75.
49. It took a major "revitalization movement" among the Five Nations, i.e., the creation of the League (Wallace 1958).
50. Dragoo 1976, p. 20; the evidence is indirect: an increase in warfare, the effects of which show up archaeologically in fortified villages.
51. They held out for a remarkably long time; see Rountree forthcoming.

Chapter 5: Sex Roles and Family Life

1. Cooperation here is probable, not documented; see chap. 2.
2. Strachey 1953 [1612], p. 74. He gives no details about the ritual restrictions commonly placed on Indian women while staying in the menstrual house, though in calling the Powhatan structure a "Gynaeceum," he hints that it served as a sort of clubhouse for women.
3. Smith 1986b [1612], p. 162 (copied in Smith 1986c [1624], p. 116); Strachey 1953 [1612], p. 81, 114.
4. Spelman 1910 [1613?], p. cxii.
5. 1969c [1607], p. 103.
6. Smith 1986b [1612], p. 162 (copied in Smith 1986c [1624], p. 116); copied by Strachey 1953 [1612], p. 81.
7. Smith 1986b [1612], p. 162 (copied in Smith 1986c [1624], p. 116); Strachey 1953 [1612], p. 114; Spelman 1910 [1613?], p. cxii.
8. Spelman 1910 [1613?], pp. cvi–cvii; Pargellis 1959, p. 232.
9. Strachey 1953 [1612], p. 115.
10. Spelman 1910 [1613?], p. cxiii.
11. See chap. 6.
12. Smith 1986b [1612], p. 162 (copied in Smith 1986c [1624], p. 116); paraphrased by Strachey (1953 [1612], p. 81).
13. Strachey (1953 [1612], p. 115) wrote that people hid in caches "Their Corne and (indeed) their Copper, hatchetts, Howes, beades, perle and most things with them of value according to their owne estymation."
14. The currency was probably shell beads, judging from surviving records of Indian transactions as well as the scarcity of English coinage among the colonists. See Rountree forthcoming.
15. Pargellis 1959, p. 232.
16. Service 1966, p. 13.
17. Strachey was the most explicit: "they wyn the loves of their women who wilbe the sooner contented to live with such a man . . . they perceaue they are likely to be fedd with well" (1953 [1612], p. 84).
18. Europeans themselves had the practice in the Middle Ages; it was only in the urbanization that occurred during the Renaissance that women became more confined to the house and less economically productive and dowries became common (Herlihy 1978, p. 60).
19. This paragraph and the next are a composite picture, drawn from Strachey (1953 [1612], p. 112) on the James and York River region and Spelman (1910 [1613?], p. cvii) on either the upper Chickahominy region or Patawomeck. A later account, concerning the Por-

tobacco on the Rappahannock River, differs: the groom built the bride a house, the village gathered, he gave the bride a deer's foot, the bride gave him an ear of corn (symbolizing their roles in the marriage), and the ceremony was over (Durand de Dauphine 1934 [1687], pp. 153–54).

20. The evidence is negative evidence: the seventeenth-century English, who usually made economically based marriages themselves, said nothing about the Powhatan doing any differently.

21. Strachey and Spelman are specific on the point: Powhatan marriage was virilocal; it may have been patrilocal as well. Recorded cases of virilocal marriage: Powhatan's wives, who were not sisters, adding weight to virilocality (Strachey 1953 [1612], p. 61); Pipsco's stolen wife (ibid., pp. 64–65); and a younger daughter of Powhatan (Hamor 1957 [1615], pp. 41–42).

22. Strachey 1953 [1612], p. 112. My interpretation; Feest (personal communication 1984) feels that all wives after the first, even for a *weroance,* were "hired." Strachey is ambiguous: "the weroances after this manner [i.e., bride-wealth payments] may haue as many as they can obteyne, howbeit all the rest, whome they take after their first Choise, are (as yt were) mercinary." The women involved may have been past child-bearing age. Purchas heard from Wingfield that "their elder women are cookes, Barbers, and for service, the younger for dalliance" (1614, p. 768). Strachey assumes that all decisions in the relationship were made by the man, which may not have been the case.

23. Strachey 1953 [1612], p. 116.
24. Ibid., p. 123.
25. Pargellis 1959, p. 234; the phrasing used by that anonymous writer of the 1680s was "They put away their wives at pleasure, and take others."
26. Pargellis 1959, p. 234. Banister (1970, p. 381) does not mention the option of sons staying with their fathers.
27. See Rountree forthcoming.
28. Strachey 1953 [1612], pp. 64–65.
29. Ibid., p. 62.
30. For more details, see Rountree forthcoming.
31. Bland 1911 [1651], pp. 13–14.
32. 1953 [1612], pp. 112–13; corroborated by Archer 1969c [1607], p. 104. Purchas heard from Wingfield that men "have one wife, many loves, and are also sodomites" (1614, p. 768).
33. Spelman 1910 [1613?], p. cxi; he could be speaking of either the Patawomecks or the Powhatan heartland.
34. Strachey 1953 [1612], pp. 112–13.
35. 1986c [1624], p. 128.
36. Archer 1969c [1607], p. 104.
37. Spelman 1910 [1613?], p. cviii.
38. Smith 1986c [1624], p. 128. This could be considered further evidence of adultery by women not being a capital offense, though Powhatan had the power to make his own rules in such matters.
39. John Pory, in Smith 1986c [1624], p. 291; Pory wrote of the Eastern Shore groups, but the mainland people probably followed the same rules.
40. Archer 1969c [1607], p. 103; he said that he was guessing, but he happened to be right.
41. The anonymous author of the 1680s (Pargellis 1959, p. 240). Information from that late in the seventeenth century, when "the Indians of Virginia" might include a variety of non-Algonquians, must be suspect; I quote it here for what it is worth.
42. 1958, especially chaps. 8 and 9.
43. In Samoa, the most elaborate of the societies in this category, there was no family

specialization, and village specialization was rare (Sahlins 1958, p. 214). There was, however, some craft specialization (ibid., p. 30).
44. 1968, pp. 270–75.
45. 1961, p. 96.
46. Nancy O. Lurie, repeated personal communications since 1971.
47. Smith 1986b [1612], pp. 174 (general principle of brothers to sisters to eldest sister's children) and 247 (list of Powhatan's actual heirs, including "my two sisters, and their two daughters"). (Copied in Smith 1986c [1624], pp. 127 and 196, respectively.)
48. Spelman 1910 [1613?], p. cx. I disagree with Feest, who states (1978, p. 262) that "after death, property was passed on in the male line." Spelman merely happened to be writing about a deceased person who was male.
49. Martin and Voorhies 1975.
50. Strachey 1953 [1612], Appendix.
51. Strachey's list is by far the longest; considering his interest in other aspects of Indian life and his willingness to write what details he learned, his omission of any mention of how relatives outside the nuclear family were named must be taken as evidence that he did not ask his informants about it.
52. 1953 [1612], p. 116.
53. Smith 1986b [1612], p. 162 (copied in Smith 1986c [1624], p. 116); closely paraphrased by Strachey 1953 [1612], p. 113.
54. Wallace 1970, pp. 34–35.
55. That is probably what their general statements to the English were. Toughness and endurance could have been valued qualities in women as well as men.
56. Smith 1986b [1612], p. 162 (copied in Smith 1986c [1624], p. 116); copied by Strachey 1953 [1612], p. 113.
57. 1947 [1705], pp. 171–73. He also says children were bound naked onto their cradle boards at all seasons, which may be doubted in the case of newborns, at least.
58. Hulton 1984, p. 65.
59. Similar wrapping for carrying is reported for the Algonquians of New York: Danckaerts 1913 [1679–80], p. 56.
60. Smith 1986b [1612], p. 162 (copied in Smith 1986c [1624], p. 116); copied by Strachey 1953 [1612], p. 113.
61. 1968 [1687], p. 434. Clayton was probably, but not necessarily, writing about the Powhatans.
62. Pargellis 1959, p. 241. The caution given in the above note applies here as well.
63. Strachey 1953 [1612], p. 85.
64. Ibid., p. 84 and 84n.
65. Culin 1975 [1903], pp. 616–17, 622; John Swanton (1969 [1946], p. 676) erroneously identified the game as rackets, the ancestor of lacrosse.
66. Pargellis 1959, p. 232. The wording "he wins that drives [the ball]" indicates that the game was played by males; Strachey does not indicate the sex of the players.
67. Spelman 1910 [1613?], p. cxiv; Strachey 1953 [1612], p. 84. Strachey indicates that only kicking was acceptable: "they only forceably encounter with the foote to carry the Ball."
68. Spelman 1910 [1613?], p. cxiv.
69. Pargellis 1959, p. 232.
70. 1953 [1612], p. 84.
71. Pargellis 1959, p. 232; the writer does not mention whence the challenge of the game came. However, John Lawson observed a similar game among the Siouans to the southwest in which a player held fifty-one reeds and then suddenly grabbed and threw some of them to an opponent. He won if he guessed correctly "by feel" how many reeds he had thrown so quickly (cited in Swanton 1969 [1946], p. 685). Culin (1975 [1903], p. 232) classes the game as a stick game.

72. Clayton 1965 [1687], pp. 38–39.
73. Beverley 1947 [1705], p. 221.
74. Strachey 1953 [1612], p. 85.
75. Ibid., p. 71.
76. Percy 1969a [1608?], p. 136; Smith 1986b [1612], p. 170 (copied in Smith 1986c [1624], p. 123).
77. Smith 1986b [1612], p. 167 (copied in Smith 1986c [1624], p. 120); copied by Strachey 1953 [1612], p. 85; Spelman 1910 [1613?], p. cxiv.
78. Strachey 1953 [1612], p. 96. Accounts of rattles being used in conjuring: Percy 1921–22 [1612], p. 277; Smith 1986b [1612], p. 170 (copied by Strachey 1953 [1612], p. 97). Accounts of rattles being used in curing: Smith 1986a [1608], p. 59; Smith 1986b [1612], p. 168 (copied by Strachey 1953 [1612], p. 111); Spelman 1910 [1613?], pp. cix–cx.
79. Smith 1986b [1612], p. 167 (copied in Smith 1986c [1624], p. 120). Spelman (1910 [1613?], p. cxiv) calls it a "pipe."
80. Strachey 1953 [1612], p. 85; partially copied from Smith, previous reference.
81. Percy 1969a [1608?], p. 137.
82. Smith 1986b [1612], p. 167 (copied in Smith 1986c [1624], p. 120).
83. Strachey 1953 [1612], p. 109.
84. Banister 1970, p. 382; copied by Beverley (1947 [1705], p. 224).
85. 1953 [1612], p. 86.
86. Lenape use: Kinietz 1946, p. 37 and Flannery 1939, p. 85; analogy with Powhatans: Christian F. Feest and Nancy O. Lurie, personal communications 1984.
87. See the White paintings of a dance and what appears to be a "community sing" (Hulton 1984, pp. 69, 70). No upright posts at a dance ground are recorded for the Powhatans.
88. Strachey 1953 [1612], pp. 86–87; Spelman 1910 [1613?], p. cxiv; Percy 1969a [1608?], p. 136.
89. Mentioned only in Strachey's account.
90. Mentioned only in Spelman's account but corroborated by Beverley (1947 [1705], p. 189), who probably never saw Spelman's manuscript.
91. Mentioned only in Percy's account.
92. Smith 1986c [1624], pp. 147–48.
93. Smith 1986b [1612], pp. 235–36 (copied in Smith 1986c [1624], pp. 182–83). In his later account, Smith said that Pocahontas had been there to calm the initially alarmed English, but in neither account did he identify the dance's "leader."
94. 1910 [1613?], p. cxiv.
95. Strachey 1953 [1612], p. 86.
96. Beverley 1947 [1705], p. 224.
97. Strachey 1953 [1612], p. 86.

Chapter 6: Social Distinctions

1. Beverley (1947 [1705], p. 226) wrote that there was a lower stratum still, "inferiour to the Commons," called "black boys." The term "black boys" applied early in the seventeenth century to candidates for the *huskanaw*; Beverley's use of the term does not ring true, either for traditional Powhatan culture or for the conditions under which the Powhatans were living in his time.
2. The only mentions of the "better sort," by Archer (1969c [1607], pp. 102–103), Smith (1986b [1612], pp. 160–61 [copied in Smith 1986c (1624), p. 115]), and Strachey (1953 [1612], p. 71) concerned items of clothing; Spelman (1910 [1613?], p. cxiii), an erstwhile resident of chiefly households, wrote of etiquette in eating, while Percy (1969a [1608?], p. 135) contrasted "chiefest" people to the "meanest sort" at a formal feast. These are minutiae, not general statements on social ranking.
3. Always men: Beverley 1947 [1705], p. 214.

4. Smith 1986b [1612], p. 172 (also 1986c [1624], p. 125: "Quiyoughcosughes" or gods); almost exactly copied by Strachey 1953 [1612], p. 100 ("half Quiyoughcosughes"). Smith's interviews were primarily with rulers, while Strachey's main informants, Kemps and Machumps, were commoners; the difference shows. Late in the seventeenth century Clayton (1965 [1687], p. 21) wrote that priests were outranked by the Indians' "great War-Captain," a situation that was probably much changed after the Powhatans' defeats at English hands, which the priests had not predicted.

5. Beverley 1947 [1705], 212–13.

6. Strachey 1953 [1612], p. 88.

7. Spelman 1910 [1613?], p. cxiii. This hairstyle differs from the North Carolina Algonquian one pictured in fig. 20; I am led to wonder if Beverley, who let his illustrator copy de Bry, had ever actually seen an Indian priest.

8. Smith 1986b [1612], p. 170 (copied in Smith 1986c [1624], pp. 122–23); paraphrased by Strachey 1953 [1612], p. 95.

9. Strachey 1953 [1612], p. 96.

10. Ibid., p. 95. Beverley speaks instead of a special priestly "hanging of his Cloak, with the Fur reverst and falling down in flakes, looks horridly shagged." (1947 [1705], p. 212).

11. Smith 1986a [1608], p. 59; Smith 1986b [1612], p. 170 (copied in Smith 1986c [1624], p. 123); closely paraphrased by Strachey 1953 [1612], pp. 95–96.

12. 1947 [1705], p. 212.

13. 1986b [1612], p. 170 (copied in Smith 1986c [1624], pp. 122–23); closely paraphrased by Strachey 1953 [1612], p. 95.

14. Hariot 1972 [1590], pp. 48, 54 (de Bry edition of separate pictures of a priest and a conjurer).

15. Beverley 1947 [1705], p. 212.

16. Beverley 1947 [1705], p. 213.

17. Pargellis 1959, p. 236.

18. Strachey 1953 [1612], pp. 94–95.

19. Whitaker 1936 [1613], p. 26.

20. Purchas 1617, p. 955. Purchas's source was the priest Uttamatomakkin, and he reports (perhaps accurately) that priests would normally demand in their god's name any "good deere" killed by a commoner and then enjoy it themselves.

21. Beverley 1947 [1705], p. 226, 213.

22. Purchas 1617, p. 955.

23. Smith 1986b [1612], p. 146 (copied in Smith 1986c [1624], p. 103); copied by Strachey 1953 [1612], p. 69 (cawcawwasoughs); Strachey 1953 [1612], pp. 58 and 67 (cronoccoes).

24. Smith 1986c [1624], p. 127; Bland 1911 [1651], p. 9; Banister 1970, p. 354 (copied in Beverley 1947 [1705], pp. 149, 226).

25. Strachey 1953 [1612], p. 69. He presumably knew what the word meant; the passage in Smith is unclear: "the Priestes and their Assistants [or] their Elders called . . ."

26. 1986c [1624], p. 127.

27. 1970, p. 354.

28. Strachey 1953 [1612], pp. 71–72; copied with additions from Smith 1986b [1612], pp. 160–61 (copied in Smith 1986c [1624], p. 115).

29. Strachey 1953 [1612], p. 65 (both the quotation and the reference to being carried ashore).

30. Smith 1986b [1612], p. 174 (copied in Smith 1986c [1624], p. 127).

31. Analysis of the picture in Feest 1967a, p. 10.

32. 1983.

33. From either "*Saxidomus aratus* or *S. graciles*": Feest 1983, p. 136.

34. Ibid., p. 134.

35. Banister 1970, p. 378; the garment is described as "a very rich Deer match coat

taken belonging to Quoiccos or God, painted with puccoon, & embroydered with peak & some fine pearls."

36. Smith 1986b [1612], p. 174; Smith's 1624 version (1986c [1624], p. 127) additionally reads "commander, which commonly they call Werowance, or Caucorause, which is Captaine"; copied by Strachey 1953 [1612], p. 59.

37. "Powhatan" was the name he used in his youth and the name still used by "foreign" Indian groups for him in 1607 (Strachey 1953 [1612], p. 56).

38. Strachey 1953 [1612], p. 56.

39. Smith 1986c [1624], p. 151.

40. 1910 [1613?], p. cxiii; "sic" is mine; other brackets are Arber's.

41. Smith 1986b [1612], p. 173 (copied in Smith 1986c [1624], p. 126).

42. Strachey 1953 [1612], p. 78.

43. Spelman 1910 [1613?], p. cvi.

44. Smith 1986a [1608], p. 53; the event described is Smith's first meeting with Powhatan in January 1608.

45. Smith 1986b [1612], p. 216 (copied in Smith 1986c [1624], p. 155).

46. Smith 1986a [1608], p. 53; Smith 1986c [1624], p. 150 (detail of the raccoon tails).

47. Smith 1986b [1612], p. 173 (copied in Smith 1986c [1624], p. 126).

48. Smith 1986a [1608], p. 51.

49. Smith 1986b [1612], p. 173 (elaborated in Smith 1986c [1624], p. 126 [the mode of hallooing]); almost exactly copied by Strachey 1953 [1612], p. 59.

50. At Kecoughtan, in their first sight of the English: Percy 1969a [1607], p. 135.

51. At Arrahateck when another weroance arrived: Archer 1969a [1607], p. 84.

52. At Werowocomoco, on Smith's second visit: Smith 1986a [1608], p. 65.

53. Smith 1986b [1612], pp. 167–68 (copied in Smith 1986c [1624], pp. 120–21); almost exactly copied by Strachey 1953 [1612], pp. 84–85. Later in the century Clayton wrote that when "the Indians" decided to break their silence and give utterance, their words were "vehement & Emphatical & allways attended with strong gesticulations" (1965 [1687], p. 39).

54. Smith 1986a [1608], p. 65. In his 1624 account, Smith cited her serving him in early January (1986c [1624], p. 151), during his captivity, as proof of the initial friendliness of Powhatan; he gave no physical description of her there, which has led his editor, Barbour, to identify her with Opossunuqounuske (p. 151n).

55. Archer 1969a [1607], p. 92.

56. Percy 1969a [1608?], p. 136; Archer 1969a [1607], p. 84; Hamor 1957 [1615], pp. 39–40. Tobacco was also smoked when a female ruler was the host, though the English witness (Archer 1969a [1607], p. 92) does not say specifically that she joined in the smoking.

57. Smith 1986b [1612], p. 168 (copied in Smith 1986c [1624], p. 121); closely paraphrased by Strachey 1953 [1612], p. 85.

58. Smith 1986a [1608], pp. 65–69.

59. Smith 1986c [1624], p. 148.

60. Ibid., p. 150.

61. Ibid.

62. Hamor 1957 [1615], pp. 43, 45–46.

63. Kingsbury 1906–35, 3: 438; the writer was recording a story heard secondhand at best, and the annual progress may have been an assumption based on an analogy with English royalty of the time.

64. Spelman 1910 [1613?], p. cxiii.

65. Smith 1986a [1608], p. 69.

66. Strachey 1953 [1612], p. 87; his editors, Wright and Freund, define "cades" as "caddies, small boxes or chests."

67. 1986b [1612], p. 174 (copied in Smith 1986c [1624], p. 127).

68. Strachey 1953 [1612], pp. 63, 87.

69. Ibid., p. 87.

70. Smith 1986b [1612], pp. 158−59.

71. Smith 1986b [1612], p. 169; paraphrased by Strachey 1953 [1612], p. 95.

72. 1953 [1612], p. 87.

73. Spelman 1910 [1613?], p. cxii; he was not a witness, since the first fields of the year were planted in April, and he left Powhatan's household in March 1610.

74. Archer 1969a [1607], p. 93.

75. Spelman speaks only of corn in his account.

76. Smith 1986b [1612], p. 173 (copied in Smith 1986c [1624], p. 126); copied by Strachey 1953 [1612], p. 62.

77. Spelman 1910 [1613?], p. cv. Clayton understood that the corn in question was "provision[s]" of some kind (1968 [1687], p. 436.

78. Strachey 1953 [1612], p. 107.

79. Smith 1986a [1608], pp. 81, 93.

80. Strachey 1953 [1612], pp. 56−57.

81. Fausz 1977, pp. 70, 76.

82. Sahlins 1958.

83. Smith 1986b [1612], p. 163; paraphrased by Strachey 1953 [1612], p. 80.

84. Spelman 1910 [1613], p. cx.

85. This paragraph is a composite picture drawn from Strachey 1953 [1612], pp. 61−62, and Spelman 1910 [1613?], pp. cvii−cviii.

86. Only Spelman's account mentions such rapid turnover; the retention of Winganuske comes from Strachey's account.

87. Strachey 1953 [1612], p. 62.

88. Spelman 1910 [1613?] p. cviii.

89. Strachey 1953 [1612], p. 62.

90. Hamor 1957 [1615], pp. 41−42.

91. Strachey 1953 [1612], p. 62.

92. This paragraph is a composite picture drawn from Smith 1986b [1612], p. 169 (copied in Smith 1986c [1624], p. 122); Strachey 1953 [1612], p. 94; Spelman 1910 [1613?], p. cx, and Pargellis 1959, pp. 231−32. The anonymous writer of the 1680s (Pargellis 1959, pp. 231−32) gives a classic account of secondary burial, with a bone bundle the end product.

93. Strachey and also Hariot in the Pamlico region (1972 [1590], p. 72) write as though the scaffold episode were omitted and the bone-scraping done immediately; Smith speaks of drying "on hurdles," and it is Spelman who actually mentions the scaffold. Hariot adds that the body's skin was retained as the first wrapping of a still-articulated skeleton, a practice (if he is accurate) that is not attested to by Virginia writers.

94. Kingsbury 1906−35, 4: 10. It is possible that his bone bundle was merely being moved from temple to temple, though no English document indicates a movement of either holy places or major Indian towns in that year.

95. And yet Beverley (1947 [1705], p. 196) found a disarticulated bone bundle in a Chickahominy(?) temple (see chap. 8).

Chapter 7: Law, Politics, and War

1. See Rountree forthcoming.

2. Smith 1986b [1612], p. 174 (copied in Smith 1986c [1624], p. 127); paraphrased by Strachey 1953 [1612], p. 87.

3. Smith 1986b [1612], p. 160 (copied in Smith 1986c [1624], p. 115).

4. The evidence for this assertion is very sketchy. It consists of Strachey's remarks on the assignment of Quiyoughcohannock to a new ruler (1953 [1612], p. 65), as well as the moving about of the conquered Kecoughtans (see below).

5. See Rountree forthcoming.

6. Beverley 1947 [1705], pp. 225–26.

7. Strachey 1953 [1612], p. 77; copied, with additions, from Smith 1986b [1612], p. 174 (copied in Smith 1986c [1612], p. 127).

8. Smith 1986a [1608], p. 49.

9. Glover 1904 [1676], p. 26.

10. Pargellis 1959, p. 243.

11. Smith 1986b [1612], p. 146 (copied in Smith 1986c [1624], p. 103); closely paraphrased by Strachey 1953 [1612], p. 69; Hamor 1957 [1615], p. 14 (eight elders).

12. Archer 1969a [1607], p. 90.

13. Strachey 1953 [1612], p. 60; copied, with additions, from Smith 1986b [1612], p. 175 (copied in Smith 1986c [1624], pp. 127–28).

14. 1969c [1607], p. 102.

15. Strachey 1953 [1612], p. 75.

16. Archer 1969c [1607], p. 103.

17. Smith 1986a [1608], p. 81.

18. Ibid., p. 93.

19. 1986b [1612], p. 160 (copied in Smith 1986c [1624], p. 115); Strachey 1953 [1612], p. 76.

20. Monetary reparations became the rule in Powhatan-English assault and murder cases later in the seventeenth century (see Rountree forthcoming); however, there is no record of paying reparations in cases involving only Indians. Instead, one writer (Glover 1904 [1676], p. 26) states that murder was revenged by the victim's family, a practice that may not have existed in the short-lived heyday of strong native rulers in eastern Virginia.

21. Spelman 1910 [1613?], pp. cx–cxi.

22. The male hairstyle was believed to be supernaturally ordained for "real" men; see chap. 3.

23. Smith 1986b [1612], p. 174 (copied in Smith 1986c [1624], p. 127); Strachey 1953 [1612], p. 60.

24. Strachey 1953 [1612], p. 62.

25. Smith 1986b [1612], pp. 174–75 (copied in Smith 1986c [1624], p. 127); Strachey 1953 [1612], p. 60.

26. Strachey 1953 [1612], p. 60; Smith (1986b [1612], p. 175 [copied in Smith 1986c (1624), p. 127]) says "notorious enimie or malefactor."

27. Purchas 1617, p. 955.

28. The English word "son" may be too restrictive. The Powhatan kinship terminology system may have been such that certain nephews or other relatives were classificatory "sons."

29. Since these men and two "sisters" were Powhatan's heirs and the English accounts make it clear that lateral succession through children of the same mother was the norm (see below), then the three men were probably Powhatan's brothers or half-brothers (if gossipy Strachey had told us about the husbands of *weroansquas*, we could guess which) or else a combination of his male siblings and children of his mother's sisters(s).

30. Strachey 1953 [1612], pp. 62, 65, 67, 69.

31. John Pory, in Smith 1986c [1624], p. 291. Their sibling status may have been classificatory.

32. Strachey 1953 [1612], p. 63; she was a tough, hostile, mannish woman (Archer [1969a (1607), p. 92] described her as "a fatt lustie manly woman"), and the town she ruled, at the junction of the Appomattox and James rivers, was an important one, the gateway to Appamattuck territory beyond. Her sibling status with Coquonasum may have been classificatory.

33. Strachey 1953 [1612], p. 46; Argall 1904–6 [1613], p. 93. Their sibling status may have been classificatory. In 1624 the Patawomeck *weroance* was also referred to as a "brother" of Powhatan's brother and successor, Opitchapam (Smith 1986c [1624], p. 308), though the reference is set in a rhetorical context that may not indicate real kinship.

34. Archer 1969a [1607], p. 93.
35. Later in the century two positions were passed down patrilineally. These were the Chiskiack chieftainship in the 1650s (Mason 1946–48, frontispiece) and the Eastern Shore "emperorship" in 1657 (Wachiawamp, to his daughter and then to his brother's son: Northampton County, Virginia, *Deeds, Wills, Etc.*, 9: 5) and 1673 (Tapatiaton to his daughter: Accomac County, Virginia, *Wills* 1673–76, p. 33). Earlier accounts of these chiefdoms omit mention of chiefly inheritance, so I am not certain that a change to patrilineality had occurred because of English influence.
36. 1953 [1612], pp. 63–66.
37. Smith 1986b [1612], p. 173 (copied in Smith 1986c [1624], p. 126); copied by Strachey 1953 [1612], p. 57. Smith (p. 147 [copied in Smith 1986c (1624), p. 104]) and Strachey (pp. 43–44, paraphrasing Smith) give another list, which includes Werowocomoco and Chiskiack; the status of these two groups as ancestral inheritances is actually uncertain.
38. Strachey 1953 [1612], p. 57.
39. Or Lin Stuchans (Nugent 1934, 30, 75), assuming the Eastern Shore king of 1635 was the same as the "Laughing King of Accomac" of 1621 (there is no proof). An Eastern Shore historian (Upshur 1901–02, p. 89), who has been used extensively since, confused the "Laughing King" with Tapatiaton ("Debbedeavon"), whose first appearance was in 1648 as a lesser ruler in Occohannock territory (Rountree MS A).
40. This name has been anglicized to Kiptopeke and remains as a place-name near Cape Charles.
41. John Pory, in Smith 1986c [1624], p. 291. Pory's wording is unclear, so the text is my interpretation. His visit to the Eastern Shore took place in 1621; the two brothers became well known to the English only in the 1620s.
42. Hamor 1957 [1615], p. 10.
43. Purchas 1617, p. 956; paraphrased in Purchas 1904–6, 19: 118.
44. Kingsbury 1906–35, 3: 73–74.
45. Fausz (1977, p. 322; 1981, p. 27; 1985, p. 243) claims it was. However, it could just as easily have been Powhatan putting a good face on it, as the Accomac *weroance* did, and letting his brother rule while keeping the title himself.
46. Purchas 1617, pp. 956–57.
47. The offer may have been real, or it may have been a trap. See Rountree forthcoming.
48. Strachey 1953 [1612], pp. 44, 68.
49. Ibid., pp. 57–58.
50. Ibid., p. 44.
51. Ibid., pp. 68–69.
52. Archer 1969a [1607], p. 82.
53. See Rountree forthcoming.
54. Strachey 1953 [1612], pp. 58–59.
55. The only clear reference is in Hamor (1957 [1615], p. 6), who says of Powhatan after Pochahontas's capture that he "could not without long aduise & delibertion [*sic*] with his Councell, resolue vpon any thing."
56. Clayton 1968 [1687], p. 435; all spellings *sic*.
57. The word means literally "a great house" (Strachey 1953 [1612], p. 188) and idiomatically "Their Church and Storehouse" (Smith 1986c [1624], p. 265 margin). The council meeting held in the temple became known as a "*matchacomoco*" by 1651 (Meade 1857, 2: 478; spelled "*machcomacoi*"), and that term was used in a law of 1663 (Hening 1809–23, II: 194), an account of 1676 (*Virginia Magazine of History and Biography* 17: 420; spelled "*matcha comicha wee whio*"), Banister's account (1970, p. 381), and Beverley's book (1947 [1705], p. 192).
58. Strachey 1953 [1612], p. 104; copied with additions from Smith 1986b [1612], p. 165 (copied in Smith 1986c [1624], p. 119).
59. Banister 1970, p. 381.

60. The latter two occupied territories southwest of the James River, along the rivers bearing their names; they were coastal plain people in both Virginia and North Carolina. Major sources on them are Binford 1961 and 1967, Boyce 1978, and Rountree 1987.

61. Bland 1911 [1651], p. 13.

62. Strachey 1953 [1612], pp. 35, 106; see Rountree forthcoming.

63. Sainsbury 1860, 3: 56; Smith 1986c [1624], p. 305.

64. The spelling of the latter is Smith's (1986a [1608], pp. 55, 67); Strachey's spelling is "Bocootawonauk" (1953 [1612], p. 35).

65. Hoffman 1964b (Erie); W. W. Tooker (Ottawa), cited in Fausz (1985, p. 265).

66. Smith first met them not on the Potomac River but up at the head of Chesapeake Bay, at or near the mouth of the Susquehanna River (1986b [1612], pp. 230–31 [closely copied in Smith 1986c (1624), pp. 170–71]). That, of course, does not prove that they had come there via the Susquehanna. Yet with the exception of the Patawomecks, the tribes that Smith lists as having been terrorized by the Massawomecks are those living in the headwaters of the Bay, who lived less dispersed than the Powhatans, while the Susquehannocks (farthest north) lived in palisaded towns (Strachey 1953 [1612], p. 48). As though to confuse matters for us, Smith wrote later that the Massawomecks lived "beyond the mountaines from whence is the head of the river Patawomecke . . . upon a great salt water" (1986b [1614], pp. 165–66 [copied in Smith 1986c (1624), p. 119]), and the Smith map (Smith n.d. [1608]) clearly shows their homeland to the west of the head of Chesapeake Bay. Strachey agrees that they lived to the northwest and served as a source of copper for the Powhatans (1953 [1612], p. 35).

67. Among the Virginia Algonquian groups, the Patawomecks are known to have been raided by them (Spelman 1910 [1613?], p. cxiv), and the Kecoughtans heartily feared them (Smith 1986b [1612], p. 229 [copied in Smith 1986c (1624), p. 169]).

68. Strachey 1953 [1612], pp. 104–5. Strachey, who may not have known what he was talking about, mentions their having a *weroance*, indicating that the Chesapeakes were a chiefdom.

69. The timing is a matter of controversy among scholars (notably, between David B. Quinn and me) involving other issues, such as the identity of the Indians who attacked the Jamestown colonists on their arrival in Virginia in April 1607 and the possibility that refugees from the Roanoke Colony of the 1580s were still living among the Chesapeakes when they were exterminated by Powhatan. See Rountree forthcoming.

70. Strachey 1953 [1612], p. 108; he speaks of "new Inhabitants . . . togither with the Weroances of *Nandsamund Warraskoyack* and *Weanock*," which indicates that the neighboring Nansemonds may not have taken over the territory. However, if the new inhabitants evolved a "tribal" name, the English never learned it before the territory was abandoned and taken over by English settlers.

71. Strachey 1953 [1612], p. 104; copied in part from Smith 1986b [1612], p. 165 (copied in Smith 1986c [1624], p. 119).

72. Smith 1969b [1612], p. 166 (copied in Smith 1986c [1624], p. 119); copied by Strachey 1953 [1612], p. 109.

73. Opechancanough invoked the rule when he invited the English to assist him in 1619 in making war on the Monacans for "murthering certaine woemen of his[,] Contrary to ye law of Nations" (Kingsbury 1906–35, 3: 228). The English first broke the rule in 1610, after which Powhatan raids on them assumed a new and different tone; see Rountree forthcoming.

74. Barbour, followed by Mossiker and Fausz.

75. Smith 1986c [1624], p. 151.

76. See the discussion of the historical problems with the "rescue incident" in Rountree forthcoming.

77. Smith 1986c [1624], p. 151.

78. Strachey 1953 [1612], p. 104.

79. Ibid., p. 107.

80. Ibid., p. 69.

81. Ibid., p. 107.

82. Smith 1986a [1608], p. 67; Smith, as an emissary of Captain Christopher Newport, was allotted "a great house sufficient to lodge mee."

83. 1953 [1612], p. 62.

84. Smith 1986c [1624], p. 144. This incident appears only in Smith's 1624 version; earlier versions speak only of Kecoughtan unwillingness to trade and derision toward the famished English. The authenticity of the incident must thus be questioned.

85. This formation was used against the English in preparing for an attack in 1609 (Smith 1986b [1612], p. 255).

86. Smith 1986b [1612], pp. 166-67 (copied in Smith 1986c [1624], p. 120); Strachey 1953 [1612], pp. 109-10.

87. Strachey 1953 [1612], p. 44.

88. Archer 1969c [1607], p. 103.

89. Ibid.; Spelman 1910 [1613?], pp. cxiii-cxiv.

90. Archer 1969a [1607], p. 96.

91. 1910 [1613?], pp. cxiii-cxiv.

92. Archer 1969a [1607], p. 98.

93. Smith 1986a [1608], p. 87.

94. Spelman 1910 [1613?], p. cxiv.

95. The description is from Callahan 1981, pp. 238-44, in the absence of clear contemporary descriptions. Callahan found this kind of "sword" useful in chopping thatch.

96. Percy (1969a [1608?], p. 138) saw such "swords" at Appamattuck.

97. 1947 [1705], facing p. 182; textual description on pp. 196-97. Callahan (1981, p. 240) feels that this kind of weapon would have been of limited use and that therefore Beverley's account should be taken "with a grain of salt."

98. Strachey 1953 [1612], pp. 86, 109, 192, 203; Smith 1986b [1612], p. 136 (copied in Smith 1986c [1624], p. 130). Feest feels (personal communication 1984) that "monohacan" applied to English swords, yet Strachey speaks on p. 86 of Thomas Savage's "bright sword" as a "monnacock." Feest thinks (personal communication 1986) that the original word "tomahacan" referred to English iron hatchets, while another word, *cussenagwus* (Strachey 1953 [1612], p. 187) meant Indian hatchets made of other materials. Siebert (1975) does not list the latter word among the entries in Strachey that he can identify as an authentic Algonquian word.

99. Among the early settlers, only Spelman uses that term (1910 [1613?], p. cxiii), and he uses it erroneously for "shield." The term became general for Powhatan war-clubs later in the century, and Beverley uses it for the *monacock* illustrated in his book.

100. Smith 1986b [1612], p. 163 (copied in Smith 1986c [1624], p. 116); Strachey 1953 [1612], p. 109; both writers say the latter but not the former was used as well in felling trees.

101. Smith 1986a [1608], p. 87 ("cudgels"); Smith 1986b [1612], p. 175 (copied in Smith 1986c [1624], p. 127) ("clubbes"); Strachey 1953 [1612], p. 60 ("Clubbs" for executions, "Cudgells" for beating but not killing).

102. Spelman 1910 [1613?], p. cxiii.

103. Feest 1967a, p. 25.

104. Strachey 1953 [1612], p. 109; which groups used them went unrecorded.

105. Ibid.; copied with additions from Smith 1986b [1612], p. 163 (copied in Smith 1986c [1624], p. 116).

106. Spelman 1910 [1613?], p. cxiii.

107. Smith 1986b [1612], p. 154 (copied in Smith 1986c [1624], p. 110); copied by Strachey 1953 [1612], p. 122.

108. Hariot 1972 [1590], p. 24.

109. The following English accounts are the only records of trophy taking by anyone in Virginia before 1610; it was not, in fact, until 1623 that the English began taking trophies of their own. The English, instead, offended Indians by killing women and children, beginning

in 1610 (see Rountree forthcoming). For a larger-scale discussion of scalping as an aboriginal custom in North America, see Axtell 1981, pp. 16–35.

110. Smith 1986b [1612], p. 161 (copied in Smith 1986c [1624], p. 115); Strachey 1953 [1612], p. 74.

111. Smith 1986b [1612], p. 175 (copied in Smith 1986c [1624], p. 128); paraphrased in Strachey 1953 [1612], p. 44.

112. Clayton 1968 [1687], pp. 435, 436, and 1965 [1687], p. 23.

113. Clayton 1968 [1687], p. 436.

114. Percy 1921–22 [1612], p. 276.

115. 1986a [1608], p. 47.

116. 1986c [1624], pp. 147–48.

117. 1947 [1705], p. 194.

118. Tooker 1978, pp. 422–23.

119. The English recorded such gifts on two occasions, in 1607 and early 1608; see Rountree forthcoming.

120. Smith 1986c [1624], p. 179.

121. Both incidents occurred in January 1609: Smith 1986b [1612], p. 249 (copied in Smith 1986c [1624], p. 198); Smith 1986b [1612], p. 255 (copied in Smith 1986c [1624], p. 205).

122. Hamor 1957 [1615], pp. 38–39.

123. 1969a [1608?], p. 38. Beverley had his illustrator, Gribelin, engrave a peace pipe he had seen among unidentified Indians (1947 [1705], p. 169). It had a long stem carved in a spiral and what appear to be bird wings attached near the bowl.

124. Strachey 1953 [1612], p. 116.

125. Percy 1969a [1608?], p. 143.

126. Strachey 1953 [1612], p. 116.

Chapter 8: Medicine and Religion

1. Clayton (1968 [1687], p. 436) spoke of priests being "very reservd even amongst themselves." Banister said (1970, p. 378) that he had been told that the Indians considered it "part of their religion to conceal" the herbal remedies they knew about, while Beverley wrote (1947 [1705], p. 195) that in his time it was "reckon'd Sacriledge, to divulge the Principles of their Religion." The parallel with modern Pueblo feelings is obvious.

2. Beverley (1947 [1705], p. 218) said that common people knew only about snakeroot.

3. Clayton 1965 [1687], p. 22.

4. Ibid., p. 23.

5. Archer 1969c [1607], p. 102.

6. Banister 1970, p. 378; paraphrased by Beverley (1947 [1705], p. 218). Banister was more explicit: "any kind of medicine, be it simple or compound."

7. 1975, pp. 180–81.

8. Strachey 1953 [1612], p. 81.

9. Banister 1970, p. 378.

10. Archer 1969a [1607], p. 90.

11. Percy 1969b [1608?], p. 146.

12. Corroborated in Merrill and Feest 1975, p. 177; white plantain and persicary identifications are by them; "Indian weed" and "self-heal" identifications are by Clayton's 1965 editors, the Berkeleys.

13. Clayton 1965 [1687], p. 23.

14. Banister 1970, p. 378; copied by Bevereley (1947 [1705], p. 218).

15. 1986b [1612], p. 168 (copied in Smith 1986c [1624], p. 121); Strachey 1953 [1612], p. 111.

16. 1953 [1612], p. 110.
17. Clayton 1965 [1687], p. 38.
18. Clayton 1968 [1687], p. 432.
19. 1986b [1612], p. 168 (copied in Smith 1986c [1624], p. 121); Strachey 1953 [1612], p. 111.
20. See Hudson 1979. Merrill and Feest (1975, p. 177) do not believe that this was the plant used.
21. Clayton 1965 [1687], p. 29. Corroborated by Merrill and Feest 1975, pp. 178, 180.
22. So can another "pokeroot," *Veratrum viride* Ait. (Merrill and Feest 1975, pp. 177–78).
23. Merrill and Feest 1975, p. 178.
24. Ibid.
25. Clayton 1965 [1687], p. 28. Corroborated by Merrill and Feest (1975, p. 178), who suggest *Apocynum cannabinum* L.
26. Clayton 1965 [1687], p. 33.
27. Beverley 1947 [1705], p. 217–18.
28. Clayton 1965 [1687], pp. 28–29.
29. Klimas and Cunningham 1974, passim.
30. See Rountree forthcoming. The cure came after a vicious practical joke played on an Indian by an Englishman.
31. Banister 1970, p. 379; the Indians were probably the Tuscaroras.
32. Beverley 1947 [1705], p. 217; he has paraphrased and added to the passage in Banister, cited above, possibly indicating that he knew of cauterization among the Powhatans.
33. Clayton 1965 [1687], p. 27.
34. Lederer 1975 [1681], p. 153.
35. 1986b [1612], p. 168 (copied in Smith 1986c [1624], p. 121); Strachey 1953 [1612], p. 111.
36. Smith 1986b [1612], p. 168 (copied in Smith 1986c [1624], p. 121).
37. Banister 1970, p. 378; copied almost exactly by Beverley (1947 [1705], p. 217). Neither author mentioned the fang being hafted.
38. Banister 1970, p. 378; copied almost exactly by Beverley (1947 [1705], p. 217).
39. Clayton 1965 [1687], pp. 30–31.
40. Lederer 1975 [1681], pp. 154–55. Feest identifies the *Esula* as either wild ipecac or flowering spurge.
41. Smith 1986b [1612], p. 168 (copied in Smith 1986c [1624], p. 121); Strachey 1953 [1612], p. 111.
42. Beverley 1947 [1705], pp. 217, 218–19.
43. Banister 1970, p. 379; paraphrased by Beverley (1947 [1705], p. 218).
44. The term is Banister's, from whose account (1970, pp. 379–80) the following details are drawn unless otherwise noted.
45. Beverley mentioned only men; Banister said that "6 or 8 or as many as can sit round" used the sweathouse and that both sexes sweated (together?): "they come out of the stoves naked as the back of a mans hand, both men & women."
46. Banister 1970, p. 46.
47. Puccoon was used not only as a pigment but also as "an emulgent root of much afficacy [sic] for swellings & aches" (Banister 1970, p. 263).
48. Insect repellent after sweating: Banister 1970, p. 380.
49. Banister 1970, p. 46; the gentleman is not identified.
50. 1947 [1705], p. 217.
51. Pargellis 1959, p. 233.
52. These identifications are mine, based on entries in Miller 1976.
53. 1953 [1612], p. 113.
54. Archer 1969c [1607], p. 104.

55. There is a controversy over whether syphilis was a native American malady passed to Europeans for the first time in 1492 or whether the syphilitic epidemics that struck Europe immediately after that time were caused instead by a coincidentally timed spontaneous mutation of the Old World relatives of the disease. See Crosby 1972, chap. 4.

56. Pargellis 1959, p. 233; when two or more priests cured a patient, they divided the fee.

57. See, for example, Park 1938.

58. 1986a [1608], p. 59.

59. Pargellis 1959, p. 233.

60. 1910 [1613?], p. cix–cx.

61. Pargellis 1959, p. 233.

62. Strachey 1953 [1612], p. 97.

63. Pargellis 1959, pp. 232–33.

64. Smith 1986b [1612], p. 169 (copied in Smith 1986c [1624], p. 122); copied by Strachey 1953 [1612], p. 88.

65. Pargellis 1959, pp. 235–36.

66. Also implied in the wording of Strachey 1953 [1612], p. 95.

67. Purchas 1617, pp. 954–55. Remember that Purchas gives more details in a spirit of greater toleration in that edition of his *Pilgrimage* than he does in the 1625 edition, after the Indian attack of 1622.

68. Banister 1970, p. 378; Purchas (1617, p. 954) received the same impression.

69. Beverley 1947 [1705], p. 191.

70. Purchas 1617, p. 955.

71. Smith 1986b [1612], p. 170. Fausz errs in saying that the ceremony was to "purify him for having shed Pamunkey blood" (1977, p. 237). No purification ritual was ever recorded for the Powhatans. The following account of divining is a composite drawn from Smith (1986a [1608], p. 59); Smith (1986b [1612], pp. 170–71); Strachey (1953 [1612], pp. 96–97); and Smith (1986c [1624], pp. 149–50). Where contradictions occurred, I placed more weight on Smith's earlier account, because it was written sooner after the events.

72. These events occurred "three or foure dayes after my taking," while nonpriestly men were still on their communal hunt ("Each morning . . . the principall to the number of twentie or thirtie [i.e., *weroance*s and councillors of the tribes involved] assembled themselues in a round circle a good distance from the towne, where they told me they there consulted where to hunt the next day") (Smith 1986a [1608], p. 59). The Indians did not alter their seasonal round in order to take Smith to a village temple for the divining ritual.

73. Pargellis 1959, p. 232.

74. 1986b [1612], p. 171 (copied in Smith 1986c [1624], p. 124); Strachey (1953 [1612], p. 98) adds that *wisakon* was also offered.

75. The planter was William Byrd II; see Rountree forthcoming.

76. Percy 1921–22 [1612], p. 277; Whitaker 1964 [1611], pp. 498–99.

77. The anonymous writer of the 1680s (Pargellis 1959, p. 232) understood that storms could be raised by "drawing circles, muttering words, by making a dreadful howling and using stranger gestures and various rites, upon which the wind ariseth, etc."

78. This was Machumps, Powhatan's brother-in-law and one of Strachey's two main informants.

79. Percy 1921–22 [1612], pp. 277–78; Whitaker 1964 [1611], pp. 498–99.

80. 1921–22 [1612], p. 272.

81. Smith 1986b [1612], pp. 169–70 (copied in Smith 1986c [1624], p. 122); copied by Strachey 1953 [1612], p. 95.

82. Spelman 1910 [1613?], p. cv.

83. Strachey 1953 [1612], pp. 88–89, 95; copied in part from Smith 1986b [1612], p. 169 (copied in Smith 1986c [1624], p. 122). Dimensions are from Strachey, p. 88.

84. Strachey 1953 [1612], p. 88.

85. Among the North Carolina Algonquians, Hariot wrote that in "some *Machicomuck* we haue seene but on[e] *Kewas,* in some two, and in other some three" (1972 [1590], p. 26). No Virginia writer indicates more than one image per temple.

86. This description contrasts with the Pamlico practice (Hariot 1972 [1590], pp. 72–73; White painting, shown in Hulton 1984, p. 68), which called for a high scaffold on which both "bodies" and image were kept while a priest lived below.

87. Pargellis 1959, p. 235.

88. Smith 1986b [1612], p. 173–74 (copied in Smith 1986c [1624], p. 126); closely paraphrased by Strachey 1953 [1612], p. 62.

89. Beverley 1947 [1705], p. 196.

90. Percy 1921–22 [1612], pp. 263, 272.

91. Smith 1986c [1624], p. 144.

92. Beverley 1947 [1705], pp. 196–98. Judging by where Beverley lived and the fact that he went into the temple while "the Indians" were away negotiating about a new reservation, it is probable that the temple belonged to the Chickahominies, who lived on the upper Mattaponi River in the last decades of the seventeenth century. They are the only Indian group who formally requested new lands after 1670, as far as the surviving records show.

93. Purchas 1617, p. 955.

94. Beverley 1947 [1705], pp. 200–201. Part of the man's emotions may have been a reaction to Beverley's tampering with a temple to begin with.

95. Smith 1986b [1612], p. 169 (copied in Smith 1986c [1624], pp. 121–22); closely paraphrased by Strachey 1953 [1612], p. 88.

96. Purchas 1614, p. 765, quoted (from 1613 ed.) in Barbour 1986, 3: 318. Purchas learned of the incident from Smith.

97. For local variants of that term, see the note below. There is a note in Spelman's manuscript consisting of a list: "*Caukewis, Manato, Taukingesouke, Quoiuassack.*" The note may have been made by Spelman, whose experience was in Virginia, or by someone else whose knowledge covered Virginia and New England. Lederer, who in the early 1670s definitely knew other Indians as well as the Powhatans, recorded the terms "*Quiacosough* and *Tagkanysough*" for "lesser deities" and *Okaee* or *Mannith* for the powerful creator deity (1958 [1672], p. 13). The correspondence between the two lists is indicative. Clayton (1968 [1687], p. 435) recorded the major "Indians'" deity's name as "Tanto," a term derived from the northern Algonquian word "manitu."

98. Strachey 1953 [1612], pp. 88–89; copied in small part from Smith 1986b [1612], p. 169 (copied in Smith 1986c [1624], pp. 121–22). Direct quotation from Smith.

99. Beverley 1947 [1705], pp. 195, 200–201.

100. For two alternate accounts of the world's creation, see below.

101. Beverley 1947 [1705], p. 201.

102. Strachey 1953 [1612], p. 89.

103. Purchas 1617, p. 955.

104. Strachey 1953 [1612], p. 89.

105. Smith 1986b [1612], p. 169.

106. Smith 1986c [1624], p. 122.

107. Strachey and Purchas in their works.

108. Banister 1970, p. 378; copied in Beverley 1947 [1705], p. 198.

109. Spelman 1910 [1613?], p. cv.

110. Ibid.

111. Hariot 1972 [1590], p. 71.

112. The first scholar to make this connection was Christian Feest (1966b, pp. 1–2).

113. Strachey 1953 [1612], p. 89.

114. Purchas 1617, p. 955. Late in the century the anonymous writer heard that offerings left in the temple were burned after a time (Pargellis 1959, p. 235).

115. No English writer even hints about whether the blood was animal or human blood.

116. Smith 1986b [1612], p. 171 (copied in Smith 1986c [1624], p. 124); copied by Strachey 1953 [1612], p. 97.

117. Beverley wrote (1947 [1705], p. 214) that there was a small bird called by the same name because its call sounded like the word. The bird was solitary and "only heard in the twilight. They say that this is the Soul of one of their Princes" and therefore they would do it no harm; Beverley heard about a "profane *Indian*" who was bribed to kill one and who "was taken away" a few days thereafter.

118. Smith 1986b [1612], p. 171 (copied in Smith 1986c [1624], p. 123); copied by Strachey 1953 [1612], p. 97. Late in the seventeenth century, Banister wrote of some offerings being made on "three pyramidal stones, which (as they do themselves) they bedaub with paint & puccoon, & adorn them with peak & roanoake, giving them all outward signs of worship and devotion, not as God (say they) but as an Hieroglyphick of the permanency & immutability of the Deity" (1970, pp. 377–78; paraphrased by Beverley 1947 [1705], p. 213).

119. Beverley 1947 [1705], p. 213; see also Smith 1986c [1624], pp. 123–24.

120. Smith 1986b [1612], pp. 174–75 (copied in Smith 1986c [1624], p. 127); Strachey 1953 [1612], p. 60.

121. Beverley 1947 [1705], p. 127.

122. Banister 1970, p. 377; copied, with additions (such as "five feet asunder") by Beverley 1947 [1705], pp. 211–12.

123. Percy 1969a [1608?], pp. 143, 145–46; Strachey 1953 [1612], pp. 97–98. No later English writer mentions sun veneration; in fact the anonymous writer of the 1680s specifically denies it (Pargellis 1959, p. 236).

124. Smith 1986b [1612], p. 170 (copied in Smith 1986c [1624], p. 123); Strachey 1953 [1612], p. 96.

125. Pargellis 1959, p. 235.

126. Beverley 1947 [1705], p. 210; his mention of going to war makes me question whether he is speaking of the Powhatans of his time.

127. Feest (personal communication 1986; see also his 1966a, p. 76) disagrees, saying that "Okeus was clearly associated with hunting—woods—war—coercion—maleness—perhaps fire." Yet Okeus made crops fail and people become sick, attributes not connected with Feest's list except for the coercion part. If Okeus could make crops fail, then it is logical (to this Anglo-American, at least) that he should be thanked when he let them thrive. If Okeus is actually a collection of deities, as I suggest tentatively above, then some deity in the collection would definitely be receiving the thanks. In general, I find Feest's position on Okeus as a male-world god to be rather extreme and not well proved by the documents available to us.

128. Purchas 1617, p. 952.

129. Ibid., p. 955.

130. Smith 1986b [1612], p. 172 (almost exactly copied in Smith 1986c [1624], p. 125); closely paraphrased by Strachey 1953 [1612], p. 101 (whence the identification of which Quiyoughcohannock *weroance* it was); paraphrased also in Smith 1986b [1612], p. 266 ("his gods were angrie all the time") (almost exactly copied in Smith 1986c [1624], p. 215).

131. Strachey 1953 [1612], p. 89.

132. Purchas 1617, pp. 954–55.

133. Strachey 1953 [1612], p. 102. Purchas (1614, p. 767) also interviewed Spelman. His account is different and much shorter than Strachey's, probably because he collected his information and wrote it up much later than Strachey did, and someone's memory had lapsed. Purchas's account is this: "a Hare came into their Countrey and made the first men, and after preserued them from a great Serpent: and when two other Hares came thither, that Hare for their entertainment killed a Deer, which was then the only Deere that was, and strewing the haires of that Deeres hide, euery haire prooued a Deere." I follow Strachey in my text.

134. The anonymous writer of the 1680s heard that "the Indians" had a tradition of the world being flooded and everyone drowned except for "a few that were saved, to wit, about seven or eight in a great canoro"; for that reason they had only seven "great men," or coun-

cillors, in each nation besides their "king" (Pargellis 1959, pp. 236, 235). Feest (personal communication 1986) suggests that the connection between "seven or eight" survivors and eight Chickahominy councilmen may indicate that some Virginia Algonquians had the myth. I am very dubious, indeed, about that, having watched too many students indulging in wishful thinking about the universality of a flood myth in human societies. I suspect that the evangelistic English of Virginia and the Carolinas (wherever the anonymous writer met Indians) were capable of the same thing.

135. E. Randolph Turner, personal communication 1984; one or more ossuaries have been found at unpublished sites on the Chickahominy River (Stephen Potter, personal communication 1985).

136. Smith (1986b [1612], p. 169 [copied in Smith 1986c (1624), p. 122]) and Strachey (1953 [1612], p. 95), who wrote of primary inhumations, both knew the James-York region best; Spelman's account of secondary inhumation (1910 [1613?], p. cx) could come from either that region or the Patawomeck territory. Thomas Glover's statement that the dead were cremated and their ashes kept in mats in relatives' houses (1904 [1676], p. 25) may not be wholly accurate. See also the execution of criminals (chap. 7), whose bodies were burned.

137. The anonymous writer of the 1680s, who spoke of corpses buried "standing upright," facing the setting sun, was almost certainly off the mark, if speaking of the Powhatans.

138. Smith 1986b [1612], p. 262 (copied in Smith 1986c [1624], p. 211).

139. Ubelaker 1974. Examination of bones from these two ossuaries shows that some corpses were clean bones (carelessly gathered up: small bones were few in the ossuaries) when buried, while ligaments still articulating bones show that others were only partially decomposed. Ubelaker did not speculate on the time involved in his published report; however in a preliminary report on the site at a conference (see 1973 Proceedings of the Fourth Middle Atlantic Archaeological Conference) he estimated the time as five to ten years.

140. Smith 1986b [1612], p. 172 (copied in Smith 1986c [1624], p. 125 with addition of "but rot in their graves like dead dogs"); Strachey 1953 [1612], p. 100. Archer (1969c [1607], 104), whose brief account mentions no status differences, could have interviewed either rulers or nonrulers, but interpreting was very poor in 1607.

141. Samuel Argall and Henry Spelman, in Strachey 1953 [1612], pp. 102–3.

142. Strachey 1953 [1612], p. 100.

143. Archer 1969c [1607], p. 104.

144. Purchas 1617, p. 955. The question mark is Purchas's.

145. Spelman repeated the story to Strachey: 1953 [1612], pp. 102–3.

146. See Rountree forthcoming.

Epilogue: The Powhatans as a Chiefdom of Coastal Algonquians

1. For a briefer summary of the traits making Powhatan's organization a chiefdom and an account of its history to 1646, see Turner 1985.

2. Strachey 1953 [1612], p. 37; alternately spelled Tsenacommacah (p. 56). The meaning of the name is uncertain.

3. Strachey 1953 [1612], p. 69.

4. Smith 1986a [1608], p. 91.

5. Smith 1986b [1612], p. 150; copied by Strachey 1953 [1612], p. 49.

6. Smith 1986c [1624], p. 291. E. Randolph Turner feels that the economic differences between the Eastern Shore and the mainland were exaggerated in English minds, the reasons being that the mainland people, pressured to trade by the hungry English colony, misled the English about how little corn they produced, while the most distant Eastern Shore people could afford to speak accurately about their harvests. The Eastern Shore soils, Turner points out, are no better than those on the mainland, and the early Contact Period population densities are low. I counter the last assertion by noting the epidemic that happened on the Eastern Shore before 1608 (see below).

7. On Powhatan's orders, the Patawomecks, Onawmanients, and Sekakawons gave the

English a hostile reception in 1608, while the Moyaones acted friendly (Smith 1986b [1612], p. 291. The Patawomecks continued trading with Englishmen and harbored the English refugee Henry Spelman after Powhatan broke off diplomatic relations with the English in 1610; they also assisted in the capture of Pocahontas (Rountree forthcoming). Potomac River groups were neutral during the Powhatans' major attack of 1622 (Rountree forthcoming).

8. See, for instance, Ashburn 1947, Crosby 1972 (especially chap. 2), and Dobyns 1983.

9. Hariot 1972 [1590], p. 28.

10. Smith 1986b [1612], p. 247 (almost exactly copied in Smith 1986c [1624], p. 196).

11. Smith 1986b [1612], p. 225 (almost exactly copied in Smith 1986c [1624], p. 163).

12. E. Randolph Turner, personal communications 1984, 1985.

13. Dobyns 1983.

14. 1617: ". . . a great mortality among us, far greater among the Indians and a morrain [sic] amongst the deer" (Kingsbury 1906−35, 3: 92). 1619: "they have been much distempord by reason of an intemporate heate not onely hapninge vnto them but chiefly amongst the Indians" (1: 310). Why worse among the natives, unless these were European "bugs"? Living conditions for the James River groups had not become drastically worse, and their being pushed back from the James actually meant living along less brackish streams (see Rountree forthcoming).

15. Gottfried 1982, chap. 5 (especially pp. 97−103); Deaux 1969, chap. 7.

16. Rountree forthcoming.

17. Knowles 1940.

18. Massawomeck: Smith 1986b [1612], pp. 149−50 (copied with additions by Strachey 1953 [1612], pp. 107−8). Pocoughtaonack: Smith 1986a [1608], pp. 55, 67; Strachey 1953 [1612], pp. 35, 36, 57; Barbour 1969, p. 267.

19. Smith 1986b [1612], pp. 230−31; during both expeditions, visits to the Kecoughtans showed that they were eager for the annihilation of the Massawomecks (pp. 229, 230).

20. Spelman 1910 [1613?], p. cxiv; the fight took place in "a marish ground full of Reade," indicating that the Massawomecks had arrived by water.

21. Archer 1969c [1607], p. 102.

22. 1961, p. 89. Binford divides the coastal plain rivers into three zones, as opposed to Lippson and Lippson's four. Binford's "transitional" zone appears to cover all the latters' "brackish" zone and the upper part of the "moderately salty" zone.

23. E. Randolph Turner, personal communication 1985.

24. Strachey 1953 [1612], p. 56. He must have heard this at second- or third-hand.

25. See Rountree forthcoming.

26. Strachey 1953 [1612], p. 62; close paraphrase of Smith 1986b [1612], p. 173.

27. 1982, chap. 6; his list is based, with his own additions, on the work of Robert A. Dahl ("The Concept of Power," in Roderick Bell et al., eds., *Political Power: A Reader in Theory and Research* [New York: Free Press, 1969], pp. 79−93) and John C. Harsanyi ("Measurement of Social Power, Opportunity Costs, and the Theory of Two-Person Bargaining Games," in the same collection, pp. 226−38).

28. Smith 1986b [1612], p. 161; paraphrased by Strachey 1953 [1612], p. 71.

29. For a description of the incident and its causes, see Rountree forthcoming.

30. Ibid.

31. Haas 1982, p. 76; Service 1975, p. 304; Sahlins 1958.

32. 1976, 1986, and personal communications 1985.

33. Virginia is a "transitional" area between "northeastern" and "southeastern" climatic and biotic zones, and no one, as far as I can discover, has yet wanted to tackle its complexities.

34. Peebles and Kus 1977, p. 431; Turner 1986.

35. Ibid.

36. Personal communication 1985.

37. Rainey 1936; Flannery 1939.

38. See, for instance, Champlain 1907 [1604−18], pp. 65−75.

39. De Laet 1909 [1625, 1630], pp. 39–43.

40. 1907 [1604–18], p. 96.

41. Mourt 1963 [1622], p. 51.

42. Ibid., pp. 57, 66.

43. Winslow 1971 [1624], pp. 360–61.

44. 1970 [1792], pp. 7–10, 20. Gookin speaks of the Pokanockets as having their maximum power before the epidemics. He lists seven petty sachems and refers to "several others" under the "chief sachem."

45. Wood 1977 [1636], pp. 97–98.

46. Denton 1937 [1670], p. 6.

47. Williams 1973 [1643], p. 202; Brinley 1900 [1696], p. 73.

48. Williams 1973 [1643], p. 203.

49. Simmons and Aubin 1975.

50. Winslow 1971 [1624], p. 361.

51. 1978, p. 168. As far as I can determine, Salwen is the first scholar to deal with the differences in the early and late accounts.

52. 1924, p. 191.

53. 1964 [1946], passim.

54. 1975, vol. 4.

55. 1977, pp. 412–13.

56. 1947, p. 94.

57. After carefully examining both the seventeenth-century sources and Speck's fieldnotes, I find his work to be careless on both fronts. See my comments on him in Rountree forthcoming.

58. 1939, pp. 167–76; I am relying, somewhat unwillingly, on her labeling of certain traits as "diagnostically" "southeastern" or "northen Algonquian."

59. As far as I know, only one other scholar (Kupperman 1980) has arrived (independently) at the same conclusion.

60. See Rountree forthcoming.

Bibliography

Accomac County, Virginia
   1670 to present.   County Records. Accomac, Virginia (copy in Virginia State
      Library, Richmond).
Alexandria Drafting Company
   N.d.   *Salt Water Sport Fishing and Boating in Eastern Virginia.* Alexandria, Va.
Anonymous
   1900–1901   Two Tragicall Events: The Voyage of Anthony Chester, Made in
      the Year 1620. . . . *William and Mary Quarterly,* 1st ser., 9:203–14.
Anonymous
   1947   [1610]   A True Declaration of the Estate of the Colonie in Virginia. . . .
      In Peter Force, ed. *Tracts and Other Papers.* New York: Peter Smith. Vol. 3,
      no. 1.
Anonymous
   1969   [1608]   Map of Virginia [the so-called Zúñiga map]. In Philip L. Barbour,
      ed. *The Jamestown Voyages Under the First Charter.* Cambridge: Hakluyt
      Society. 2d ser. Vol. 137, facing p. 239.
Archer, Gabriel
   1969a   [1607]   Relatyon of the Discovery of Our River. In Philip L. Barbour,
      ed. *The Jamestown Voyages Under the First Charter.* 2d ser. 136:80–98.
   1969b   [1607]   Description of the River and Country. In Philip L. Barbour, ed.
      The Jamestown Voyages Under the First Charter. Cambridge: Hakluyt So-
      ciety. 2d ser. 136:98–102.
   1969c   [1607]   Description of the People [authorship uncertain]. In Philip L.
      Barbour, ed. *The Jamestown Voyages Under the First Charter.* Cambridge:
      Hakluyt Society. 2d ser. 136:102–4. (Note: 1969b–c are also published in
      David B. Quinn, ed. *New American World: A Documentary History of North
      America to 1612.* New York: Arno Press. Pp. 174–76.)
Argall, Samuel
   1904–1906   [1613]   A Letter of Sir Samuel Argall touching his Voyage to
      Virginia, and Actions there: Written to Master Nicholas Hawes. In Samuel
      Purchas, ed. *Hakluytus Posthumus or Purchas His Pilgrimes.* Glasgow: James
      MacLehose and Sons. 19:90–95.
Ashburn, Percy M.
   1947   *The Ranks of Death: A Medical History of the Conquest of America.*
      New York: Coward-McCann.
Axtell, James
   1981   *The European and the Indian: Essays in the Ethnohistory of Colonial
      North America.* New York: Oxford University Press.

Banister, John
1970 John Banister and His Natural History of Virginia, 1678–1692. Edited
by Joseph and Nesta Ewan. Urbana: University of Illinois Press.
Barbour, Philip L.
1964 The Three Worlds of Captain John Smith. Boston: Houghton Mifflin.
1970 Pocahontas and Her World. Boston: Houghton Mifflin.
1971 The Earliest Reconnaissance of the Chesapeake Bay Area: Captain John
Smith's Map and Indian Vocabulary, Part I. Virginia Magazine of History and
Biography 79: 280–302.
1972 Further Notes on Bison in Early Virginia. Quarterly Bulletin of the
Archeological Society of Virginia 27: 100.
1980 The Riddle of the Powhatan "Black Boyes." Virginia Magazine of History and Biography 88: 148–54.
———, ed.
1969 The Jamestown Voyages Under the First Charter. 2d ser. Cambridge:
Hakluyt Society.
1986 The Complete Works of Captain John Smith (1580–1631). 3 vols. Chapel
Hill: University of North Carolina Press.
Beverley, Robert
1947 [1705] The History and Present State of Virginia. Edited by Louis B.
Wright. Chapel Hill: University of North Carolina Press.
Binford, Lewis
1961 Archaeological and Ethnohistorical Investigation of Cultural Diversity
and Progressive Development Among Aboriginal Cultures of Coastal Virginia
and North Carolina. Ph.D. diss., University of Michigan.
1967 An Ethnohistory of the Nottoway, Meherrin and Weanoc Indians of
Southeastern Virginia. Ethnohistory 14: 103–218.
Bland, Edward, et al.
1911 [1651] The Discovery of New Brittaine. . . . In Alexander S. Salley, ed.
Narratives of Early Carolina, 1650–1708. New York: Barnes and Noble.
Pp. 5–19.
Boyce, Douglas W.
1978 Iroquoian Tribes of the Virginia–North Carolina Coastal Plain. In Bruce
G. Trigger, ed. Handbook of North American Indians. Vol. 15, Northeast.
Washington: Smithsonian Institution. Pp. 282–89.
Brasser, T. J.
1978 Mahican. In Bruce G. Trigger, ed. Handbook of North American
Indians. Vol. 15, Northeast. Washington: Smithsonian Institution. Pp. 198–212.
Brickell, John
1968 [1737] The Natural History of North Carolina. Murfreesboro, N.C.:
Johnson Publishing Co.
Bridenbaugh, Carl
1968 Vexed and Troubled Englishmen, 1590–1642. New York: Oxford University Press.
Brinley, Francis
1900 [1696] Francis Brinley's Briefe Narrative of the Nanhiganset Countrey.
Rhode Island Historical Society Publications 8: 69–93.
Brown, Alexander
1964 [1890] The Genesis of the United States. 2 vols. New York: Russell and
Russell.

Bushnell, David Ives
    1937   Indian Sites Below the Falls of the Rappahannock, Virginia. Smithsonian
        Miscellaneous Collections. Vol. 96, no. 4.
Byrd, William
    1966   *The Prose Works of William Byrd of Westover.* Edited by Louis B.
        Wright. Cambridge: Harvard University Press.

Callahan, Errett H., Jr.
    1981   Pamunkey Housebuilding: An Experimental Study of Late Woodland
        Construction in the Powhatan Confederacy. Ph.D. diss., Catholic University
        of America.
Campbell, Marius
    1927   The Meaning of Meanders in Tidal Streams. *Bulletin of the Geological
        Society of America* 38: 537–56.
Ceci, Lynn
    1975a   Fish Fertilizer: A Native North American Practice? *Science* 188:26–30.
    1975b   [Reply to letters on 1975a] *Science* 189:946–49.
Cedarstrom, D. J.
    1945   Structural Geology of Southeastern Virginia. *Bulletin of American Asso-
        ciation of Petroleum Geologists* 19: 71–95.
Champlain, Samuel de
    1907   [1604–18]   *Voyages of Samuel de Champlain.* Edited by W. L. Grant.
        New York: Barnes and Noble.
Clayton, John
    1965   [1687]   The Aborigines of the Country: Letter to Dr. Nehemia Grew. In
        The Reverend John Clayton. Edited by Edmund Berkeley and Dorothy S.
        Berkeley. Charlottesville: University of Virginia Press.
    1965   [1694]   Seven Severall Sorts of Snakes—and Vipers Most Deadly. In
        The Reverend John Clayton. Edited by Edmund Berkeley and Dorothy S.
        Berkeley. Charlottesville: University of Virginia Press. Pp. 105–21.
    1968   [1687]   Another Account of Virginia. Edited by Edmund Berkeley and
        Dorothy S. Berkeley. *Virginia Magazine of History and Biography* 76:415–36.
Cope, Walter
    1969   [1607]   Letter to Lord Salisbury. In Philip L. Barbour, ed. The James-
        town Voyages Under the First Charter. Cambridge: Hakluyt Society. 2d ser.
        136:108–10.
Crosby, Alfred
    1972   *The Columbian Exchange.* Westport, Conn.: Greenwood Press.
Culin, Stewart
    1975   [1903]   *Games of the North American Indians.* New York: Dover.
        Originally in 24th Annual Report of Bureau of American Ethnology.
Culliford, S. G.
    1965   *William Strachey, 1572–1621.* Charlottesville: University of Virginia
        Press.

Danckaerts, Jaspar
    1913   [1679–80]   *Journal of Jaspar Danckaerts, 1679–1680.* Edited by
        Bartlett Burleigh James and J. Franklin James. New York: Scribner's.
Day, Gordon M.
    1953   The Indian as an Ecological Factor in the Northeastern Forest. *Ecology*
        34:329–46.

Deaux, George
  1969   *The Black Death, 1347.* New York: Waybright and Talley.
Denton, Daniel
  1937 [1670]   *A Brief Description of New-York with the Places Thereunto Adjoining, formerly Called The New Netherlands, Etc.* New York: Columbia University Press.
Dobyns, Henry F.
  1983   *Their Number Become Thinned: Native American Population Dynamics in Eastern North America.* Knoxville: University of Tennessee Press.
Dragoo, Don W.
  1976   Some Aspects of Eastern North American Prehistory: A Review 1975. *American Antiquity* 41: 3–27.
Driver, Harold
  1961   *Indians of North America.* Chicago: University of Chicago Press.
Dunbar, Gary S.
  1964   Some Notes on Bison in Early Virginia. *Quarterly Bulletin of the Archeological Society of Virginia* 18:75–78.
Durand de Dauphine
  1934 [1687]   *A Huguenot Exile in Virginia . . . from the Hague Edition of 1687.* New York: Press of the Pioneers.

Earle, Carville V.
  1979   Environment, Disease, and Mortality in Early Virginia. In Thad W. Tate and David L. Ammerman, eds. *The Chesapeake in the Seventeenth Century: Essays on Anglo-American Society.* Chapel Hill: University of North Carolina Press. Pp. 96–125.
Edwards, Andrew C.
  1978   Excavations at 44Pg3. *Quarterly Bulletin of the Archeological Society of Virginia* 33:75–78.
Elliott, Charles F.
  1976   *Fox Hill: Its People and Places.* Hampton, Va.: privately printed.
Emerson, Everett H.
  1967   Captain John Smith as Editor: The Generall Historie. *Virginia Magazine of History and Biography* 75:143–56.

Fausz, J. Frederick
  1977   The Powhatan Uprising of 1622: A Historical Study of Ethnocentrism and Cultural Conflict. Ph.D. diss., College of William and Mary.
  1981   Opechancanough: Indian Resistance Leader. In David G. Sweet and Gary B. Nash, eds. *Struggle and Survival in Colonial America.* Berkeley: University of California Press. Pp. 21–37.
  1985   Patterns of Anglo-Indian Aggression and Accommodation Along the Mid-Atlantic Coast, 1584–1634. In William W. Fitzhugh, ed. *Cultures in Contact: The European Impact on Native Institutions in Eastern North America, A.D. 1000–1800.* Washington: Smithsonian Institution. Pp. 225–68.
Fausz, J. Frederick, and Jon Kukla
  1977   A Letter of Advice to the Governor of Virginia, 1624. *William and Mary Quarterly,* 3d ser., 34: 104–29.
Feest, Christian F.
  1966a   Virginia Indian Miscellany I. *Archiv für Völkerkunde* 20:1–7.

1966b   Powhatan, a Study in Political Organisation. *Wiener Völkerkundliche Mitteilungen* 13:69–83.
1967a   The Virginia Indian in Pictures, 1612–1624. *Smithsonian Journal of History* 2:1–30.
1967b   Virginia Indian Miscellany II. *Archiv für Völkerkunde* 21:5–15.
1972   Virginia Indian Miscellany III. *Archiv für Völkerkunde* 26:1–14.
1973   Seventeenth Century Virginia Algonquian Population Estimates. *Quarterly Bulletin of the Archeological Society of Virginia* 28:66–79.
1978   Virginia Algonquians. In Bruce G. Trigger, ed. *Handbook of North American Indians*. Vol. 15, *Northeast*. Washington: Smithsonian Institution. Pp. 253–70.
1979   Pictographic Skin Painting in Eastern North America: Facts and Fiction. *Archiv für Völkerkunde* 33:85–104.
1983   "Powhatan's Mantle" and "Skin Pouch" [the "Virginia Purse"] In Arthur MacGregor, ed. *Tradescant's Rarities*. Oxford: Clarendon Press. Pp. 130–37.
1987   Ethnohistory and Archaeology: A View from Coastal Virginia and Maryland. In Karl Wernhart, ed. *Ethnohistory in Vienna*. Aachen: Edition herodot im Rader Verlag. Pp. 87–100.

Fenton, William
1978   Northern Iroquoian Culture Patterns. In Bruce G. Trigger, ed. *Handbook of North American Indians*. Vol. 15, *Northeast*. Washington: Smithsonian Institution. Pp. 296–321.

Flannery, Kent V., and Michael D. Coe
1968   Social and Economic Systems in Formative Mesoamerica. In Sally R. Binford and Lewis R. Binford, eds. *New Perspectives in Archeology*. Chicago: Aldine. Pp. 267–83.

Flannery, Regina
1939   *An Analysis of Coastal Algonkian Culture*. Anthropological Series, No. 7. Washington, D.C.: Catholic University of America.

Glenn, Keith
1944   Captain John Smith and the Indians. *Virginia Magazine of History and Biography* 52:228–47.

Glover, Thomas
1904   [1676]   *An Account of Virginia, Its Scituation, Temperature, Inhabitants and Their Manner of Planting and Ordering Tobacco, etc.* Oxford: Blackwell. Originally published in *Philosophical Transactions of the Royal Society*.

Gookin, Daniel
1970   [1792 (written before 1674)]   *Historical Collections of the Indians in New England: Of Their Several Nations, Numbers, Customs, Manners, Religion and Government, Before the English Planted There*. New York: Towtaid.

Gottfried, Robert S.
1982   *The Black Death: Natural and Human Disaster in Medieval Europe*. New York: Free Press.

Haas, Jonathan
1982   *The Evolution of the Prehistoric State*. New York: Columbia University Press.

Hamor, Ralph
  1957 [1615] *A True Discourse of the Present State of Virginia.* Richmond:
    Virginia State Library.
Hariot, Thomas
  1972 [1590] *A Briefe and True Report of the New Found Land of Virginia.*
    New York: Dover.
Harshberger, John W.
  1958 [1911] *Phytogeographic Survey of North America.* New York: Hafner
    Publishing Co.
Harvill, A. M., Jr.
  1970 *Spring Flora of Virginia.* Parsons, W. Va.: Privately printed.
Hening, William Waller, Comp.
  1809–23 *The Statutes at Large, Being a Collection of all the Laws of Virginia
    from the First Session of the Legislature.* 13 vols. New York: R. & W. &
    G. Bartow.
Herlihy, David
  1978 The Natural History of Medieval Women. *Natural History* 87:56–67.
Hoffman, Bernard G.
  1964a An Unusual Example of Virginia Indian Toponymics. *Ethnohistory* 11:
    174–82.
  1964b *Observations on Certain Ancient Tribes of the Northern Appalachian
    Province.* Bureau of Ethnology Bulletin 191:195–206. Washington, D.C.:
    U.S. Government Printing Office.
Huden, John C., Comp.
  1962 *Indian Place Names of New England.* Contributions, Vol. 18. New
    York: Heye Foundation.
Hudson, Charles M.
  1979 *Black Drink.* Athens: University of Georgia Press.
Hulton, Paul
  1984 *America 1585: The Complete Drawings of John White.* Chapel Hill:
    University of North Carolina Press.

Kinietz, W. Vernon
  1946 Delaware Culture Chronology. *Indiana Historical Society, Prehistory
    Research Series* 3(1):1–143.
Kingsbury, Susan Myra, comp.
  1906–35 *Records of the Virginia Company of London.* 4 vols. Washington,
    D.C.: Library of Congress.
Klimas, John E., and James A. Cunningham
  1974 *Wildflowers of Eastern North America.* New York: Knopf.
Knowles, Nathaniel
  1940 The Torture of Captives by the Indians of Eastern North America. *Pro-
    ceedings of the American Philosophical Society* 82:151–225.
Krech, Shepard, III, ed.
  1981 *Indians, Animals, and the Fur Trade: A Critique of "Keepers of the
    Game."* Athens: University of Georgia Press.
Kroeber, Alfred L.
  1947 *Cultural and Natural Areas of Native America.* 2d ed. Berkeley: Univer-
    sity of California Press.

Kupperman, Karen Ordahl
   1980   Settling With the Indians: The Meeting of English and Indian Cultures in
      America, 1580–1640. Totowa, N.J.: Rowman and Littlefield.

Laet, Johan de
   1909   [1625, 1630]   From the "New World," by Johan de Laet, 1625, 1630,
      1640. In J. Franklin Jameson, ed. Narratives of New Netherland, 1609–1664.
      New York: Scribner's. Pp. 29–60.
Lahontan, Louis Armand de Lom d'Arce de
   1905   [1703]   New Voyages to North America by the Baron de Lahontan.
      Reuben Gold Thwaites, ed. 2 vols. Chicago: A. C. McClurg. [Translator's
      name not given.]
Lamb, H. H.
   1963   On the Nature of Certain Climatic Epochs Which Differed from the
      Modern (1900–1939) Normal. In Changes of Climate: Proceedings of the
      Rome Symposium. Paris: UNESCO. Pp. 125–50.
Lawson, John
   1967   [1709]   A New Voyage to Carolina. Edited by Hugh T. Lefler. Chapel
      Hill: University of North Carolina Press.
Leacock, Eleanor.
   1954   The Montagnais "Hunting Territory" and the Fur Trade. American An-
      thropological Association, Memoir 78.
Lederer, John
   1958   [1672]   The Discoveries of John Lederer. Edited by William P. Cumming.
      Charlottesville: University of Virginia Press.
   1975   [1681]   Another French Account of Virginia Indians by John Lederer
      [authorship probable]. Edited by Christian F. Feest. Virginia Magazine of His-
      tory and Biography 83:150–59.
Lewis, Clifford M., and Albert J. Loomie
   1953   The Spanish Jesuit Mission in Virginia, 1570–1572. Chapel Hill: Uni-
      versity of North Carolina Press.
Lippson, Alice Jane, and Robert L. Lippson
   1984   Life in the Chesapeake Bay. Baltimore: Johns Hopkins University Press.

MacCord, Howard A., Sr.
   1965   The DeShazo Site, King George County, Virginia. Quarterly Bulletin of
      the Archeological Society of Virginia 19:98–104.
Martin, Calvin
   1978   Keepers of the Game. Berkeley: University of California Press.
Martin, M. Kay, and Barbara Voorhies
   1975   Female of the Species. New York: Columbia University Press.
Mason, Polly Cary, comp.
   1946–48   Records of Colonial Gloucester County, Virginia. Newport News,
      Va.: Privately printed.
McCary, Ben C.
   1958   The Kiskiack (Chiskiack) Indian Site Near Yorktown, Virginia. Quarterly
      Bulletin of the Archeological Society of Virginia 13: part of issue; unpaginated.
   1964   An Indian Dugout Canoe, Reworked by Early Settlers, found in Pow-
      hatan Creek, James City County, Virginia. Quarterly Bulletin of the Archeo-
      logical Society of Virginia 19:14–19.

1981   The Location of Werowocomoco. *Quarterly Bulletin of the Archeological Society of Virginia* 36:77–93.
McCary, Ben Clyde, and Norman Barka
1977   The John Smith and Zúñiga Maps in the Light of Recent Archeological
Research along the Chickahominy River. *Archaeology of Eastern North
America* 5:73–86.
McIlwaine, H. R., comp.
1924   *Minutes of the Council and General Court of Virginia, 1622–1632,
1670–1676.* Richmond: Virginia State Library.
McIntyre, Andrew, et al.
1976   The Glacial North Atlantic 18,000 Years Ago; A CLIMAP Reconstruc-
tion. In R. M. Cline and J. D. Hays, eds. *Investigation of Late Quaternary
Paleoceanography and Paleoclimatology.* Boulder, Colorado: Geological So-
ciety of America, Memoir 145.
Meade, William
1857   *Old Churches, Ministers and Families of Virginia.* Philadelphia:
Lippincott.
Merrill, William L., and Christian F. Feest
1975   An Exchange of Botanical Information in the Early Contact Situation:
Wisakon of the Southeastern Algonquians. *Economic Botany* 29: 171–84.
Miller, Sigmund Stephen
1976   *Symptoms: The Complete Home Medical Encyclopedia.* New York:
Crowell.
Morgan, Edmund S.
1975   *American Slavery, American Freedom.* New York: Norton.
Mossiker, Frances
1976   *Pocahontas: The Life and Legend.* New York: Knopf.
Mourt, G.
1963   [1622]   *A Journal of the Pilgrims at Plymouth: Mourt's Relation.* Edited
by Dwight B. Heath. New York: Corinth Books.
Murdock, George P., and Timothy J. O'Leary, Comps.
1975   *Ethnographic Bibliography of North America.* 5 vols. New Haven, Conn.:
Human Relations Area Files Press.

Northampton County, Virginia
1632 to present   County Records. Eastville, Virginia (copy at Virginia State Library, Richmond).
Nugent, Nell Marion, comp.
1934   *Cavaliers and Pioneers: Abstracts of Virginia Land Patents and Grants,
1623–1800.* Vol. 1. Richmond, Va.: Dietz Press.
1977   *Cavaliers and Pioneers: Abstracts of Virginia Land Patents and Grants,
1623–1800.* Vol. 2. Richmond: Virginia State Library.
1979   *Cavaliers and Pioneers: Abstracts of Virginia Land Patents and Grants,
1623–1800.* Vol. 3. Richmond: Virginia State Library.

Oaks, Robert Q., Jr., and Nicholas K. Coch
1963   Pleistocene Sea Levels, Southeastern Virginia. *Science* 140:979–83.

Painter, Floyd E.
1980   The Great King of Great Neck: A Status Burial from Coastal Virginia.
The Chesopean 18:74–75.

Palmer, Ralph S.
    1954   *The Mammal Guide.* Garden City, N.Y.: Doubleday.
Pargellis, Stanley, ed.
    1959   The Indians of Virginia. *William and Mary Quarterly,* 3d ser., 16:
           228–53.
Park, Willard Z.
    1938   *Shamanism in Western North America.* Evanston, Ill.: Northwestern
           University Press.
Peck, Rodney M.
    1984   Stone Fish Traps on the Pee Dee River in North Carolina. *Indian-Artifact
           Magazine* 3:4–5, 58.
Peebles, Christopher S., and Susan M. Kus
    1977   Some Archaeological Correlates of Ranked Societies. *American Antiquity*
           42: 421–48.
Percy, George
    1921–22 [1612]   A Trewe Relacyon. *Tyler's Quarterly* 3:259–82.
    1969a   [1608?]   Observations Gathered out of a Discourse of the Plantation of
           the Southern Colonie in Virginia by the English 1606. In Philip L. Barbour,
           ed. *The Jamestown Voyages Under the First Charter.* Cambridge: Hakluyt
           Society. 2d ser. 136:129–46.
    1969b   [1608?]   Fragment Published in 1614. In Philip L. Barbour, ed. *The
           Jamestown Voyages Under the First Charter.* Cambridge: Hakluyt Society.
           2d ser. 136:146–47.
Perkins, Francis
    1969   [1608]   Letter of March 18, 1608. In Philip L. Barbour, ed. *The James-
           town Voyages Under the First Charter.* Cambridge: Hakluyt Society. 2d ser.
           136:158–62.
Pollard, John Garland
    1984   *The Pamunkey Indians of Virginia.* Bureau of American Ethnology Bul-
           letin 17. Washington, D.C.: U.S. Government Printing Office.
Potter, Stephen R.
    1982   An Analysis of Chicacoan Settlement Patterns. Ph.D. diss., University of
           North Carolina.
    1984   Baubles and Burials: An Analysis of Nineteenth Century Archeological
           Discoveries in the Vicinity of Potomac Creek, Virginia. Paper read at the
           Middle Atlantic Archeological Conference.
    In press   Early English Effects on Virginia Algonquian Exchange and Tribute in
           the Tidewater Potomac. In Peter Wood, Gregory Waselkov, and Thomas
           Hatley, eds. *Powhatan's Mantle: Indians in the Colonial Southeast.* Lincoln:
           University of Nebraska Press.
Pough, Richard H.
    1953   *All the Birds of Eastern and Central North America.* New York: Au-
           dubon Guide Series.
Purchas, Samuel, comp. and ed.
    1614   *Purchas His Pilgrimage.* 2d ed. London.
    1617   *Purchas His Pilgrimage.* 3d ed. London.
    1904–6   [1625]   *Hakluytus Posthumus or Purchas His Pilgrimes.* 20 vols.
           Glasgow: James MacLehose and Sons.

Rainey, Froelich G.
    1936   A Compilation of Historical Data Contributing to the Ethnography of

Connecticut and Southern New England Indians. *Bulletin of the Archaeological Society of Connecticut* 3:1–89.
Robinson, Gary G.
1984 The Glass Bead Collection from the Heretick Site (44Pg62). *Quarterly Bulletin of the Archeological Society of Virginia* 39:14–23.
Rountree, Helen C.
1986 Ethnicity Among the "Citizen" Indians of Virginia, 1800–1930. In Frank W. Porter, III, ed. *Strategies for Survival.* New York: Greenwood Press. Pp. 173–209.
1987 The Termination and Dispersal of the Nottoway Indians of Virginia. *Virginia Magazine of History and Biography* 95:193–214.
Forthcoming *The Powhatan Indians of Virginia Through Four Centuries.* Norman: University of Oklahoma Press.
MS A (with Martha McCartney). Powhatan Words and Names.
MS B On the Nature of Ethnicity.
Rozwenc, Edwin C.
1959 Captain John Smith's Image of America. *William and Mary Quarterly,* 3rd. ser., 16:27–36.

Sahlins, Marshall
1958 *Social Stratification in Polynesia.* Seattle: University of Washington Press.
Sainsbury, W. Noel, Comp.
1860 *Calendar of State Papers, Colonial Series.* 27 vols. London: Longman, Green and Roberts.
Salwen, Bert
1978 Indians of Southern New England and Long Island: Early Period. In Bruce G. Trigger, ed. *Handbook of North American Indians.* Vol. 15, *Northeast.* Washington: Smithsonian Institution. Pp. 160–76.
Schmitt, Karl, Jr.
1965 Patawomeke: An Historical Algonkian Site. *Quarterly Bulletin of the Archeological Society of Virginia* 20:1–36.
Service, Elman R.
1966 *The Hunters.* Englewood Cliffs, N.J.: Prentice-Hall.
1975 *Origins of the State and Civilization: The Process of Cultural Evolution.* New York: Random House.
Sheehan, Bernard W.
1980 *Savagism and Civility: Indians and Englishmen in Colonial Virginia.* New York: Cambridge University Press.
Siebert, Frank T., Jr.
1975 Resurrecting Virginia Algonquian from the Dead: The Reconstituted and Historical Phonology of Powhatan. In James M. Crawford, ed. *Studies in Southeastern Indian Languages.* Athens: University of Georgia Press. Pp. 285–453.
Simmons, William S.
1978 Narragansett. In Bruce G. Trigger, ed. *Handbook of North American Indians.* Vol. 15, *Northeast.* Washington: Smithsonian Institution. Pp. 190–97.
Simmons, William S., and George F. Aubin
1975 Narragansett Kinship. *Man in the Northeast* 9: 21–31.
Smith, John
n.d. [1608] *Virginia Discouered and Described by Captayn John Smith, 1606.* Map, in various editions. Richmond: Virginia State Library.

1986a [1608] A True Relation. In *The Complete Works of Captain John Smith (1580–1631)*. Edited by Philip L. Barbour. 3 vols. Chapel Hill: University of North Carolina Press. 1:3–118.

1986b [1612] A Map of Virginia. Historical section compiled from various texts by William Simmond. In *The Complete Works of Captain John Smith (1580–1631)*. Edited by Philip L. Barbour. 3 vols. Chapel Hill: University of North Carolina Press. 1:119–90.

1986c [1624] The Generall Historie of Virginia, New England, and the Summer Isles, 1624. In *The Complete Works of Captain John Smith (1580–1631)*. Edited by Philip Barbour. 3 vols. Chapel Hill: University of North Carolina Press. 2:25–488.

Smithsonian Institution
1893   *U.S. National Museum Annual Report*. Washington, D.C.

Snow, Dean R.
1978   Late Prehistory of the East Coast. In Bruce G. Trigger, ed. *Handbook of North American Indians*. Vol. 15, *Northeast*. Washington: Smithsonian Institution. Pp. 58–69.

Speck, Frank G.
1924   The Ethnic Position of the Southeastern Algonkian. *American Anthropologist* 26: 184–200.
1928   Chapters on the Ethnology of the Powhatan Tribes of Virginia. *Indian Notes and Monographs*. Vol. 1, no. 5.
1950   *Penobscot Man*. New York: Octagon Press.

Spelman, Henry
1910   [1613?] Relation of Virginea. In Edward Arber and A. G. Bradley, eds. *The Travels and Works of Captain John Smith*. New York. Pp. ci–cxiv.

Spencer, Robert F., and Jesse D. Jennings, Eds.
1977   *The Native Americans*. 2d ed. New York: Harper and Row.

Spindler, Louise S.
1978   Menominee. In Bruce G. Trigger, ed. *Handbook of North American Indians*. Vol. 15, *Northeast*. Washington: Smithsonian Institution. Pp. 708–24.

Stith, William
1969   [1747] *The History of the First Discovery and Settlement of Virginia*. New York: Johnson Reprints.

Strachey, William
1953   [1612] *The Historie of Travell into Virginia Britania*. Edited by Louis B. Wright and Virginia Freund. Cambridge: Hakluyt Society. 2d ser. Vol. 103.
1964   [1610] A True Reportory of the Wreck and Redemption of Sir Thomas Gates. . . . In Louis B. Wright, ed. *A Voyage to Virginia in 1609, Two Narratives*. Charlottesville: University of Virginia Press. Also published in David B. Quinn, ed. *New American World: A Documentary History of North America to 1612*. New York: Arno Press. Pp. 288–301.

Swanton, John R.
1964   [1946] *Indians of the Southeastern United States*. New York: Johnson Reprints. Originally published as Bulletin 137 of Bureau of American Ethnology.

Tanner, Adrian
1979   *Bringing Home Animals: Religious Ideology and the Mode of Production of the Mistassini Cree Hunters*. New York: St. Martin's Press.

Thwaites, Reuben Gold, ed.
1897–1901   *The Jesuit Relations and Allied Documents.* 73 vols. Cleveland: Burrows Brothers Co.
Tindall, Robert
n.d.   [1608]   *Tyndall's Draughte of Virginia 1608.* Copy in Virginia State Library, Richmond.
Tooker, Elisabeth
1978   The League of the Iroquois: Its History, Politics, and Ritual. In Bruce G. Trigger, ed. *Handbook of North American Indians.* Vol. 15, *Northeast.* Washington: Smithsonian Institution. Pp. 418–41.
Trumbull, James Hammond
1870   *The Composition of Indian Geographical Names, Illustrated from the Algonkin Languages.* Collections of the Connecticut Historical Society 2(1).
1974 [1881]   *Indian Names in Connecticut.* Hamden, Conn.: Archon Books.
Turner, E. Randolph
1976   An Archaeological and Ethnohistorical Study on the Evolution of Rank Societies in the Virginia Coastal Plain. Ph.D. diss., Pennsylvania State University.
1978   An Intertribal Deer Exploitation Buffer Zone for the Virginia Coastal Plain–Piedmont Regions. *Quarterly Bulletin of the Archeological Society of Virginia* 32: 42–48.
1982   A Reexamination of Powhatan Territorial Boundaries and Population, ca. A.D. 1607. *Quarterly Bulletin of the Archeological Society of Virginia* 37: 45–64.
1985   Socio-Political Organization Within the Powhatan Chiefdom and the Effects of European Contact, A.D. 1607–1646. In William W. Fitzhugh, ed. *Cultures in Contact: The European Impact on Native Cultural Institutions in Eastern North America, A.D. 1000–1800.* Washington: Smithsonian Institution, Pp. 193–224.
1986   Difficulties in the Archaeological Identification of Chiefdoms as Seen in the Virginia Coastal Plain During the Late Woodland and Early Historic Periods. In Jay F. Custer, ed. *Late Woodland Cultures of the Middle Atlantic Region.* Newark: University of Delaware Press. Pp. 19–28.
Tyler, Lyon G., ed.
1907   *Narratives of Early Virginia, 1606–1625.* New York: Barnes and Noble.

Ubelaker, Douglas H.
1974   Reconstruction of Demographic Profiles from Ossuary Skeletal Samples: A Case Study from the Tidewater Potomac. Smithsonian Miscellaneous Collections, No. 18.
Upshur, Thomas T.
1901–2   Eastern Shore History, an Address Delivered at Accomack Courthouse on June 9, 1900, Being the Occasion of the Dedication of the New Courthouse at that Place. *Virginia Magazine of History and Biography* 9: 89–99.

Wallace, Anthony F. C.
1958   The Dekanawideh Myth Analyzed as the Record of a Revitalization Movement. *Ethnohistory* 5(2): 118–30.
1970   *The Death and Rebirth of the Seneca.* New York: Knopf.

Whitaker, Alexander
  1936 [1613] *Good Newes from Virginia.* New York: Scholars' Facsimiles &
    Reprints.
  1964 [1611] Letter to Releigh Croshaw. In Alexander Brown, ed. *The Gene-
    sis of the United States.* New York: Russell and Russell. Pp. 497–500.
White, Andrew
  1910 [1634] A Briefe Relation of the Voyage Unto Maryland by Father An-
    drew White, 1634. In C. C. Hall, ed. *Narratives of Early Maryland, 1633–
    1684.* New York: Barnes and Noble. Pp. 29–45.
White, William
  1969 [1608?] Fragments Published Before 1614. In Philip L. Barbour, ed.
    The Jamestown Voyages Under the First Charter. Cambridge: Hakluyt So-
    ciety. 2d ser. 136:147–50.
Williams, Roger
  1973 [1643] *A Key Into the Language of America.* Edited by John J. Teunissen
    and Evelyn J. Hinz. Detroit: Wayne State University Press.
Williamson, Margaret Holmes
  1979 Powhatan Hair. *Man* (n.s.) 14:392–413.
Winfree, R. Westwood
  1969 Newington, King and Queen County. *Quarterly Bulletin of the Archeo-
    logical Society of Virginia* 23:160–224.
Wingfield, Edward Maria
  1969 [1608] Discourse. In Philip L. Barbour, ed. *The Jamestown Voyages
    Under the First Charter.* Cambridge: Hakluyt Society. 2d ser. 136:213–34.
    (Note: also published in David B. Quinn, ed. *New American World: A
    Documentary History of North America to 1612.* New York: Arno Press.
    Pp. 276–85.)
Winslow, Edward
  1971 [1624] Winslow's Relation. In Alexander Young, ed. *Chronicles of the
    Pilgrim Fathers, 1602–1625.* New York: Da Capo Press. Pp. 269–375.
Wood, William
  1977 [1634] *New England's Prospect.* Amherst: University of Massachusetts
    Press.
Wright, David, and Dennis A. Andrejko
  1982 *Passive Solar Architecture.* New York: Van Nostrand Reinhold.
Wynn, Peter
  1969 [1608] Letter of November 16, 1608. In Philip L. Barbour, ed. *The
    Jamestown Voyages Under the First Charter.* Cambridge: Hakluyt Society.
    2d ser. 136:245–46.

Index

Acclimatizing: 69 & n., 78, 94
Accohannock Indians: *see* Occohannock
  Indians
Accomac (capital town): 9
Accomac, chief of: 117, 118
Accomac County, Va.: 9
Accomac Indians (district chiefdom): 7, 9,
  13, 14, 31, 35, 56, 57, 82, 117, 141; less
  warlike than mainland groups, 14
Acorns: 41, 44, 53
Adoption procedure: 121–22; gauntlet-like
  procedure in *huskanaw*, 81
Adultery: *see* marital relations
Advancement, social: 79; *see also* status
  symbols
Afterlife: only for high-status people, 100,
  139, 145–146; no heaven or hell, 139;
  James River tribes' accounts, 139; Pa-
  tawomeck account, 139
Alder, leaves of: 76
Algonquian-speaking Indians: 6, 7, 8, 9,
  16; *see also* Chowanoc; Piscataway;
  names of specific groups of Powhatans
Altar-stones (*pawcorances*): 50, 117, 121,
  136 & n.; crystal altar-stone, 136; an-
  other sacred stone, 136–37
Amarice (Indian man): 116
Ambushes: *see* warfare, tactics
American nightshade: 127
Amnesia, induced: *see* huskanaw
Amonute: *see* Pocahontas
Ancestors, spirits of: 125, 139, 146
Angelica: 39, 41–42, 128, 129
Animals, attitude toward: 40
Annual round: 41, 44–46, 47, 49
Anoeg Indians: 145
Anonymous writer of 1680s: 6, 65, 129,
  130
Antimony ore (*matchqueon*): 55, 76, 77,
  144
Antler, use of: 42, 70, 76, 81, 98, 124

Apones (bread): *see* food preparation
Appalachian Mountains: 18, 22, 71, 145
Appamattuck (capital town): 11
Appamattuck, chiefs of: district *weroance*
  (Coquonasum), 15, 108, 117, 142; petty
  weroansqua (Opussunoquonuske), 69,
  108, 117, 142
Appamattuck Indians (district chiefdom): 5,
  6, 8, 13, 15, 55, 56, 69, 117, 118, 125,
  127, 144
Appomattox Indians: *see* Appamattuck
  Indians
Appomattox River: 6, 11, 22, 110
Archaeology: 8 n., 16, 32, 38 & n., 40, 42,
  53 n., 58 n., 63 & n., 65, 70 n., 71, 72 n.,
  78, 130, 139 n., 144, 149–50, 151, 152
Archaic Period: 40
Archer, Gabriel: 5 & n., 60, 61, 88, 108,
  116, 126, 130, 139
Armor, English: 133
Armor, Powhatan, lack of: 124
Armories: 122
Arrohateck (capital town): 11, 53, 126
Arrohateck Indians (district chiefdom): 14,
  42, 56, 57, 118, 144
Arrow arum (tuckahoe or wild potato):
  44–45, 52–53; berries of (*ocoughtam-
  nis*), 52
Arrows: 42, 98, 106, 123, 125, fig. 10
Ashmolean Museum: 103
Assentamens (small beans): 47
Astronomy: 49–50
Atlantic Ocean: 13, 17, 18, 49
Attack of 1622: 5
Augurers, Roman: 130
Austria: 102
Axes, stone: 32, 34, 47; for digging, 76

Bacon's Rebellion: 103
Bags: 65, 101, 103, figs. 10, 15, 20, 22; implements in making, 65, fig. 16

Banister, Rev. John: 6, 39, 40, 49, 62, 63, 65, 71, 73, 101, 128
Baraconos (Indian town): 11 n.
"Barbecuing": 51
Barbour, Philip L.: 5 n., 80 n.
Bark: house sheathing, 55, 57, 60–61, 144; shields, 77, 124; bandages, 127
Baskets: 49, 51, 65, 88, 109, 110, 116, fig. 15; implements in making, 65, fig. 16
Bast, for cordage: 35, 63
Beads: *see* copper; shell
Beans: 47, 52, 53, 109, 110
Beards: 65, 70 & n.
Bears: 27, 39, 57, 70, 76, 129
Beavers: 27, 39; teeth of, 32, 42
Bedding: 62, 90
Beds: *see* houses, furnishings
Belts: 69, 98
"Better sort, the": 100 n., 101–102
Beverley, Robert: 6, 34, 73, 100, 101, 125, 129, 131, 134–35, 151
Bible, Holy: 131
Binford, Lewis R.: 14, 93, 143
Birds: connected with religion, 78, 136 n.; available to Indians, *see* Virginia, coastal plain of
Birth, customs surrounding: 94
Birth rate: 94
Bison, not used: 27
"Black boys": 80 & n., 100 n.; making of, *see* huskanaw
"Black drink": 127
Bloodroot (*musquaspenne*): 76, 124
Bloodwort: 126
Blue Ridge Mountains: 18
Bodyguard for paramount chief: 106, 109, 143
Bone tools: 65, figs. 7, 16
Boundaries of chiefdoms: 29, 40
Bows: 42, 79, 98, 106, 125, fig. 10; compared to English firearms, 42
Bread: *see* food preparations; butter for, *see* suet
Bride-wealth: 90
Bridges: 63
Bristol Parish: 6
"Bruff Mask": 73, 78 n., fig. 19
Burden-carrying: tumplines, 65; women as usual carriers, 88
Burials: *see* mortuary practices
Byrd, William: 5, 6

Caches: 49, 56, 89 n.
Calendar: *see* time, calculation of
Callahan, Errett H., Jr.: 60–61, 124 n.
Camden, Va.: 24
Canada: 55
Cannibalism, Iroquoian: 142
Canoes: 27, 32, 34, 64, 133, fig. 8
Cantaunkack (Indian town): 11 n.
Capahosic (Indian town): 122
Caposepock (Indian town): 11 n., 60 n.
Carolina (region) Indians: 35, 42, 47 n., 49, 55, 58, 61, 63, 82, 84, 96, 113 n., 124, 128, 136
Caroline County, Va.: 12
Carrot, wild: 52
Cassapecock (Indian town): 11 n.
Cattapeuk (spring): 49
Cauterization: 128
Cawcawwasough: *see* cockarouse
Cedar trees, red: 60
Cekakawon: *see* Sekakawon
Censers: 133
Ceramics: *see* pottery
Ceremonies: *see* rituals
Champlain, Samuel de: 150
Charles City County, Va.: 9, 11, 58 n.
Chechinquamins: *see* chinquapins
Chepeco (Indian town): 11 n., 60 n.
Cheriton, Va.: 9
Cherry, wild: 52
Chesapeake (capital town): 9, 24
Chesapeake, Va.: 13, 120
Chesapeake Bay: 13, 15, 18, 22, 24, 28–29, 38, 57, 73, 120, 142
Chesapeake Indians: 9, 24, 55, 56, 120–21, 120 n., 140, 142
Chesterfield County, Va.: 11
Chestnut trees: 44, 61
Chickacoan: *see* Cekakawon
Chickahominy Indian "language" [actually dialect]: 8
Chickahominy Indians (tribe): 6, 8–9, 11, 29, 41, 56, 100, 114, 115, 119, 122, 134 n., 138, 140, 141, 148
Chickahominy River: 11, 22, 57, 110
Chief, paramount (status): luxurious lifestyle, 15, 106, 108, 138; ceremony in daily life, 54–55, 78, 101–102; monopoly on English copper and weapons, 55, 111, 116, 145; rewarding services by subjects, 55, 79, 80, 85, 91, 101, 111, 119, 122, 146; how addressed, 106; in-

formality in lifestyle, 106, 109, 143; houses kept for in inherited chiefdoms, 106; fields planted for, 110; steward over land (possible), 114; partial abdication, 118 & n., steward for deity over valuable gifts presented to him, 133–34; powers of, *see* power of paramount chief; *see also* chiefs; deference shown to chiefs; visiting by chiefs; Powhatan (the man)

Chiefdom, paramount (organization): 7, 13–14, 15, 22, 29, 38, 40, 148; Chicka-hominies as allied tribe, 8, 119, 140; groups included in by 1607, 9–12, 140–41; name of territory occupied by, 13, 140; newness and development of, 13, 14, 87, 118–19, 140; three-tiered structure of, 15, 117, 142; single *husk-anaw* for, 80, 82; matrilineal succession in, 88, 93, 112–13, 117; groups inherited by man Powhatan, 118, 140; chiefs' relatives as subordinate rulers, 117–18, 142; non-relatives as subordinate rulers, 118; reasons for formation of, 141–42, 143–44, 148–51; *see also* power of paramount chief

Chiefdoms, distribution in Virginia: 8

Chiefs, district: 8, 25; lifestyle, 46, 80, 86, 90, 101–102, 110, 111, 115–16, 138, 143; relatives as subordinates and successors, 86, 117, 142; competition and conflict among, 91, 100, 114; wives of, 91, 92, 94, 102, 108; stewards for deity over gifts presented, 103 n.; probably collectors of tribute, 109; ranking among, 117, 142; *see also* chief, paramount; deference shown to chiefs

Child-rearing: 41, 47, 79, 89, 94, 96; for boys, 38, 79–80, 85; for girls, 44; fig. 21

Chincoteague Island: 22

Chinquapins: 44

Chiskiack (capital town): 11

Chiskiack Indians (district chiefdom): 8, 11, 41, 56, 117 n., 118 n., 141

Chowanoc Indians: 11, 91, 120, 145

Chowanoc language: 8

Civet cats: 27

Clams: 38, 50; shells of, 63, 71, 73

Claremont, Va.: 9

Class system: *see* social differentiation

Claws, as ornaments: 70–71

Clayton, Rev. John: 5, 39, 41, 62, 96, 119, 124, 127, 128

Clothing: children's, 69 & n.; men's, 69, fig. 10; women's, 69, fig. 21; decorated, 69, 71, 102, 103; leggings, 69; moccasins, 69; acclimatization, 69; winter coverings, 69, 96, 103, fig. 21; "dressing up," 69, 102, 106

Clubs: *see* warclubs

Coan River: 12

Cockarouse: 101, 103 n.

Cohattayough (summer): 49

Cohonks (winter): 49

Collars (of *peak*): 73

Columbus, Christopher, 130

Combs: 70

Compensation, legal: 115

Conch shells: 71, 73

Confederacy, miscalled: 7, 117

Contact Period: 7, 58 n., 63, 73, 152

Contagious distribution system: 93

Continental shelf: 17

Cooking and cooking utensils: *see* food preparation

Copper: payment for military services, 55, 80, 111, 119, 122, 140; component of tribute, 55, 109, 110, 144; decoration of tobacco pipes, 63; decoration of clothing, 69; jewelry, 70–71, 98, 102, 106, 134, fig. 17; valuable commodity, 86, 116, 139; offerings to deities, 132, 133–34

Coquonasum (Indian man): 15, 108, 117, 142

"Coral": 71

Cordage: 35, 63, 88, 97; *see also* bags

Corn: 41, 44, 47, 51–52, 53, 88, 89, 108, 109, 110, 116, 132, 138, 139; husks, 65; stalks, 123

Coronets: 73

Corrotoman: *see* Cuttatawomen (lower)

Cougars (probable): 71, 134

Council of elders (Chickahominy): 8

Councils to chiefs: duties, 41, 106, 119, 120, 125, 142–43, fig. 24; personnel, 80, 100, 101, 142–43; perquisites, 82, 111, 143, 145; deliberations, 119–20

Courtship: *see* marital relations

Crabs: 44, 109

Cradle boards: 94 & n., 96, fig. 21

Creation accounts: 41, 135, 137–38, 138 n.

Cronoccoe: see cockarouse

Crystal: 136

Culture-areas: 151–52

Cups: 63, fig. 7

Cuttanemons (*ocoughtamnis*): 52
Cuttatawomen (lower) (capital town): 12
Cuttatawomen (upper) (capital town): 12,
   63 n.; *see also* DeShazo site
Cuttatawomen Indians (lower) (district
   chiefdom): 12, 56, 77
Cuttatawomen Indians (upper) (district
   chiefdom): 12, 56
Cutting tools: 32, 34, 47, 58, 63, 71, fig. 7,
   11; *see also* arrows; axes; beavers, teeth
   of; mussels, shells; reeds
Cypress trees: 27, 34

Dancing: to entertain foreign visitors in
   chief's absence (girls), 70, 77, 98; to begin *huskanaw*, 76–77, 80–81, 98;
   nightly social dances, 77, 96, 98–99;
   other occasions, 80, 89, 133, 137, fig.
   12; welcome dance, 97–98; war dance
   before raid, 77, 120; movements in general, 98; victory dance, 98, 121, 124–
   25; to honor visitors, 99, 108; belief in
   doing it in afterlife, 139
Debbedeavon: *see* Tapatiaton
De Bry, Theodor: 34, 35, 101
Deer: 27, 38–41, 57, 101 n., 109, 113,
   138; skins, 60, 69, 102, 103 & n., 113,
   138, 147; hair, 70; scapulae, 63; *see also*
   antlers; suet; venison
Deference shown to chiefs: 79, 85, 101,
   110, 116, 147; use of subchief's wife as
   servant, 108; *see also* servants
Deities: Okeus, 39, 70, 78, 100, 103 n.,
   122, 126, 130, 131–32, 133–34,
   135–36, 137, 137–38, 139, 145; rulers
   and priests as semi-deities, 100, 115,
   145; sun, 125, 137, 139; Ahone, 135,
   137–38; others, 135, 136, 139; Okeus
   connected with storms, 136; various
   names for Okeus, 136; polytheistic attitudes, 137; Great Hare, 138, 139; four
   winds (giants), 138
Delmarva Peninsula: *see* Eastern Shore of
   Virginia
DeShazo site: 60 n.
Dialects: *see* language
Digging tools: 47, 63, 76, 138
Dignified behavior: of a chief's favorite
   wife, 102; of commoners, 96; *see also*
   chief, paramount; chiefs, district
Diseases: 91, 128–30; *see also* epidemics;
   syphilis
Dishes: 54, 63, 69; *see also* platters

Districts: boundaries, 8, 29; list of, 9–12;
   names of, given to rivers, 31
Divorce: *see* marital relations
Dobyns, Henry F.: 33
Dogbane: *see* "silk grass"
Dogs, domesticated: 27–28, 41
Dragon Swamp: 18
Drought: *see* Virginia, coastal plain of
Drums: *see* music, instruments
Dutch language: 8

Eagles: 70
Earle, Carville V.: 45
Earth, use of: 34 n., 53, 58
Eastern Shore of Virginia: 7, 9, 13, 14, 17,
   22, 24, 50, 57, 73, 117 n., 120, 141, 145
Eating: 29, 89, 54–55, 102; etiquette on
   formal occasions, 54–55, 88, 102, 108
Eating utensils: 54, 63, fig. 7
Eiakintonomo (Indian man): 65, 102–103,
   fig. 10
Elders, rule by: 11
Elizabeth River: 9, 22, 24
Elm trees: 57
Enemies: 15, 41, 46, 58, 79, 85, 87, 111,
   121, 123, 149–50; intruders (into
   houses), 62; listed, 120, 148
England, voyages to: by Machumps, 4; by
   Uttamatomakkin, 5, 49, 131–32
English boats, compared to canoes: 34
English language: 8
English opinions of Powhatans: 3, 5, 32,
   114, 126
English people: *see* foreigners
English-speaking Indians: Kemps, 4; Ma-
   chumps, 4
English trade goods, use of: 32, 47, 55–56,
   63, 71, 73, 135; plenty of "hatchetts"
   (English?) in afterlife, 139
Epidemics: 7, 15, 87, 141–42; in North
   Carolina, 141; in New England, 151
Erie Indians: 120
Esmy Shichans (Indian man): 118 & n.
Essex County, Va.: 12
Ethnicity: 12–13, 14, 141
Exchange Branch (of Nansemond River): 9
Executions: of criminals, 116–17; of male
   war captives, 84, 117
Exmore, Va.: 9

Fabrics: *see* textiles
Fall line: 13, 17–18, 22, 41, 46, 65,
   149–50

Farming: clearing of fields, 32, 46–47, 88; crops raised, in annual cycle, 44, fig. 12; annual production, 45–46, 54; size of fields, 45–46; location of fields, 46, fig. 12; non-use of fertilizer, 47; planting, 47; tools used in planting (aboriginal and European), 47, 63; weeding and scarecrows, 49, fig. 12; harvesting, 49; fields planted for chiefs, 110, 144
Fausz, J. Frederick: 13, 77, 78 n.
Feasts, given by chiefs: obligation to provide, 15, 80, 106, 138; procurement of food for, 41, 46, 109; disposal of leftovers, 55, 108–109, 111; food served, 108; frequency of, 111
Feasts, given by commoners: 80, 90, 137
Feather mantles: 69, 100, 102
Feathers, use of: 42, 69, 70, 77–78, 98, 100, 102, 123, 139, figs. 10, 12, 20, 24
Feest, Christian F.: 7, 13, 15, 90 n., 93 n., 103, 126
Fertilizer, non-use of: 47
Feverwort: 128
Fields: see farming
Fire: 40, 47, 54, 58, 61, 80, 98, 133; as cutting tool, 34, 47; kept constantly in houses, 51, 62; in sacrificing designated boys, 81 n.; in disposing of tortured enemies, 84; in executing criminals, 116; kept constantly in temples, 134; see also food preparation; food storage; cauterization
Fire making: 62
Firewood: 47, 58, 60, 61 n., 89, 109; see also food preparation, boiling
Fishhooks: see fishing, angling
Fishing and shellfishing: 34–38, 44; angling, 34; fire-fishing, 34, fig. 8; netting, 34–35, fig. 8; spearing, 35, fig. 8; traps, 35; weirs, 35, 38, 44, figs. 8, 9; diving (for mollusks), 38; poisoning, 61
Fishnets: see fishing, netting
Flannery, Kent V., and Michael D. Coe: 92–93
Flannery, Regina: 151–52
Fleas: 62, 129
Flood story: 138 & n.
Florida: 152
Flowerdew Hundred: 58 n.
Flowering spurge: 127–28
Food preparation: boiling, 38, 50–53, 63 & n., 109; roasting, 50, 51, 109; eating raw, 50; baking, 51, 53; cooking meat and vegetables together, 51 n., 54 n.; sea-

soning and buttering, 52, 53; menus of meals, 53–54; liquids drunk, 53–54; utensils listed, 63, 88, figs. 7, 14; women's work, 88–89; calling English spices "medicinal," 126
Food storage: drying of corn, 49, 50, 51, 62; places for storing food, 49, 109–10, 144; drying of meat and fish, 50, 51, 62, 111; rendering of oil, 53; deer suet made into cakes, 57; drying of fruit, 91
Foreigners (non-Powhatans): attitude toward, 56, 86, 116, 117; divining purpose of, 121, 132; attempts to neutralize firearms, 132–33; (late 17th century) impossible to divine plans of, 132; initial fear of strange possessions, 135; see also warfare, treatment of captives
Foxes: 27, 44, 98
Fredericksburg, Va.: 18
Frumentry: 51
Fuel: see firewood
Funerals: see mortuary practices
Funnels: 63
Fur: see skins, animal; names of individual animals
Fur-trading era: 40, 142

Games: 137; stickball, 96; football, 96; gambling with reeds, 96–97
Garbage disposal: 78
Gathering of wild plants: 44
"Generall Historie": 3
German language: 8
Gestures, hand: 106, 125
Gibbon, John: 77
Gift exchange: 56, 90
Gloucester County, Va.: 11
God, Christian, attitude to: 137
Gods: see deities
Gookin, Daniel: 150
Gooseberries: 52
Gosnold, Bartholomew: 5
Gourds: 47, 49, 53, 63, 97, 110
Grass seeds (sp. unknown): 53
Great Bear (constellation): 49
Great Dismal Swamp: 27
Great Lakes: 152
Great Neck site: 58 n.
Great Wicomico River: 18, 24
Grinding stones: 63, fig. 14
Ground nuts: 45, 52, 91
Gulf States: 152
Gulf Stream: 17

Haas, Jonathan: 146, 147
Hair, animals': 77, 96; *see also* fur; hair-
    styles, men's
Hair, Indians': 65; plucking, 69, 70; *see
    also* beards
Hairstyles: children's, 69; men's, 69–70,
    78, 116, 131, figs. 10, 24; women's, 69,
    102, fig. 21; women barbers, 70, 88;
    priests', 100
Hakluytus Postumus: 5
Hallooing: 106
Hamlets: 60, 143
Hammer stones: 63, 65, fig. 14
Hamor, Ralph: 109
Hampton, Va.: 11
Hampton Creek: 11
Hampton Roads: 17, 22
Handbook of North American Indians: 151
Hariot, Thomas: 34, 58, 101, 113 n.
Harris Creek: fig. 2
Hartleberries: 52
Hatchets: for cutting trees, 47; for digging,
    76; iron ones, *see* English trade goods;
    see also warclubs
Hawks: 70
Heating: *see* houses, heating in
Heaven and hell: *see* afterlife
Hemp, Indian: *see* "silk grass"
Henrico County, Va.: 11
Herons: 77
Hickory, roots of: 52
Hiding of valuables: 49, 56, 89 n.
Hoes: 63
Holly: 130; yaupon, 127
Hominy: 51
Horse gentian: 128
Horses (from Europeans): 27 & n., 135
Horseshoe crabs: 29
House of Burgesses: 6
Houses, chiefs': 61, 106
Houses, ordinary: construction, 32, 60–62,
    fig. 12; continual fire kept in, 51, 62;
    sturdiness, 58, 61; called a *yi·hakan,* 60;
    number of occupants, 60, 90; lighting in,
    61; heating in, 61 & n.; adapted to Vir-
    ginia climate, 61; furnishings in, 61, 62
    & n.; ease of moving, 61–62; sleeping
    arrangements in, 62, 65; cleanliness, 62,
    129; usually built by women, 62, 88–89;
    possibly owned by women, 88–89; for
    newlyweds, built by man's family, 90;
    disposal after death of male owner, 93

Houses, temporary: 34, 41, 62
Hunting: overkill, 15, 40, 57; attitude to-
    ward, 38; profession for most men, 38,
    79, 87, 88; trapping, 39; stalking, 39–
    40, 41–42; surround or communal or
    "fire hunting," 40–41, 57, 132 n.; of
    squirrels, 44; of wild turkeys, 40, 44;
    hairstyle for, 70; involvement of Okeus,
    136; training for, *see* childrearing, boys;
    hunting territory
"Hunting root": 39, 41–42
Hunting territory: paramount chief's, 15,
    109, 144, 146; lack of for commoners,
    40 & n.
Huskanaw: preliminaries, 70, 76–77,
    80–81, 121; purpose, 80, 82; timing, 80;
    mortality, 80, 82; seclusion period,
    81–82, fig. 20; absence on Eastern
    Shore, 82, 141; for both sexes in Caro-
    lina (late 17th century), 82, 84

Images, manmade: of humanoids, 76, 103,
    134; of god Okeus, 76, 122, 133, 134–
    35; of animals, 134
Indian Field Creek: 11
"Indian weed": 127
Indians: *see* (for Algonquian-speaking
    groups) Accomac, Appamattuck, Ar-
    rohateck, Chesapeake, Chickahominy,
    Chiskiack, Chowanoc, Cuttatawomen,
    Kecoughtan, Mattaponi (Mattapanient),
    Moraughtacund, Nandtaughtacund,
    Nansemond, Occohannock, Onawma-
    nient, Opiscopank, Pamunkey, Pas-
    pahegh, Patawomeck, Piankatank,
    Piscataway, Pissaseck, Powhatan,
    Quiyoughcohannock, Rappahannock,
    Sekakawon, Warraskoyack, Werowoco-
    moco, Weyanock, Wiccocomico,
    Youghtanund; (for Iroquoian-speaking
    groups) Meherrin, Nottoway, Tuscarora;
    (for Siouan-speaking groups) Man-
    nahoac, Monacan
Inheritance: *see* kinship
Initiation into manhood: *see huskanaw*
Inkberry: 76
Inns of Court: 4
Interpreters: 8; *see also* English-speaking
    Indians; language, learned by Englishmen
Intoxicants, use of: 82 & n.; calling English
    wine and spices "[bitter] medicine," 126

Iopassus (Japazaws, Indian man): 4, 86, 112, 117, 139, 142
Ipecac, wild: 127
Iris, dwarf: 128
"Irish, the": 69
Iron, possession of at coming of English: 55, (possible) 76
Iroquoian-speaking Indians: 6, 142; see also Nottoway; Meherrin; Tuscarora
Iroquois Indians (Five Nations): 46, 61, 94, 142
Isle of Wight County, Va.: 9

Jack of the Feather: see Nemattanew
James I, King of England: 110, 133
James City County, Va.: 11
James City Parish: 5
James River: 3, 4, 5, 8, 11, 13, 16, 18, 22, 25, 31, 35, 45, 51, 55, 56, 57, 60n., 61, 69, 76, 113, 118, 130, 136, 137, 139, 149
James River, falls of: 4, 7, 11, 18, 22, 45, 56, 71, 120, 133, 136
Jamestown Colony (English colony in Virginia): 3, 7, 9, 22, 40, 45, 86, 120, 125, 134
Jamestown fort and "cittie": 4, 5, 16, 25, 55, 56, 109, 112, 119, 147
Jamestown Island: 22, 61
Japazaws: see Iopassus
Jesuit mission of 1570: 7
Jewelry, in general: 69, 70–71, 73, 113, 134, 138; see also copper; feathers; pearls; shell
Jimson weed: 82, 127
Jonson, Ben: 4

Kecoughtan (capital town); 4, 11, 60, 61, 119, 122, 134
Kecoughtan, chiefs of: 117, 142
Kecoughtan Indians (district chiefdom): 11, 56, 80, 117, 118–19, 120n., 140
Kekataugh (Indian man): 117; full or half-brother of Powhatan, 117n.
Kemps (Indian man): 4
King and Queen County, Va.: 11, 115
King George County, Va.: 12
Kings Creek: 9
King William County, Va.: 11, 115
Kinship: 60, 77, 92–94, 117n.; inheritance (commoners), 57, 93–94; chiefly succes-

sion, 93, 112–13; status of chief's children, 112–13
Kiptopeke (Indian man): 117, 118
Kiskiack: see Chiskiack
Kocoum (Indian man): 91, 112, 113
Kroeber, Alfred L.: 151
Kupperman, Karen O.: 152n.
Kwiocos (pl. kwiocosuk): 135, 136

Ladles: 54, 63
Lagrange Creek: 12
Lahontan, Baron Louis Armand de Lom d'Arce de: 6
Lamb's Creek: 58n.
Lancaster County, Va.: 12
Land: ownership of, 29, 40, 46, 57, 114–15; annual allocation of, 114; usufruct system, 114–15
Land patents, Virginia colonial: 62
Language: 4, 7–8, 13, 15–16; learned by Englishmen, 4, 7, 11, 109; words borrowed into English, 27; "general [archaic?] language," 131; New England relatives, 150
"Laughing King of Accomac": see Esmy Shichans
Law: execution of foreigner, 84, 116; civil, 85, 86, 87, and see also marital relations; kinship; vindictiveness; criminal law, 85, 86, 87, 136; personal revenge by commoners, 85, 115; customary law, 114, 115; enforced by chiefs and priests, 85, 92, 115, 116–17, 146; disobeying chief, 86n., 115, 116–17, 121; theft, 116; infanticide, 116; murder, 116
Lawson, John: 96n.
Leaves, use of: 40, 51, 52, 62, 69, 76, 78, 98, 147
Lederer, John: 50, 128–129
Leedstown, Va.: 12
Leggings: 69
Lenape Indians: 97
Length of Algonquian occupation of Virginia: 8
Lice: 62, 129
Lighting, artificial: 61, 99
Lineages, probable presence of: 92–94
"Little Ice Age": 17
Little Wicomico River: 12
Liverwort: 126
Locust trees, black: 60
Loincloths: 69

London, England: 4, 102
Long Island, N.Y.: 150
Long Island, Virginia Beach, Va.: 60 n.
Lower Peninsula (or The Peninsula): 22
Lurie, Nancy O.: 93
Luxury goods: 32, 55–56, 57
Lynhaven Bay: 24

Machumps (Indian man): 4, 112
Magic: 80
Mahican Indians: 61
Mamanatowick: 16, 106; *see also* chief,
    paramount; Powhatan (the man)
Manguahaian (constellation): 49
Manitu (northern Algonquian word): 135 n.
Manliness, conceptions of: 38, 79, 85,
    86–87, 91, 99, 115, 116; *see also* status
    symbols
Mannahoac Indians: 87, 120, 148
Manosquosick (Indian town): 60 n.
Mantles: 69, 96, 102, 103 & n., 106, figs.
    10, 21; feather mantles, 69, 102
Maple trees, red: 60
"Map of Virginia": 3, 4, 5
Maracock (passion flower): 47, 52
Marginella shells: 73
Marital relations, chiefs': authority of
    chiefly husbands, 86; favoritism, 91, 112;
    divorcing wives, 91, 112; duties, 106,
    109; forbidding of wives' extramarital re-
    lations, 92, 93–94, 112; acquiring wives,
    111–12, 143; living arrangements, 112;
    disposal of children, 112
Marital relations, commoners': polygyny,
    79, 82, 90–91, 90 n., 101, 111–12; vir-
    ginity probably not demanded, 89, 91,
    108; qualities preferred in spouses, 90,
    101; courtship, 90; marriage ceremony,
    90 & n.; virilocal residence, 90, 92;
    spouses by temporary contract, 90; ex-
    tramarital relations, 90, 91–92, 93–99,
    108; connection of such relations with
    syphilis, 91; divorce, 91
Marjoram, wild: 53
Martens: 27
Martin, Calvin: 40
Martinez, Bartolomé: 7
Martins, purple: 49
Mask: *see* "Bruff Mask"
Massachusett Indians: 150
Massacre of 1622: *see* Attack of 1622
Massasoit (Indian man): 150
Massawomeck Indians: 120 & n., 142, 148

Matachanna (Indian woman): 101
Matchacomoco: 119 & n.
Matchcoats: *see* mantles
Matchqueon: see antimony
Matoaka: *see* Pocahontas
Mats: 51, 60, 61, 62, 62–63, 65, 76, 81,
    88, 90, 102, 108, 113, 134, 138, figs. 15,
    24
Mattapanient: *see* Mattaponi
Mattaponi (capital town): 11
Mattaponi Indians (district chiefdom): 11,
    41, 56, 118, 122, 141, 144
Mattaponi River: 6, 15, 18, 149, fig. 3
Mattoume (grass): 53
"May—umps": 13, 118
Medicine: in general, 5, 126; term *wisakon,*
    126; herbalism, 126–28; cauterization,
    128; cupping, 128; lancing, 128; sweat-
    ing, 128–29; curing with supernatural
    aid, 130
Meherrin Indians: 120 & n.
Menapacunt (Indian town): 11 n.
Men's work: English attitudes toward, 38,
    44, 46, 47, 79, 87, 88, 89, 110; recipro-
    cal with women's work, 89; paramount
    chief able to perform, 106
Menstrual practices: 88 & n.
Merrill, William L.: 126
Mesoamerica: 92
Microenvironment reduction system:
    92–93
Middle Peninsula: 13, 15, 18
Middlesex County, Va.: 11, 12
Middle Woodland: 71
Mink: 27
Mnemonic devices: 5, 13, 60
Moccasins: 63, 69 & n., 71, 106
Monacan Indians: 5, 55, 87, 120, 148;
    name applied to losing side in mock
    battle, 122–23
Monacock: see warclubs
Monahassonugh Indians: 145
"Money": 89, 130; *see also* shell, in beads
Monohominy (acorn oil): 53
Moons (lunar months): 49
Morattico: *see* Moraughtacund
Moraughtacund (capital town): 12
Moraughtacund, chief of: 91
Moraughtacund Indians (district chiefdom):
    26, 56, 119
Mortars: 41, 51, 63, 88, 90
Mortuary practices: for commoners, 65,
    113, 138–39; mourning, 76, 80, 81,

138; for tortured war captives, 84; for chiefs, 110, 111, 113 & n., 133, 134–35, 138–39, 149; for criminals, 116

Mosco (Indian man): 56

Mosquitoes: 61, 62

Moss, use of: 62, 69 n., 79, 81, 129, 134

Mourning: see mortuary practices

Moyaone Indians: see Piscataway Indians

Moyaons (Indian town): 13, 141 n.

Mulberry trees, red: 44, 52, 53–54, 58

Mummapacun: see Menapacunt

Murdock, George P., and Timothy J. O'Leary: 151

Music: singing, 81, 84, 89, 96, 97, 99, 123, 132, 137; instruments, 97, 130, 132, 133; expected in afterlife, 139

Muskrats: 39, 71 n., 85

Musquaspenne: see bloodroot

Mussels: for eating, 29, 38, 50, 71; shells for cutting, 32, 84; shells for *roanoke* beads, 73; see also pearls

Myrtle: 130

Name for whole Powhatan area: 13

Names, personal: "throne names" of paramount chiefs, 7, 80, 106; given in infancy, 79–80; secret, 80; earned, 80

Nandtaughtacund (capital town): 12

Nandtaughtacund Indians (district chiefdom): 12, 56

Nansemond (capital town): 9

Nansemond, chiefs of: 15, 118 (*weroance* and petty *weroances*)

Nansemond Indian "language" [actually dialect]: 8

Nansemond Indians (district chiefdom): 9, 13, 14–15, 45, 56, 125, 132–33

Nansemond River: 9, 22

Nanzatico (place and people): 12

Narragansett Indians: 62, 150, 151

Natural resources: see Virginia, coastal plain of

Neals Point: 12

Necklaces: see jewelry

Nemattanew (Jack of the Feather, Indian man): 77–78, 78 n., 84–85, 85 n.

Nepinough (season of ripening corn): 49

Nets: see bags; fishing

New England Algonquian Indians: 45, 150–51, 152

New Kent County, Va.: 11, 115

Newport, Christopher: 5 n.

New York Algonquian Indians: 150

Nomini: see Onawmanient

Nomini Bay: 12

Norfolk, Va.: 17, 18, 120

Northampton County, Va.: 9

North Carolina: 8, 27, 49

"Northeastern" Indians: 151–52

Northern Neck: 12, 18, 77, 124

North star: 49

Northumberland, Earls of: 5

Northumberland County, Va.: 12

Northwest Passage: 3

Nottoway Indians: 9 n., 120 & n.

Numbering system: 49 & n.

Nutritional status: 45, 54, 65, 94

Oak species: 44, 91–92; white oak, 60

Oath-taking: 125

Occohannock (capital town): 9

Occohannock, chief of (Kiptopeke): 117, 118

Occohannock Indians (district chiefdom): 7, 9, 13, 56, 57, 82, 117, 118 n., 120, 141; less warlike than mainland groups, 14

Ochahannauke (Indian town): 11 n.

Ocoughtamnis (arum berries): 52

Offerings to deities: 54, 132, 133–34, 136 & n., 137

"Of the Natives": 6

Oholasc (Indian woman): 117

Oil: from bears, 50, 76, 129; from acorns, 50, 53; to soften dried food, 50, 53; as insect repellent, 62, 76; for warmth, 69, 76, 94; for sleek hair, 70; to keep out summer heat, 76, 94; from hickory nuts, 70, 76; as base for body paint, 76, 78, 98, 108, 139; as base for ashes in mourning, 76; as base for ointment, 128; see also suet

Okeus: see deities

Old age: 70, 90, 139

Omens: 39, 62, 81 n., 130

Onawmanient (capital town): 12

Onawmanient Indians (district chiefdom): 12, 56, 141 n.

Onions, wild: 52

Opechancanough (Indian man): 91, 108–109, 115, 117, 118, 120, 124, 147; full or half-brother to Powhatan, 117 n.

"Opechancanough" (Indian town): 60 n.

Opiscatumek Indians: see Opiscopank Indians

Opiscatumek River: see Rappahannock River

Opiscopank (capital town): 12
Opiscopank Indians (district chiefdom): 12, 31, 56
Opitchapam (Indian man): 108, 117 & n., 118; full or half-brother to Powhatan, 117n.
Opossums: 27
Opossunoquonuske (Indian woman): 69, 108, 117, 142
Orapax (Indian town): 4, 110, 133, 134, 136
Oratory: 108, 119
Ossuaries: 139 & n.
Ottaniack (paramount chief's title): 106
Ottawa Indians: 120
Otters: 27, 39, 98
Overkill: *see* hunting
Oxford University: 5, 103
Oysters: 29, 38, 44, 50, 57, 109; shell, 42

Pacific Ocean: 3
Paddles: 34
Pagan River: 13
Painting: materials used, 39, 76; "winter-count," 50, 103; as insect repellent, 62; of mats and baskets, 65, 76; of clothing, 69; of body, daily, 65, 76, 94, 129; of body, on ceremonial occasions, 76–77, 77n., 81, 98, 106, 122; of shields, 76, 124; color symbology, 76–77; of body, for war, 77, 84, 123; of body, by priests, 78, 100; of images, 134
Palisades: 46, 58 & n.
Pamareke (Indian town): 11n., 60n.
Pamlico region: *see* Carolina (region) Indians
Pamunkey, a chief of (probably Opitchapam): 117
Pamunkey (capital town): 11, 60n.
Pamunkey Indian "language" [actually dialect]: 8
Pamunkey Indian Reservation (modern): 61
Pamunkey Indians (district chiefdom): 6, 11, 27n., 41, 50, 100, 103, 106, 116, 117, 118, 141, 144
Pamunkey Neck: 6, 18, 143, 144
Pamunkey River: 11, 18, 31, 60 & n., 112, 133, 149
Parahunt (Indian man): 91, 117, 142
Parokonoso: *see* Baraconos
Paspahegh (capital town): 11, 135
Paspahegh, chief of (Wowinchopunck): 76, 122

Paspahegh Indians (district chiefdom): 8, 11, 41, 47, 56, 80, 119, 122, 141
Passapatanzy (Indian town): 4, 86, 117
Passion flower (*maracock*): 47, 52
Pataunck: *see* Potauncak
Patawomeck (capital town): 12, 46, 58n., 73, 78n., 85, 142
Patawomeck, chiefs of: district *weroance*, 86, 117 & n., 142; petty *weroance* (Iopassus), 4, 86, 112, 117, 139, 142
Patawomeck Indians (district chiefdom): 4, 12, 14, 56, 85, 86, 88, 113, 117, 120 & n., 136, 138, 141n., 148
Pausarowmena (corn and bean dish): 51, 52
Pawtucket Indians: 47n.
Peak (*wampum peak*): 71, 73, 103n., 125
Pearls, freshwater mussel: preparation, 71; use, 56, 70, 71, 80, 102, 103 & n., 106, 109, 110, 125, 144, figs. 10, 17
Pellitory: 82n.; identified, 82n.
"Pembroke side": 55
Peninsula, The: *see* Lower Peninsula
Pepiscunimah: *see* Pipsco
Pequot Indians: 150
Percy, George: 5, 42, 70, 76, 126, 133
Persicary: 127
Persimmons: 52
Personality, male: *see* manliness
Pestles: 63–65, 90, fig. 14
Physique: 45, 65, 70, 76, 94, 135
Piankatank (capital town): 11, 22
Piankatank Indians (district chiefdom); 11, 15, 56, 119, 123, 124, 140, 141, 146, 147
Piankatank River: 11, 18, 22, 109
Pigs (from Europeans): 135
Pilgrims: 47n., 150
Pine barrens: 25, 76
Pine trees: yellow, 60; "shivers," 34n.
Pipes, tobacco: 63 & n., 113
"Pipsco, Captain": 27n.
Pipsco (properly Pepiscunimah, Indian man): 69, 71, 91, 102, 137, 146, 147
Piscataway Indians (Maryland): 4, 13, 120, 141n., 148
Piscataway Indians (Virginia): *see* Opiscopank
Pissaseck (capital town): 12
Pissaseck Indians (district chiefdom): 12, 56
Plants available: *see* Virginia, coastal plain of

Plants used by Powhatans: *see* individual
    entries
Platters: 51, 88, 97; *see also* dishes
Plymouth colonists: *see* Pilgrims
Pocahontas (Indian woman): 7, 49, 76 n.,
    80 & n., 81 n., 91, 112, 113, 121, 131,
    137, 141 n.
Pochins (Indian man): 117, 119
Pocoughtaonack (or Bocootawonauk) In-
    dians: 55, 120, 142, 148
Poison: in fishing: 34; on arrowheads, 42
Pokanocket Indians: 150, 151
Pokeberry: 127
Poles, for canoes: 34
Polio: 129
Pomonkey Creek: 13
Popanow (winter): 49
Popcastle Turn: 12
Population: distribution, 15, 29, 109, 143,
    figs. 1, 6; size, 15, 143
Portobacco (Indian town at Nandtaughta-
    cund): 60, 90 n.
Portobago Bay: 12
Port Royal, Va.: 24
Potato, wild: *see* arrow arum
Potauncak (Indian town): 11 n.
Potomac Creek: 12
Potomac Indians: *see* Patawomeck Indians
Potomac River: 8, 13, 14, 18, 22, 31, 34 n.,
    35, 56, 113, 118, 120, 141
Potter, Stephen R.: 149
Pottery: 8 n., 35, 63, 65, 88, 97, 106, fig. 13
Poultices: *see* medicine
Powcohicora (walnut milk): 53, 108, 139
Powells Creek: 9
Power of paramount chief, analyzed: by
    strength of economic power base, 146;
    by strength of positive and negative sanc-
    tions, 146; by scope of power, 146–47;
    by amount of obedience exacted, 147; by
    costs of holding and using power, 147;
    by compliance costs for subjects, 147; by
    refusal costs for subjects, 147–48
Power of paramount chief, described: in-
    complete power over subjects, 13, 85,
    115, 119, 147, 148; incomplete power
    over district chiefs, 13, 114, 119, 122,
    141, 145, 147; power to order communal
    hunt, 41, 123; in general, 114; life-and-
    death, over subjects, 114, 115–16, 146;
    still bound by customary law, 114, 115;
    incomplete power over heirs, 118; ability
    to move whole populations around,

118–19; having to call council sessions,
    119; ability to make policy in council
    cession, 119; ability to have warriors at-
    tack subject chiefdom, 119, 123, 147;
    ability to have warriors exterminate for-
    eign chiefdom, 120–21; ability to order
    men into war, 122
Powhatan (as name): pronunciation, 7 n.; of
    Virginia Algonquians: 7, 13; of para-
    mount chief, 7; of district chiefdom, 7; of
    language, 7–8
Powhatan (capital town near falls of James
    River): 7, 11, 56, 60 n.
Powhatan, chief of (Parahunt): 91, 117, 142
Powhatan (the man): 4, 5, 7, 13–15, 17,
    29, 38, 41, 55, 60, 73, 85, 87, 91, 92,
    93, 101, 103, 106, 109, 110, 111, 112,
    113, 116, 117, 118–19, 120–22,
    121–22, 124, 125, 133, 134, 136,
    140 ff., 146–48
Powhatan Indians (district chiefdom): 11,
    56, 117, 118, 120, 144
Powhatan River: *see* James River
"Powhatan's Mantle": 76, 103, fig. 23
Prestige: *see* status symbols
Priests: appearance, 70, 78, 100, fig. 20;
    training, 80, 101, 126; possible involve-
    ment in *huskanaw*, 81; at least part-time
    specialists, 88, 145; ranked, 100–101,
    132; status in society, 100–101, 111,
    119, 120; as keepers of temples, 100,
    133; as prescribers of offerings, 100,
    101 n., 136; ability to marry, 101; impor-
    tant priest married to paramount chief's
    daughter, 101; as enforcers (with chiefs)
    of law, 115, 116, 117; as diviners, 116,
    119, 120, 121, 131, 132; as allies of
    chiefs, 119–20, 136, 142–43, 145; se-
    cretiveness, 126 & n., 131; as curers,
    129, 130; communicating with deities,
    130–32; as bringers of rain, 131,
    132–33, 137; as quellers of storms, 131,
    132; as finders of lost articles, 131;
    (probable involvement), as causing dis-
    orientation of enemies, 131, 133; as ma-
    nipulators of image of Okeus, 135; *see
    also* Uttamatomakkin
Prince George County, Va.: 9, 58 n.
Prophecies: by priests, 120; by Okeus,
    131–32
Public works: 148, 149; *see also* houses,
    chiefs'; temples
Puccoon: 26, 55, 56, 69, 76, 77, 103 n.,

Puccoon (*continued*)
  106, 108, 109, 113, 129, 132, 133, 136,
  139, 144
Pueblo Indians: 126n.
Pungnough (ashes of corncobs): 51
Purchas, Rev. Samuel: 5, 49, 77, 101, 117,
  131, 137, 139
Purchas His Pilgrimage: 5
Purses: in general, *see* bags; "Virginia
  Purse," 103, fig. 22
Purtan Bay: 11
Pushemins or putchamins: *see* persimmons

Quahogs: 24, 71, 73
Quails: 40
Quinn, David B.: 120n.
Quiocosin houses: see temples
Quivers: 42, 98, fig. 10
Quiyoughcohannock (capital town): 4, 9
Quiyoughcohannock, chiefs of: Pipsco (de-
  posed *weroance*), 71, 91, 102; Ta-
  tahcoope and Oholasc (new *weroance*
  and regent), 117, 142
Quiyonghcohannock Indians (district
  chiefdom): 9, 80, 117
Quiyounghcosugh: *see kwiocos*

Rabbits: 40
Rabbit tobacco: 127
Raccoons: 27, 44, 70, 106
Ramages, probable lack of: 92–94
Rappahannock (capital town): 12
Rappahannock, chief of: 56, 76, 77, 91
Rappahannock Indians (district chiefdom):
  12, 119
Rappahannock River: 12, 13, 14, 18, 22,
  25, 31, 35, 56, 58n., 90n., 119, 120
"Rat": 71
Rattles: *see* music, instruments
Rattlesnakes: 70, 98, 128
Rebecca: *see* Pocahontas
Redistribution: 14–15, 111, 144–45, 148
Reeds: as cutting tools, 32 & n., 128; for
  matting, 60; for whipping, 80, 81, 98; in
  gambling game, 96–97
Reid's Ferry, Va.: 9
Reincarnation: *see* afterlife
Religion: *see* deities; medicine; mortuary
  practices; priests; temples
Revenge: *see* vindictiveness
Rhode Island: 151
Richmond, Va.: 11, 17, 18, 22
Richmond County, Va.: 12

Rituals: 89; hunting (lack of data on), 41;
  thanksgiving, 41, 54, 137; at daily
  bathing, 78, 137; continence, periods of,
  94; gathering medicinal plants, 126–27;
  curing, 130; divination, 132 & n.; timing
  of, 137; *see also* priests
Rivers, naming of: 31
Roaches: *see* hairstyles, men's
Roanoke: 71, 73, 130
Roanoke Colony: 47n., 55, 120n., 141,142
Rockahominy (corn flour): 50
Rolfe, John: 5, 49, 81n., 101n., 137
Rounda: *see runtees*
Runtees: 71, 73

Sachems, New England: 150–51
"Sacrifice of children": see *huskanaw*
Sahlins, Marshall: 92
St. James's Park: 102
Salt: 52; summer "salt plug" in rivers, 45
Salwen, Bert: 353
Sanitation: 78, 89; *see also* washing
Savage, Thomas: 109
Scalps: *see* trophies
Scarecrows: 49
Scholarship, 17th and 18th century stan-
  dards of: 4, 6
Scoggins Creek: 11
Scots language: 8
Seasons: *see* time, calculation of
Secacawoni: *see* Sekakawon
Sekakawon (capital town): 12
Sekakawon Indians (district chiefdom): 12,
  56, 77, 141n.
Self-heal: 127
Servants: 54, 101, 102, 108
Settlement pattern: 46, 58
Shades (ramadas): 62
Shamanistic cures: *see* medicine
Shamapa (Indian town): 11n.
Shamapint: *see* Shamapa
Sharks' teeth: 63 & n.
Shell, use of: for cutting, 32, 34; in beads,
  55, 56, 69, 71, 73 & n., 80, 86, 90, 102,
  103, 106, 110, 116, 125, 133, 138, 139,
  144, figs. 18, 19, 22, 23; for plucking,
  70; for tinklers, 70, 98; in disks, 73; in
  digging, 76; *Saxidomus* sp., 103; *Mar-
  ginella roscida*, 103; *see also* clams;
  conchs; mussels; *peak; runtees; roanoke*
Shields: 76, 77, 124
Shooting gloves: 42
Siebert, Frank T.: 7, 15

"Silent Indian" stereotype: 96, 108 n.
"Silk grass": uses, 35, 65, 69, 127, 128; identified, 65
Simonson, Va.: 12
Sinew: 34, 73, 103
Singing: *see* music
Siouan-speaking Indians: 6, 41; *see also* Monacan; Mannahoac
Skin, Indians': 65, 76
Skins, animal: 62, 81, 102, 109, 113, 134, 138; stuffed, 39, 70, 101
Skunks: 27
Sleeping arrangements: 62, 65
Smith, John: 3–4, 5, 7, 8, 9–12, 13, 40, 41, 42, 45, 49, 60, 69, 78, 86, 92, 93, 98, 100, 101, 106, 108–109, 115, 116, 121, 121–22, 124–25, 127, 130, 132, 134, 139, 141, 143, 144
Smithfield, Va.: 9
Snakeroot: 126, 128
Snakes: various, 27, 45, 100; rattlesnakes, 70, 98, 128; greensnakes, 71
Snow, Dean R.: 46
Social differentiation: in general, 79, 93, 100, 101–102, 143, 146; "the better sort," 82, 85, 93, 101–102, 103, 106, 143; linguistic evidence, 101, 103, 106; special treatment of chiefs, *see* chief, paramount; deference shown to chiefs
Sodomy: 91 n.
Soils: *see* Virginia, coastal plain of
"Sora horses": 38 n.
Sorcer: 80
Southeastern Ceremonial Complex: 78 n.
"Southeastern" Indians: 62, 71, 127, 151–52
"Southside Virginia": 22
Spanish in Virginia: 7, 77, 142
Spears: 35, 138
Specialization of occupation, near lack of: 32, 55, 57, 93, 106, 144, 148
Speck, Frank G.: 40 n., 151
Spelman, Henry: 4, 7 n., 34, 46, 47, 54, 60, 86, 98, 106, 111, 116, 123, 130, 133, 139, 141 n., 142, 148
Spelman, Sir Henry: 4
Spencer, Robert F., and Jesse D. Jennings: 151
Spicebush: 127
Spoons: 63, 88
Squanto (New England Indian man): 47 n.
Squash (including muskmelons): 47, 52, 53, 110

Squills: 127
Squirrels: 27, 44, 70
Stafford County, Va.: 12
Status symbols: having food at all seasons, 51, 57, 79, 108; having many animal skins, 57, 69, 101–102; having bark-covered houses, 61, 106; having feather mantles, 69, 102; having blue (European) trade beads, 73; (male) having many wives, 79, 90–91, 92, 101, 143, fig. 24; (male) reputation as great hunter, 79; (male) reputation as invincible warrior, 79, 84; receiving public recognition from chief, 79, 80, 85, 101; (male) being *huskanawed* young, 80, 82; having much jewelry, 101, 102–103, fig. 24; having many houses (paramount chief), 106
Stickweed: 52
Storage pits: 49
Strachey, William: 4, 7, 9–12, 13, 14, 15, 29, 38, 40, 42, 45, 46, 54, 56, 57, 60, 61, 63, 65, 71, 86, 90, 91, 94, 98, 101, 109, 110, 112, 118, 119, 127, 129, 130, 135, 139, 143, 144, 147
Strawberry: 44, 52, 54
Sturgeons: 28, 29, 34 & n.
Succotash: 52
Suet, deer: as "butter," 52; traded, 57, 144
Suffolk, Va.: 9
Summer dispersal: *see* annual round
Surry County, Va.: 9
Susquehanna River: 18, 120
Susquehannock Indians: 120 n.
Swans: 77
Swanton, John R.: 151
Sweathouses: 62–63, 129 & n.
Sweet everlasting: 127
Swift Creek: 11
"Swords": *see* warclubs
Syphilis: 91, 129–30, 130 n.

Taboos: incest, 92; postpartum, 94; periods of continence, 94
Tanning of hides: 74–75
Tapatiaton (Indian man): 117 n., 118 n.
Tappahannock, Va.: 12
Taquitock (fall): 49
Tatahcoope (Indian boy): 117
Tattooing: 69, 73, 76 & n., 77
Temples: fig. 12; construction, 61, 100, 111, 122, 133, 134, 135; as repositories of chiefs' valuables, 103, 111, 133–34; size, 110, 110–11, 133, 134; as store-

Temples (*continued*)
  houses for tribute, 110, 111; as chiefs' sepulchers, 110, 113, 134, 134–35; as armories, 111, 122; limited access by commoners, 111, 133; abandonment of, 113, 136; most sacred temple, 117, 133; as place for council deliberations, 119; as place for semi-public ritual, 122, 135; as repositories of war trophies, 124; as repositories of valuable herbs, 126; limited access to priests at times, 132; location, 133; cleanliness, 133; as receptacle for image of Okeus, 134 (for description of image, *see* images); fire constantly kept in, 134
Terra-sigillata: 77
Territories: *see* districts
Textiles in general: 65, 88, figs. 15, 16; base for feather mantles, 69; *see also* bags; baskets; mats
Time, calculation of: 49–50, 89, 137; "winter count," 50
Tinklers: 70, 98
Tobacco: cultivation, 44, 47, 110; use, 63, 91, 108 & n., 113, 125, 132, 135, 136, 137; storage, 63; pipes, 63, 113, 125, 135
Tockwogh Indians: 145
Tomahawks: *see* warclubs
Tortoises: 44, 54; shells, 63, fig. 7
Torture: 84; Iroquoian, 142
Towns: location, 25, 26, 58, 60, 93; economic independence, 32; occupied part of year, 41, 45; palisaded, 46, 58; geographical movement through time, 46, 58, 61–62, 93; dispersed pattern, 58; underbrush cleared away near, 58, 60; size, 60, 79
Trade: 55, 144, 148; with Chowanocs, 15; ron (European), 47, 56, 63, 86, 116, 124; copper, 55, 71; antimony, 56, 76; puccoon, 56; shell for beads, 56; pearls, 56; oysters, 57; bark, 57; other foodstuffs, 57; glass beads (European), 71, 73; across fall line, 149
Trash pits: 78
Travel: by water, 34, 49; by land, 38–39; food for, 50
Trees: desired near houses, 52, 58, 61; for house frames, 60; for bark sheathing, 60–61
Tribute: 45, 55, 109–11, 144–45, 146, 148; goods collected, 38, 55, 71, 76, 109–10, 117; proportion of subjects' produce collected, 38, 109–10; partially in corvee labor, 46; disposal of, 57, 111, 148; frequency of collection, 109; storage of, 110
Trophies: 70, 84, 123, 124 & n., 125
Tsenacomoco: 13, 140
Tuckahoe: *see* arrow arum
Tulip poplar trees: 61
Tumplines: 65
Turkeys, wild: 28, 41, 44, 102, 109, 113; spurs of, 32; bone callers, 41; feathers of, 42; legs and claws of, 70
Turner, E. Randolph III: 13, 15, 40, 45, 46, 54, 57n., 141 & n., 149
Tuscarora Indians: 6, 60n., 111, 128n., 145

Underbrush: 58 & n.
Usketahamun (corn dish): 51
U.S. Route 17: 24
Uttamatomakkin (Indian man): 5, 49, 50n., 77, 101, 117, 131, 137–38, 139
Uttamussak (temple site): 110, 117, 131, 133, 136

Venison: 15, 50–51, 53, 57, 108–109, 113, 144; *see also* food preparation
Villages: *see* towns
Vindictiveness: 85, 86, 87, 115, 121
Virginia, coastal plain of: soils, 15, 18, 22; storms, 15, 17, 24, 34, 58; climate, 17, 58; climate during "Little Ice Age," 17; droughts, 17, 57, 87; location, 17; topography, 17–24, fig. 5; rivers and estuaries, 18–24, fig. 5; ecological zones (including available plants), 24–27, 144; shellfish, 24–25, 52, fig. 8; birds, 25, 28; animals, terrestrial, 27–28, 149; fish, 28–29, 149, fig. 8; summer "salt plug" in rivers, 45
Virginia Algonquians: synonym for Powhatans (Rountree), 7; as separate from Powhatans (Feest), 13
Virginia Beach, Va.: 58n., 60n., 71, 120
Virginia Capes: 22
"Vision quest," possible: 130–31
Visiting, by chiefs: eating, 55, 108–109; entertainment after meal, 85, 108; sleeping arrangements, 89, 91, 108; reception, 99, 106, 108–109, fig. 24; "progresses" of paramount chief, 109, 110

Wachiawamp (Indian man); 117n.
Wahunsenacawh (Powhatan's personal
   name): 106, 143
Walnuts: 44, 52, 57, 70, 76, 97, 108; black
   walnut trees, 61
Wampum: see peak
Warclubs: 98, 115, 120, 124 & n., 134
War cries: 123
Warfare: reasons for engaging in, 41, 85,
   86, 87, 121, 165; trophy-taking, 70, 84,
   123, 124 & n.; specialized gear (not used
   in hunting), 77, 115, 120, 124; immediate preparations, 77–78, 120, 122, 143;
   encouraged by paramount chief, 79, 85,
   87; frequency of engagements, 79, 87;
   training for, 79, 82, *see also* childrearing,
   for boys; attitude toward, 84, 137; treatment of male captives, 84, 121, 147;
   public boasting of prowess, 84–85;
   hiring warriors, 111, 119, 122, 140;
   treatment of female and child captives,
   121 & n., 123, 147; treatment of enemy
   rulers, 121, 147; tactics, 122–124; leaders in, 122, 123, 143; involuntary participation, 122, 143, 147; use of god's image
   in, 122, 134; celebrations of victory,
   124–25; peace-making procedures, 125
Warraskoyack (capital town): 9
Warraskoyack, chief of: 118
Warraskoyack Indians (district chiefdom):
   9, 15, 56
Warraskoyack River: *see* Pagan River
Washing: of bodies, 58, 78, 94, 137; of
   hands, 54, 78, 102; *see also* hair,
   plucking
Washington, D.C.: 18
Waste disposal: 78
Water, fresh: consumption of, 45, 54 & n.,
   58; from springs, 58; artificial catchment,
   lack of, 58
Wealth: *see* status symbols
Weanoc: *see* Weyanock
Weasels: 27, 100
Weroance/Weroansqua: 16, 103, 142; *see
   also* chiefs, district
Werowocomoco (paramount chief's capital
   town): 11, 15, 98, 116, 123

Werowocomoco Indians (district chiefdom):
   8, 11, 15, 56, 118n.
Westmoreland County, Va.: 12
Weyanock (capital towns): 9
Weyanock, chief of: 46, 110, 111, 118
Weyanock Indians (district chiefdom): 9 &
   n., 11, 15, 56, 119
Weyanoke Point: 9
Whitaker, Rev. Alexander: 101, 133
White, John: 35, 61, 63
White Stone, Va.: 12
Wiccocomico (capital town): 12
Wiccocomico Indians (district chiefdom):
   12, 22, 56, 77
Wicomico: *see* Wiccocomico
"Wigwam" not a Powhatan word: 60 & n.
Williamson, Margaret: 70n.
Willow: 102
Winganuske (Indian woman): 112
Wingfield, Edward Maria: 90n., 91n.
Wisakon: see medicine
Wolves: 27, 28, 44, 134
Women's status in society: 44, 89, 90; abil-
   ity to rule as chiefs, 88, 93, 112
Women's work: 41, 44, 46, 47, 62, 79, 84,
   87, 88, 88–89, 110; English attitudes to-
   ward, 89; Indian men's attitude toward,
   89; control of food, 89; reciprocal with
   men's work, 89; paramount chief able to
   perform, 106
Wood, William: 353
"Woodland" Indians: 7, 58n., 89, 152
World, view of geography of: 50 & n.
Wowinchopunck (Indian man): 76, 122
Wristguards: 42, 44, 98, fig. 10
Writing, lack of: 3; *see also* time, calculation of

Yaupon holly: 127
Yi·hacan: see houses, ordinary
York County, Va.: 11
York River: 11, 13, 16, 18, 22, 25, 31, 55,
   56, 109, 113, 118, 136, 137, fig. 4
Youghtanund (capital town): 11
Youghtanund Indians (district chiefdom):
   11, 41, 56, 60n., 118, 141, 144
Youghtanund River: *see* Pamunkey River